Ongoing Issues in Georgian Policy and Public Administration

# Ongoing Issues in Georgian Policy and Public Administration

edited by

Bonnie Stabile and Nino Ghonghadze

Westphalia Press
An Imprint of the Policy Studies Organization
Washington, DC
2017

Ongoing Issues in Georgian Policy and Public Administration



Westphalia Press
An imprint of Policy Studies Organization
1527 New Hampshire Ave., NW
Washington, D.C. 20036
info@ipsonet.org

ISBN-10: 1-63391-557-3
ISBN-13: 978-1-63391-557-2

Cover and interior design by Jeffrey Barnes
jbarnesbook.design

Daniel Gutierrez-Sandoval, Executive Director
PSO and Westphalia Press

Updated material and comments on this edition
can be found at the Westphalia Press website:
www.westphaliapress.org

We dedicate this volume to Democracy in the twenty-first century.

It is our hope and belief that scholarship can support the work of civil servants, citizens, and all who commit themselves to the achievement of a more just society for all.

And to the memory of Paul L. Posner, whose life's work contributed immeasurably to good governance.

# Contents

# Foreword: Ongoing Issues in Georgian Policy and Public Administration

**Paul L. Posner and Priscilla Regan**

In the summer of 2012, a US State Department initiative through the US Embassy in Georgia helped launch a productive partnership between the Georgian Institute of Public Affairs (GIPA) and George Mason University's Master of Public Administration program. With support from the US embassy in Tbilisi, our goal was to improve the pedagogy, curriculum, and administration of GIPA's Master of Public Administration program (MPA) and also to prepare GIPA faculty, students, and practitioners to better address the complex problems facing public administration and public policy nationally and internationally. The potential was evident from our very first conversation with a number of faculty at GIPA—including Maka Ioseliani, who was then dean of GIPA and soon became GIPA's Rector, and Nino Ghonghadze, who replaced Maka as dean. The collegiality, enthusiasm and ease that were apparent during that first teleconference foreshadowed the collaborative and rewarding relationship that GMU faculty and GIPA faculty have continued over the past five years.

During the three years of the grant, faculty exchanges expanded and deepened. In the summer of 2013, Paul Posner and Nino Ghonghadze co-taught a Public Policy course at GIPA—this was the first of ten courses that were co-taught during the grant period. Nine Mason faculty traveled to Tbilisi to collaborate with six GIPA faculty on nine different courses in their MPA program. The co-teaching model entailed Mason and GIPA faculty collaborating on the development of the course syllabi and sharing the actual teaching of the course. Between October 2012 and March 2016, there were a total of twenty-three visits by fifteen different GIPA faculty to Mason, as well as a total of thirteen visits by eleven different Mason faculty to GIPA. On average, faculty stayed for two weeks, allowing time for faculty from both schools to get to know each other well, for students at both schools to benefit from these faculty exchanges, and for faculty to work collaboratively on curriculum, administrative procedures and research. As an illustration of the latter, Mason and GIPA faculty co-authored papers at the 2014 and 2015 conferences of the American Society of Public Administration.

This volume is further and concrete evidence of the success of the GIPA and GMU partnership. Nino Ghonghadze first met Bonnie Stabile in March of 2013 during one of Nino's trips to Mason. Over the course of the next year, they identified their common interests in public administration, discussed the possibility for this volume, recruited faculty and graduate students from both GIPA and Mason, and drafted a book proposal that was accepted by the Policy Studies Organization. Bonnie and Nino worked to establish rigorous criteria for the chapters, including clear research questions, literature reviews, methodologies, theoretical frameworks, and policy implications—as well as to identify appropriate co-authors from both GIPA and George Mason. In January 2016, Bonnie traveled to Tbilisi to work with her co-editor and the GIPA authors on preparing drafts of several of the chapters.

We want to express our sincere appreciation for the time and effort that both Bonnie and Nino have devoted to this volume. Co-editing a book always entails an investment of time coordinating topics, cajoling authors, and convincing reviewers—all of which is even more challenging when working across countries, languages, and time zones. We believe that this volume, with its focus on critical issues of Georgian governance, economics and finance, will provide public administrators around the world with an understanding of and insights into the emergence of a viable and growing system of public administration in a former Soviet republic.

# Introduction

**Bonnie Stabile and Nino Ghonghadze**

Georgia is undergoing major public administration reform (PAR). It aims to transform the country's public administration system to make it more effective and efficient, and to promote and strengthen democracy and good governance. PAR is comprised of six main facets: (1) policy planning; (2) public service and human resource management; (3) accountability; (4) service delivery; (5) public finance management; and (6) local self-government. This process of reform has already brought about changes in many spheres of governance, and some major transformations are still underway.

The eight chapters introduced in this book touch upon topics directly or indirectly associated with this ongoing PAR. While the chapters describe circumstances from a unique Georgian vantage point, the problems of establishing a thriving civil service and encouraging civic engagement, combatting corruption in various forms, and managing economic crises and development are pervasive concerns, and, we believe, will hold interest for citizens and policy practitioners in Georgia and in countries around the world. The book is divided into two main sections: focusing first on general matters of **Governance** and second on issues related to **Economics and Finance**.

Chapter 1, by Ghonghadze, Dolidze and Edner, considers the **challenges to the establishment of a career civil service in Georgia**, assessing the cultural, political, legal, and professional contexts surrounding the implementation of the new Law on Civil Service. Interviews conducted with current Georgian public administrators identify several distinct classes of possible impediments to reform, including a lack of unified vision or systematic approach to public sector development and a general lack of stability and effectiveness in the public sector. This latter class of concerns encompasses the related phenomena of a perceived lack of motivation among public sector employees; a "personality-oriented" system; frequent personnel turnover; a sense of job insecurity; and a lack of public accountability. Reform will no doubt depend on civic education and democratic citizenship building, in addition to a broader cultural shift in support of democratic norms and administrative professionalism.

In Chapter 2, Koberidze thinks through **Georgian civil society's influence on government** in light of de Tocqueville's observations of civil society's role in representative democracy, particularly in tempering "the tyranny of the majority." Koberidze assesses the degree of influence civil society has on government by examining the advocacy initiatives of civil society organizations in Georgia, and identifies four key dimensions of their efforts: (1) advocacy capacity of organizations; (2) advocacy tactics; (3) funding sources of advocacy campaigns; and (4) advocacy campaign outcomes. Ultimately, the work illustrates that shifting social norms and social capital are necessary components for achieving policy successes and enhancing democratic governance.

Samadashvili and Saleem consider why **anti-favoritism policies** have not been more successfully instituted in Georgia, and explore the issue using Kingdon's Multiple Stream Framework (MSF). While acknowledging successes in establishing a functional public service and controlling corruption, in Chapter 3, they note that shortcomings remain that constitute a continuing threat to effective decision-making and civil service efficiency. Prominent among these is favoritism, "the practice of giving preferential treatment in employment and other matters to friends, relatives or associates by high officials, also known as nepotism." They conclude that meaningful agenda status and ultimate implementation of measures addressing the problem of favoritism have failed to be achieved due to shortcomings in each of the streams Kingdon deems necessary: problems, policies, and politics.

The Republic of Georgia, like so many democracies, faces challenges in sustaining and encouraging **civic engagement**. Local authorities are perhaps the most natural mechanisms for citizen engagement, as they can meet citizens closest to home, both geographically, and in terms of issues likely to have the most tangible impact on them. In Chapter 4, Sopromadze, Loladze, and Terman examine one potential instance of citizen participation—the development of **municipal budget priorities**. They investigate the degree to which citizens are currently involved in the process, and, finding participation to be minimal, make some specific recommendations for fostering citizen involvement, both to improve the responsiveness of government to citizen needs and to "create social capital and reinforce the principles of self-governance."

Tsertsvadze, Khurtsia, and Krylova in Chapter 5 examine the problem of plagiarism in Georgian higher education. The authors consider the cultural and historical roots of the problem in the Georgian context and undertake an empirical analysis to get a sense of the actual extent of plagiarism in Georgian institutions of higher education, specifically in business and public affairs. They also explore the substantial supply side of plagiarism by investigating purveyors of theses and other academic writing that students purchase and submit as their own work. Given the pervasiveness of this market, they end by recommending that schools step up enforcement mechanisms to both prevent and appropriately punish transgressors.

To kick off the section on **Economics and Finance**, Bakradze, Rusieshvili, and Birson consider the global, regional, and idiosyncratic factors that contributed to the **balance of payments shock** and subsequent **depreciation of the Georgian Lari** (GEL) versus the US dollar, which was a particularly serious challenge for both citizens and policymakers grappling with their ill effects between 2014 and 2015. Using data from the National Bank of Georgia (NBG), they chronicle the crisis. In examining the experience of other countries in the region, including Armenia, Azerbaijan, Kazakhstan, and Moldova, they conclude that NBG took constructive policy actions relative to other regional actors faced with similar circumstances. Specifically, the authors find that Georgia's monetary policy "with emphasis made on long-term development and risk mitigation" served the nation well and offers instructive policy lessons for others.

Gersamia and Shpak consider the merits and implementability of enhancements to **fiscal decentralization** and utilization of **debt financing** through **municipal bonds** to secure the financial sustainability of **regional development** in Georgia. To this end, Chapter 7 reviews best practices in developed countries and suggests that sustainable regional development can only be achieved through the bolstering of local government finances through such decentralization and debt financing. Though the Georgian government has taken some important steps in this direction, including the establishment of a "Local Self-Governance Code" in 2014, the authors note shortcomings and impediments to implementation, and advocate an incremental approach to allow regions to learn from each other in establishing best practices.

Finally, Song, Abuashvili, Akhvlediani, and Partskhaladze undertake a wide ranging analysis of **regional economic cluster development opportunities** in Georgia, reviewing the theoretical underpinnings of clusters, and analyzing revealed comparative advantage and total export share to assess Georgia's cluster opportunities. They also consider the relative merits of further developing two current industries—apparel/textile and wine tourism—and find in favor of the latter, among others that hold promise based on their findings, including the chemical and machinery sectors.

Public sector problems are pervasive and ongoing everywhere around the world. Public policies are devised to mitigate, and public servants are challenged to implement, such policies, and the problems themselves seem to evolve, with no stopping point. Perhaps, the most important aspiration of scholarly study is to be of practical use to policymakers and citizens in crafting and carrying out policies that improve the lives and circumstances of all. To that end, we offer this in-depth consideration of ongoing issues in Georgian policy and public administration at this critical and historic juncture.

# PART 1
## Governance

# CHAPTER 1

# Reforming the Georgian Public Sector from the Inside Out: Establishing a Career Civil Service

**Nino Ghonghadze, Nino Dolidze and Sheldon Edner**

## Introduction

Georgia is emerging from years of domination by Russia and is in the midst of establishing its own political and public service systems. It has been experimenting with alternative public approaches to reorder its professional public service, and these can be characterized as reflecting the New Public Management and Weberian models in the Public Administration literature. The most recent reform, adopted in 2015 and set to take effect on January 1, 2017, is intended to create a sound professional and democratic model of public management. Our research, based on data from interviews with current Georgian public administrators, seeks to assess the likelihood of success of these reforms. We focus largely on current approaches to the professional public service in Georgia, but also address the political, social, cultural, and legal/constitutional context within which the revised public service will function. We find that there will likely be significant impediments to the successful implementation of the reform, rooted in the current socio/political context of Georgian society, and its culture and political norms. Hence, despite successful change in the legal/constitutional structures of the public service, we anticipate that it will continue to function with many of the values and norms of previous political leadership.

Fundamental reforms introduced in the Georgian public sector since the 1990s have covered political, legislative, and administrative aspects of the civil service. One of the major challenges facing the government of Georgia is establishing a career civil service. Since 2004, two dominant options have appealed to Georgian political leaders: the New Public Management (NPM) model, which is competitive and entrepreneurial, or more recently, a traditional Weberian, hierarchical model (Drechsler 2005; Pollitt and Bouckaert 2011). Until 2015, the approach implemented by the previous, Saakashvili, government could be characterized as Neolibertarian, or the NPM approach. This approach, however, was not articulated in detailed legislation. The existing Law on Civil Service, adopted in 1997, was quite broad and vague, identifying only general aspects of the civil service. In 2013, as a result of work initiated by the Georgian Civil Service Bureau and refined by a network of academic and non-profit organizations, a new civil service reform concept and consequent draft law were developed. In 2015, the draft law was adopted by the parliament and is scheduled to become effective January 1, 2017, as the new Law of Georgia on Civil Service (The

Legislative Herald 2014). The first article of the draft sets out a definition of the civil service, which makes clear the legislative goals—to create a career or professional civil service, based on the following Weberian general values articulated in the European Administrative Space (EAS) as the required administrative principles for the EU member states: reliability and predictability; openness and transparency; accountability; and efficiency and effectiveness (Organization for Economic Cooperation and Development 1999). The new law also highlights the importance of establishing a uniform and impartial civil service that is politically neutral, achieved by separating politics and administration; according to the authors, civil service should be "a long-term career, which is based on clearly defined rights and duties towards the state and requires dedication and professionalism, impartiality and unity of principles" (Law of Georgia on Civil Service 2015, art. 1, para 1). In addition, it prohibits any partisan appointments and minimizes the number of short-term contracted employees in public organizations.

Until recently, civil service practices in Georgia were set up by individual agencies given a high degree of discretion and decentralized control over norms of everyday work routines and organizational structure, including working conditions and safety; performance assessment systems; and compensation, encompassing holidays, vacations, and overtime. Professional practices were established within each organization by the Minister, and any changes were to be communicated to the employees.

The new Law on Civil Service envisions the development of the civil service as a holistic process across all government agencies. It defines the basic career professional framework, principles, and long-term development expectations for all agencies. Only a very few particulars are addressed in agency administrative procedures, such as internal disciplinary and behavioral norms in the agencies providing direct services for citizens (e.g. the Public Service Hall). The unity of the civil service is reflected in a government-wide policy of employment and recruitment, applying to both central and local governments, through the creation of uniform practices, consistent in terms of management, coordination, and control. Such an approach is intended to contribute to stability, create a unified and transparent pay system, and facilitate attracting and retaining qualified staff. The law defines a model for human resource management that includes hiring and promotion based on equal opportunity principles; the establishment of common, standard job descriptions; professional qualification requirements; and a uniform evaluation process across all of the public sector. The legislation stresses the issue of political neutrality as well.

## Public Service Professionalism and Democracy

Instilling democracy in any country is far from a matter of merely planting seeds and watching them grow. Even for the developed countries of the world, supporting and maintaining democratic institutions and practices remain an ongoing challenge characterized by many missteps and confronted by forces that threaten to derail progress. In the developing countries of the world, especially those emerging from the dominance of a previous, non-democratic regime, shifting into a full blown democratic system is an evolutionary process requiring time, constant effort, support from and education of the citizenry, freedom from external contrary forces and intrigue, major social and cultural change, a stable, if not growing, economy, and much luck. One of the forces that can aid this process is a stable, professional, and ethical public service steeped in the values of democratic systems. Yet, this kind of public service must develop at the same time as the overall democratic system, complicating things considerably.

Four broad areas that play important roles in shaping the development of a country's public service system are its social/cultural, political, legal/constitutional, and professional contexts, and each is considered in turn below.

### *Social/Cultural Context*

The context of culture establishes the social value set and mores supporting society and its emergent governmental form. For a democratic society to flourish, there must be an underlying value set that establishes respect for individuals, egalitarianism, reliance on individual capability, and the encouragement of higher levels of moral development. To go beyond Hobbes' "war of all against all," humans must achieve a higher sense of social interaction that supports all six of Kohlberg's stages of moral development (Kohlberg 1981, 17–19). In this framework, at levels 1, 2, and 3, rules are obeyed to avoid punishment, for personal gain or for approval. Achievement of level 4 supports social law and order, the average attainment for most adults. Attainment of levels 5 and 6 permits the maintenance of social contracts and universal ethical principles. While it would be hard to connect this moral framework with a particular form of government specifically, it would appear that the fundamentals of democracy require respect between citizens and government, and between individual citizens. In the absence of such respect, social order would depend on government's imposition of order and not individual citizen support for order.

Seventy years of Soviet history prevented Georgia from developing democratic values and traditions, such as belief in the equality of individuals, reliance on individual capability and success, respect for government and the State, or development of a professional public service. Although the communist ideology implied universal equality, in reality, citizens were not provided equal opportunities in political, economic, or social spheres. Loyalty to the ruling party was the major determinant for an individual's opportunities in life. Much has changed since Georgia's independence in 1991, although each subsequent governmental regime has still been criticized for providing extraordinary benefits to its followers and denying benefits to opponents.

The experience of Georgia to date, from a social/cultural perspective, has not been supportive of an underlying context for social egalitarianism or social order beyond top-down, government control of society. Georgian society, long subject to monarchs and external control by other powers, had adapted to the imposition of Russian top-down control and is since in the throes of emerging as a social democracy. Fueled by the examples of other new democracies in Eastern Europe and other parts of the world, Georgian citizens have quickly sought to exploit new opportunities for social expression and individual opportunity. In the contemporary social media environment, the stimuli for this development come from many sources and provide constant challenges to the maintenance of social order independent of government. The existence of a stable social order is clear, but perhaps not yet to a point where social mores independently support order apart from government imposition.

### *Political Context*

The political traditions, behaviors, and practices of a nation set the context for the structure of government. As a nation solidifies its political sense of self and institutionalizes a form of government, its national identity emerges. For Georgia, in the past 20 years of political autonomy, the lack of a stable political identity has been reflected in its public sector development. The Georgian government is slowly moving from a model of centralized social control to reliance on the democratic expression of citizen values and the public interest, coupled with a tradition of serving the citizenry. As this new democratic political culture matures, it is expected that it will provide the basis for a political value set supportive of democratic political regimes and a professional civil service.

In the context of developing democracy, public ethical behavior is easily subverted by government and self-focused political priorities. For public servants, the interests and priorities of high-ranking governmental officials can become the dominant order of the day, often to the detriment of citizens' political engagement and transparency. The concepts of political neutrality, objectivity, and a professional civil service can remain elusive, as the maintenance of remunerative public positions can be driven by serving political masters and not citizen values and interests.

Svara observes, "Many of the basic responsibilities of administrators in a democratic society can be derived from the expectations that surround their public offices and the purposes of their organizations" (Svara 2015, 34). He identifies major responsibilities of administrators in a democratic system, such as serving the public interest, procedural fairness, obedience to the law, and responsiveness to policy decisions of political superiors, while fully examining all policy options and exercising leadership appropriate to one's position (Svara 2015, 34–35).

Furthermore, Svara adds that public administrators are obligated to promote the democratic process itself (Svara 2015, 34). These responsibilities are reasonable in a mature, stable, democratic system with a supportive culture. However, in emergent democracies such as Georgia, public servants would be a lonely voice for democracy if expected to fulfill all of Svara's expectations. Placing responsibility for a democracy's future in the hands of a professional civil service may be plausible in a stable democratic nation. It is, however, much more problematic in a new and unstable nation.

### *Legal/Constitutional Context*

A strong and positive tradition of the rule of law can set a supportive framework for an effective, responsive and responsible civil service. The existence of a predictable governmental process, and procedural and substantive due process, depends on a validating legal foundation. The basis for independent moral and accountable agency (Svara 2015, 45) on the part of public servants rests on a strong democratic process and a supportive legal system. Without these fundamental institutional supports, there is no clear basis for orderly administrative procedures or an authority outside government itself. Statute sets a basis for government action that is beyond the will of current political leaders to ensure that citizens and economic actors are treated fairly and equitably. If the legal system, and a supportive judicial system to enforce it, is not institutionalized, the whims of political leaders and current public servants can become the basis for judging the fairness of governmental action. It would make no sense to pass laws establishing the limits of public official discretion and process, if the legal system could not enforce them.

There are significant problems in Georgia's legal system. The Constitution of Georgia (Article 14) guarantees the equality of individuals before the law "regardless of race, color, language, sex, religion, political and other opinions, national, ethnic and social belonging, origin, property and title, place of residence." Yet, in practice, all facets of government have been criticized for selective justice. The judiciary suffers "from undue influence exerted by the Prosecutor's Office and the executive authority during the adjudication of criminal cases, as well as the cases where the political leadership's interests are at stake" (Transparency International, Judiciary 2011).

### *Professional Context*

The construct of a professional civil service is an outgrowth of all of the preceding factors, including rule of law, political context, and social/cultural context. It is further reinforced by expertise, independence, and objectivity as a basis for making sound, defensible decisions in support of public policy and the public interest. A permanent civil service also represents a major factor in the continuity of government knowledge and decision-making over time. The emergence of such professionalism rests, however, on the recognition and cultivation of a civil service motivation, according to Perry and Wise (1990, 367–373). It also requires the existence of a civil service value set that can be identified and adopted by public administrators (Molina and MacKeown 2012, 375–396). Also required is an identifiable basis for training, educating, and preparing a civil service corps. While it is possible for those trained in non-public technical, professional, and technological arenas to make a contribution to public affairs, a dedicated cadre of public administrators schooled in the context, traditions, and practices of public sector behavior, service, and process can clearly provide the accountability and performance expected by citizens and political officials. A trained professional civil service can also provide for the complementarity of politics and administration advocated by Svara (2015, 52–55). Lastly, a reflective professional public servant can anticipate, and potentially avoid, the perils of "administrative evil" (Adams and Balfour 2009; Jurkiewicz 2013).

The Georgian civil service has not yet achieved stability. Public servants enjoy few protections and can be easily fired from their jobs. They are mostly employed without terms, and agency heads exercise wide discretion in matters of appointment and dismissal, thus undermining the independence of the civil service. There are no operative legal mechanisms to ensure the protection of public servants. Often their job security and tenure are directly linked to the tenure of high-level officials (Transparency International, Public Administration 2011). Such instability and dependence on political appointees threatens the objectivity of career public employees and makes the continuity of government knowledge almost impossible.

## Study Objectives

This study was undertaken in order to gain some insights into progress in the development of the Georgian civil service. More specifically, the study's objectives are to:

1) Explore major problems and challenges the Georgian civil service faces, as seen by entry-, mid-, and senior-level public servants and representatives of the Legal Entities of Public Law (LEPLs). LEPLs are agencies created under governmental bodies, authorized to independently carry out political, state, social, educational, cultural, and other public activities under state control and regulated by the Law of Georgia on Legal Entities under Public Law.

2) Investigate how independent experts see and assess the problems of the Georgian civil service. For the purposes of this study, experts are representatives of local non-profit and international donor organizations that served as respondents for our research. They are recognized as experts in Georgia for their work on public administration and civil service reform issues.

3) Analyze how the new Law on Civil Service addresses problems and challenges identified by public servants, representatives of the LEPLs, as well as independent experts.

## Methodology

In-depth interviews (Rubin and Rubin 2012; Babbie 2014; Creswell 2014) were conducted with senior-level public servants (including ministers and deputy ministers) and experts (representatives of local not-for-profit and international donor organizations) in 2014 and 2015 to collect the data. A total of 17 in-depth interviews were completed with representatives of 16 different organizations, both public and non-public. Some of the respondents preferred to maintain confidentiality (see Appendix 1 for the list of in-depth interview respondents).

Focus group interviews (Babbie 2014; Creswell 2014) were used to collect information from entry- and mid-level public servants and representatives of LEPLs. Five focus groups were conducted (two in 2014 and three in 2015). The total number of respondents was 34. The respondents represented 12 different public organizations and 5 different LEPLs. To ensure openness, it was agreed that identities of all respondents would be kept confidential.

Both individual and group interviews were conducted with the use of interview guides containing a list of open-ended questions (see Appendices 2 and 3 for individual and group interview guides, respectively). All interviews were audio-recorded and transcribed.

Interviews were conducted by a group of research assistants who were trained in advance by the authors. All interviews were conducted and transcripts were made in Georgian. The research findings were also written in Georgian and translated by the authors.

## Findings

The problems and challenges identified through the interviews and focus-groups were grouped under the three major issues: (1) lack of a unified vision and systematic approach to the development of a professional public sector; (2) lack of stability and effectiveness in the public sector; and (3) political nature of civil service.

### 1. Lack of a unified vision and systematic approach to public sector development

Public servants and representatives of LEPLs claim that there isn't any long-term strategic vision for the country's development, or for the public sector. Instead, they believe specific goals and objectives are issued chaotically, and not in accordance with a shared general vision. As one public servant reported:

> In my organization we had three different ministers during a short period of time. Each had different requirements. We started from scratch every time—you cannot do any job like this. What we do depends on one single person—the minister, and each minister has a different vision. This is because there is no long-term strategy for the country that everybody would follow, regardless of who is the minister at a given time.

Senior-level public officials and heads of LEPLs also see problems emerging from the lack of a government-wide, systematic approach to the civil service. The respondents noted that there is no common political vision for the long-term development of the civil service. In the absence of a common approach, individual agencies identify concepts for their development on their own. Since its establishment in 1991, the Georgian civil service has been reformed several times, but these reforms have been largely inconsistent. Changes are often carried out on the basis of one given decision-maker's will or ideas, only in some cases accompanied by legislative support.

The absence of a unified vision and systematic approach to professional civil service development is highlighted by the representatives of donor organizations as well. They claimed that public sector reforms do not have a consistent character and have evolved sporadically, with almost unlimited discretion given to each executive agency to define and implement structural changes on their own. They reported that the level of decentralization was high, which, on the one hand, led to the development of particular agencies, but on the other hand resulted in the asymmetric development of the public sector. At the same time, the power of individual LEPLs increased as well.

### 2. Lack of stability and effectiveness of public sector

Public servants and representatives of LEPLs observed that the general instability of the public sector is connected with other problems, which we have classified in the following categories based on their responses, including a lack of motivation on the part of employees: personality-oriented systems; frequent personnel turnover; the insecurity of public servants; and lack of accountability.

### *Lack of Motivation*

Respondents observed that independence and self-motivation are key to the stability of the civil service. They expressed the view that employees are not allowed sufficient independence while fulfilling their functions. Daily, often several times a day, employees are given directions by their managers on how to conduct their work, which many believe leads them to become more passive and considerably weakens their initiative. In such circumstances, even qualified professionals can lose their sense of purpose and motivation, leading to the loss of talented personnel and the instability of the overall administrative system. Other causes of low morale, as mentioned by respondents, are: the unequal and subjective reimbursement system, low pay, significant overtime work, minimal leave, and few professional growth and promotion opportunities.

### *Personality-Oriented Systems*

According to our respondents (entry- and mid-level public servants and representatives of LEPLs), internal organizational development is rather personality-centered and, thus, the employees lack a sense of stability and job security. The instability of the system contributes to the absence of standard professional practices, as the following two quotes illustrate:

> There exists no system that will work even if people change. There is no organizational type of work. True, there are some general procedures, but when a new manager comes, employees get a sense of insecurity. How this or that department or ministry will work depends on a single person.
>
> We do not know where we are going. What we do, who does what, depends on the head and is not predetermined.

This creates problems with regard to the continuity of civil service. With a change of leadership, employees cannot continue their work; instead, they have to start from scratch and adjust to a new manager. Respondents believe that there ought to be a system that will persist beyond the views of an organization's leader at a given moment. This would make the civil service more stable and provide a greater sense of security to public servants.

### *Frequent Personnel Turnover*

Instability is great among high-level public servants. Instead of happily seeking promotion, people are often cautious and uncertain about their fate should they advance in their organization. Instead, they prefer to be specialists, avoiding greater managerial responsibility, because at lower organizational positions of responsibility there is a greater sense of stability. Heads of departments are changed more often than lower-level public servants:

> Senior level officials are changed so frequently that no one spends time on the development of professional staff and their motivation. They know tomorrow they might not be there and prefer to stay quiet, take less responsibility.

Representatives of donor organizations confirm the problem of personnel turnover. They admit that during the implementation of projects related to organizational development, they often have to deal with frequent changes of the leadership:

> We, [representatives of] international organizations, have problems connected to this all the time: for example, we visit an organization, determine the issue to work on, retrain employees accordingly, establish systems, create documents. Half a year passes and a new minister is assigned, who fires retrained personnel and then addresses us with the same request, to retrain his/her employees in the same direction.

### *Insecurity of Public Servants*

Representatives of donor and non-profit organizations (we refer to these individuals as "independent experts") also confirmed the insecurity of public servants. Because the law allows it, it is quite easy to fire public servants. This can negatively affect the quality of work, as employee motivation may decrease out of fear of being fired. Those interviewed reported that employees also feel uncomfortable complaining about issues that might be important to them. The insecurity of public servants, coupled with the frequent personnel turnover mentioned above, can be corrosive to institutional memory and optimal performance.

### *Lack of Accountability*

Respondents consider that public servants, including chief authorities, do not feel accountable to society. Fearing that with changes in political leadership they also might lose their jobs, heads of executive agencies set mainly short-term goals and try to secure their own futures, rather than being concerned with public satisfaction and trust:

> In our sector people do not feel that they have to serve people, they think they are here to make business and care about their own well-being.

Such an attitude undermines the moral and ethical values behind the notion of civil service:

> Being a public servant means influence, power and privileges. They do not know how a public servant should behave, who he/she is accountable to.

## 3. Political nature of civil service

The issues of political influence, nepotism, and favoritism were outlined by entry- and mid-level public servants alike. Respondents noted that newly appointed higher officials usually bring their own people, even to mid- and lower-level positions, as they are unsure if they can trust employees that already work in the system:

> After the election senior officials brought with them people whom they trusted. It was almost officially declared that these are the people that they trust and not you ...
>
> When a new person becomes a top manager, a lot of time is spent on issues like who is whose man.

Respondents underscore that there is no career principle in place, which would clearly chart how an individual starts from low positions and eventually grows professionally and is promoted:

> In fact, professional public servants and political positions are not separated," "on higher positions mostly people from political parties are assigned and not from inside the system.

The political nature of the civil service, with its inherent nepotism and favoritism, is exacerbated by the fact that there is no unified system of personnel recruitment, promotion, performance measurement, and reimbursement.

Representatives of donor and local not-for-profit organizations confirm that procedures for personnel recruitment are different across public organizations. Standards of qualification evaluation for recruiting new employees are inadequate or often do not exist. Many important rules, such as how an interview committee should be formed, are not established. Often nepotism is involved when it comes to recruiting personnel. Even when there is open competition, there are no mechanisms to ensure that evaluation will be performed based on predetermined criteria and will be just. How evaluation committees are formed often threatens the fairness of the process.

Some problems, for example the non-existence of uniform standards, are associated with undeserved promotion, lack of performance measurement, and unfair reimbursement of public servants. Who is promoted and who gets extra pay often depend solely on the decision of the agency head, without any objective evaluation procedures.

Public servants confirm the subjective nature of personnel recruitment:

> Nepotism is in place in eight cases out of ten: it may be a best friend, friend, son, brother, etc.
>
> I can tell how people are appointed: using old Georgian method, 90% through recommendations of acquaintances and friendship.
>
> Half of the agency is full of our head's relatives and friends.
>
> Very rarely people come to work in the ministry through competition, mostly they come through nepotism.

Public servants underline that nepotism and favoritism are involved when it comes to promotion, performance measurement, and reimbursement:

> It is easy, the minister calls and says: my close person will be promoted to this position.

Respondents note that often heads of agencies have their favorite employees, who get promotions and are afforded various possibilities for professional growth, including business trips and training.

Low- and mid-level civil servants also note that under current legislation, the hiring process for the civil service is poorly regulated and leaves room for unfairness and favoritism. In many cases, specific requirements for job openings are being adjusted to the skills and knowledge possessed by a particular person. Thus, before submitting an application for an announced vacancy, one would normally try to find out if the job opening is "fake" and whether it makes sense to apply for the job.

## Discussion: How the New Law Addresses Identified Problems and Challenges

The new Law on Civil Service will become effective in January 2017 and is intended to address problems that hinder the development of an effective Georgian public sector, some of which were raised in the interviews conducted for this study. It should be noted, however, that despite numerous public discussions organized by the Civil Service Bureau, many critical comments of independent experts were not considered in the final version of the law. We interviewed the representatives of governmental and non-governmental sectors to discover to what extent the new law is perceived to addresses identified problems, and grouped their answers under the three major issue areas outlined above: a unified vision and systematic approach to public sector development; stability of public sector; and political neutrality.

One of the solutions suggested by the law to establish a unified and systematic approach to civil service development concerns the status of the LEPLs. Under current regulations, the LEPLs are given a wide range of discretion, and for the most part, their employees are not civil servants, with the exception of the heads and their deputies. The new law will bring the majority of LEPL employees under common regulations of the civil service and give them civil servant status, rather than the fixed-term labor contracts they had under the former Labor Code. Some experts believe that this might hinder flexibility and effectiveness of the LEPLs, as it increases the number of civil servants in a sector many already believe to be inflated, and thus, too bureaucratic and inflexible. But, we have to take into account that the LEPLs are becoming part of the policy-making process, where the ministries are major policy-developers and their subordinated agencies are policy implementers. This supports the introduction of a unified political vision and common approach to maintain the integrity of the civil service system. In addition, integration of the LEPLs into the general civil service domain implies that their employees will share the same principles as central government civil servants with respect to their responsibilities and obligations. The new law makes a clear distinction between the LEPLs according to their functions; entities engaged in religious or educational fields will not be regulated by the new civil service law.

The experts are commonly of the opinion that the strong tendency toward centralization that characterizes the new law will contribute to the unified development of the public sector. The legislation equips the Civil Service Bureau with exclusive competencies and authority, assigning the functions of an "internal think-tank" and policy regulator. The Bureau is placed in charge of the hiring and promotion of public servants; creating, maintaining, and managing a civil servants' reserve; collecting and analyzing information on employees' performance for evaluation, and coordinating their professional development and training; and other official records. It is also responsible for establishing and implementing major principles of the public sector and professional civil service. It is notable that the Civil Service Bureau is the initiator and author of the new law. So, despite its intent to mitigate evident problems of the former system, centralization of authority and responsibility may, in this instance, actually increase the risk of political influence that it seeks to combat. In the worst-case scenario, some fear, the Bureau could become like an old school quasi-communist bureau controlled by the political leadership.

The experts interviewed here emphasize that the law facilitates separation of political and administrative functions by clearly distinguishing the status and function of public servants, contracted administrative employees, and political officials by differentially regulating their activities. Although some of them, especially those who support more flexible career systems, outline obvious disadvantages of the professional model as less effective and more bureaucratic. At the same time, others believe that a professional civil service system is the only way of developing the civil service in a country like Georgia.

In addition, the law clearly defines the obligation of civil servants to maintain political neutrality, which means a ban on political campaigning and the use the authority for partisan purposes. However, the experts emphasize that this restriction should not violate basic human rights of civil servants, such as the right to strike, and freedom of expression, among others. Advocates of the new law maintain that it offers several mechanisms to protect public servants and maintain their political neutrality.

First of all, it establishes a professional civil service, which, according to the legislation, is intended to prevent any partisan interference and, at the same time increase effectiveness, attractiveness of the public sector as a sector of employment. More specifically, the law provides for the following mechanisms:

(1) *A new four-stage ranking system for civil servants, with the first rank as the highest and the fourth as the lowest.* Within this system, the competition for any job opening is limited to current civil servants and is closed to outside candidates. The only entry point to the civil service is the fourth, or lowest rank, which requires candidates to have passed a certification examination checking basic skills and knowledge. In fact, a very rigid and closed system of civil service is created instead of the current, contract-based model, where external and internal candidates are equally eligible for any position at any level.

Representatives of donors and local not-for-profit organizations interviewed for the purposes of this study have varying views on this issue. Some think that it is a necessary requirement for the career system and creates stability within the sector and opportunity for fair and impartial career growth, avoiding any partisanship, favoritism, or nepotism. From this point of view, the closed civil service will decrease the employee turnover rate and provide conditions for professional and personal development. But opponents suggest that this approach establishes an extremely rigid civil service system where, due to the low competition and the lack of candidates from outside, the motivation of civil servants for personal development will significantly decrease. Besides, it violates the principle of equal accessibility to the public sector. It should be noted that this system is mainly supported by respondents employed in the civil service, while outsiders say it is too inflexible. Some even point out that the law does not consider promotion as such, but introduces an internal competition instead. They note that for a country with a small labor-market and lack of qualified candidates, limitation of external competition would further endanger the professional level of the public sector.

(2) *Evaluation of civil servants, based on performance measurement, conducted by human resources (HR) departments of relevant agencies and direct supervisors.* Evaluation will become a basis for promotion, as well as downgrading and even dismissal, but at the same time, the civil servant will have the opportunity to appeal any decision that he/she sees as unlawful or unfair. It should be noted, though, that measurable evaluation criteria have not been elaborated yet, so the implications of evaluation are not yet clear. The performance evaluation system will replace the previous model used on the basis of the old law, and is intended to be a more flexible and objective, as well as less stressful, mechanism of assessment.

(3) A *life-long labor contract.* This facet of the new law is an issue that is also differently evaluated by the respondents. On the one hand, it provides stability and protection from political influence. On the other hand, it may reduce the motivation and necessity for professional growth among employees who feel that they will be practically guaranteed life-long employment.

As for the separation of political and administrative functions, the experts point out that partisanship is natural for the public sector, which most often entails hierarchical chains of command, where the public servant is obliged to obey orders from the political leadership. Moreover, the law provides a very weak mechanism for the public servant to avoid an unwanted order; in order to do so, he or she has to provide an official letter of denial with proper arguments, but if the order is given again, then the servant is obliged to fulfill the order. The issues of responsibilities and individual decision-making capabilities are not clearly defined either. However, the new law has introduced disciplinary proceedings, which define reasons for bringing an official case against public servants, thus ensuring their responsibility and accountability, as well as effectiveness.

## Conclusion

Structural and procedural reforms reflecting a "Weberian" approach to bureaucracy are articulated in Georgia's new civil service legislation. This radical revision of current practice aims to eliminate many of the flaws found under the NPM civil service model. Ironically, both the former and the new models share a common flaw: the imposition of structure without strategies to ensure changes in the fundamental political and professional behaviors of Georgia's policy and bureaucratic actors. Furthermore, enforcement of the new legislation's professional bureaucracy model is dependent on the willingness of policy and judicial leadership to forgo reliance on traditional political and personal connections/practices in decision-making and implementation. Without fundamental changes in the political culture and traditions of Georgia, these structural changes may suffer the same fate as the NPM approach they are replacing.

Our interviews and focus group sessions produced consistent results reflecting a political culture of personal ties and connections that emphasized, "Who you know" rather than democratic professionalism in policy leadership or government practice. Successful long-term reform will require policy leaders whose decisions reflect, as we observed above, an underlying value set that establishes respect for individuals, egalitarianism, reliance on individual capability, and the encouragement of higher levels of moral development. In Svara's words, "Many of the basic responsibilities of administrators in a democratic society can be derived from the expectations that surround their public offices and the purposes of their organizations" (Svara 2015, 34). Georgia's recent emergence as a democratic nation state and its 70 year experience with Russian occupation and dominance have not set a context for democratic political practice and civil society that supports a civic culture among its elites or citizens. Until Georgia's civic culture evolves and matures to reflect contemporary democratic expectations and norms, structural reforms may continue to flounder and fail regardless of the governance logic they reflect.

We see successful long-term civil service reform as a product of both legislative action and civil political development. Such reform has taken valuable and important steps towards creating professional bureaucratic structure. However, Georgia also requires an ongoing process of civic education and democratic citizenship building to create a broad culture of support for the practice of democracy and administrative professionalism.

## References

Adams, Guy, and Danny Balfour. 2009. *Unmasking Administrative Evil.* 3rd ed. Armonk, NY: Sharpe.

Babbie, Earl. 2014. *The Basics of Social Research.* Wadsworth: CENGAGE Learning.

Creswell, John W. 2014. *Research Design: Qualitative, Quantitative and Mixed Methods Approaches.* Thousand Oaks: Sage.

Drechsler, Wolfgang. 2005. "The Rise and Demise of the New Public Management." *Post-Autistic Economics Review* 9 (14). http://www.paecon.net/PAEReview/issue33/Drechsler33.htm (accessed September 6, 2015).

Jurkiewicz, Carole J, ed. 2013. *The Foundations of Organizational Evil.* Armonk, NY: Sharpe.

Kohlberg, Lawrence. 1981. *The Philosophy of Moral Development.* New York: Harper and Row.

Law of Georgia on Civil Service. 2015.

Molina, Anthony, D., and Cassandra MacKeown. 2012. "The Heart of the Profession: Understanding Public Service Values." *Journal of Public Affairs Education* 18 (2). http://www.t.naspaa.org/JPAEMessenger/Article/VOL18-2/09_MolinaMcKeown.pdf (accessed September 10, 2016).

Organization for Economic Cooperation and Development. 1999. "European Principles for Public Administration." *SIGMA Papers, No. 27.* http://dx.doi.org/10.1787/5kml60zwdr7h-en (accessed December 1, 2015).

Perry, James L., and Lois Wise. 1990. "The Motivational Bases of Public Service." *The Public Administration Review* 45: 367–373.

Pollitt, Christopher, and Geert Bouckaert. 2011. *Public Management Reform: A Comparative Analysis: New Public Management, Governance and the Neo-Weberian State.* 3rd ed. Oxford: Oxford University Press.

Rubin, Herbert J., and Irene S. Rubin. 2012. *Qualitative Interviewing: The Art of Hearing Data.* Thousand Oaks: Sage.

Svara, James S. 2015. *The Ethics Primer for Public Administrators in Government and Nonprofit Organizations.* 2nd ed. Sudbury, MA: Jones and Bartlett.

Transparency International. 2011. *Georgia NIS Report. Judiciary.* http://transparency.ge/nis/2011/judiciary

Transparency International. 2011. *Georgia NIS Report. Public Administration.* http://transparency.ge/nis/2011/public-administration (accessed February 15, 2014).

## Appendix 1

**List of in-depth interview respondents—high-level officials (identities confidential):**

Ministry of Regional Development, 2014

Ministry of Defense, 2014

Ministry of Sports and Youth Affairs, 2014

Ministry of Education and Science, 2014

Ministry of Energy, 2014

President's Administration Office, 2014

Civil Service Bureau, 2014

Staff Member of Parliament of Georgia, 2015

**Local and international non-profit organizations**

Institute for Development of Freedom of Information (IDFI), George Kldiashvili, Director, 2014

USAID, two representatives, identities confidential, 2014

Policy and Management Consulting Group (PMCG), Aleksi Aleksishvili, Chairman of the Board, 2015

Good Governance Initiative under the USAID contract (implementer Tetra Tech Ard), Marika Gorgadze, Governance Program Manager, 2015

Open Society Georgia Foundation, Vakhtang Natsvlishvili, Local Democracy Development Program Coordinator, 2015

Transparency International, Lika Sadjaia, Project Manager, Parliamentary Secretary, 2015

Georgian Young Lawyers Association, Sopho Tchareli, Parliamentary Secretary, 2015

# Appendix 2

## Individual interview guide

1) What type of management problems do you see today in the civil service?
   a) What type of management problems do you see in your agency?
   b) In your opinion, how should these problems be solved?

2) What type of problems do you see in the decision-making process?
   a) How much decentralized/centralized is the process?
   b) Do you see any problems in how authorities are delegated?
   c) Do you see any problems in how powers are distributed in your agency?
   d) What problems do you see in how powers are distributed among different agencies?

3) What type of problems do you see in organizational structure of your agency?

4) Does your organization have an official strategy?
   a) Are the employees familiar with the strategy?
   b) What are the mechanisms of making employees familiar with the strategy?
   c) Do you see any problems in how priorities are defined in your organization?
   d) Is this process participatory?
   e) Is the strategy implementation evaluated?
   f) Are the evaluation findings introduced to the employees?
   g) What mechanisms are used?
   h) Overall, how would you characterize the evaluation process?
   i) Do you see any problems in this regard?

5) Are there any internal procedures in regard with human resources management in your agency?
   a) What is the recruitment procedure like in your organization? How effective is it?
   b) Do you see any problems in how recruitment process is organized?
   c) What is the promotion procedure like? How effective is it?

d) Do you see any problems in how promotion process is organized?

6) Is there an ethics code in your organization?

7) Do you see any problems in regard with employees' professionalism and qualification?

   a) What kind of knowledge do the employees lack?

   b) What kinds of skills do the employees lack?

8) Do you see any problems in how employees are motivated?

9) Do you see any problems in how employees' work is evaluated?

10) Is there any performance evaluation system on place?

11) Do you see any problems in regard with further professional development of employees?

12) Do you see any other problems in regard with human resources management process?

## Appendix 3

### Group interview guide

*Before the interview begins, the facilitator explains to the respondents that their identity will remain confidential. No information will be published in the final report that makes possible identification of the focus group participants.*

*Regarding every issue and problem, the facilitator should ask the respondents to give an example, explain, and express their viewpoint.*

1) How would you describe the management style in public sector?
   - What are the problems that can be identified in this regard? Please, name.
   - Please, elaborate if such problems exist in your agency (without naming the agency).
   - How would you evaluate the changes in public sector (or your particular agency) related to the issues named above, during the last year? (The facilitator should especially stress the one-year period—which is of special interest for our research.)
   - In your opinion, how these problems could be solved?
2) Please describe decision-making process in public sector/your particular agency
   - How centralized/decentralized is the process?
   - Are regular public servants somehow involved in the process and on which stages?
   - Are there any problems in regard to delegating authority?
   - Can you elaborate on any changes in the decision-making process that have taken part during the last one year in public sector in general or in your agency in particular?
   - Has the degree of public servants' involvement in the process increased or decreased?
   - What is the best way out of this problem?
3) Do you observe any problems related to the separation of the competencies in your agency?

- What are specific problems related to the separation of functions and competencies?
- Can you elaborate on any changes in this regards that have taken part during the last year in public sector in general or in your agency in particular?
- How do you see solution of these problems? (If they see any problems.)

4) Are there any problems related to the organizational structure in public sector in general or your agency in particular?
   - Can you elaborate on any changes in this regards that have taken part during the last year in public sector in general or in your agency in particular?
   - How do you see solution of these problems? (If they see any problems.)

5) Is there any strategic planning process conducted in your agency? Does your agency have a strategic plan?
   - Do the regular employees at the agency know about it? Are they familiar with the plan?
   - What is the mechanism of informing the employees on the strategy?
   - How are the priorities set within the organization? What are the problems related to this process?
   - Can this process be described as participative?
   - How is the implementation of the strategy evaluated?
   - Are the results communicated to the employees? What are the tools used to inform the employees?
   - How would you describe the process of monitoring and evaluation in your agency?
   - What are the problems related to this process?
   - Can you elaborate on any changes in this regards that have taken part during the last year in public sector in general or in your agency in particular?
   - How do you see solution of these problems? (If they see any problems.)

6) Please describe the process of hiring new employees in your agency
   - How effective do you think it is?
   - Are there any problems related to the process of hiring?

- Are there any problems of nepotism or favoritism?
- Do you have any information regarding similar problems in other public agencies?
- Can you elaborate on any changes in this regards that have taken part during the last 1 year in public sector in general or in your agency in particular?
- How do you see solution of these problems? (If they see any problems.)

7) Please describe the promotion process in your agency
   - How effective do you think it is?
   - Are there any problems related to the promotion?
   - Are there any problems of nepotism or favoritism?
   - Do you have any information regarding similar problems in other public agencies?
   - Can you elaborate on any changes in this regard that have taken part during the last year in public sector in general or in your agency in particular?
   - How do you see solution of these problems? (If they see any problems.)

8) How well, in your opinion, are ethical issues regulated in public sector? (If you can recall any ethical issue here.)
   - Can you elaborate on any changes in this regard that have taken part during the last year in the public sector in general or in your agency in particular?
   - How do you see solution of these problems? (If they see any problems.)

9) How can you describe an issue of employees' qualification and level of professionalism in your agency?
   - Can you name deficit of specific knowledge?
   - Can you name deficit of specific skills?
   - Do you have any information regarding professionalism and qualification in other public agencies?
   - Can you elaborate on any changes in this regard that have taken place during the last year in the public sector in general or in your agency in particular?
   - How do you see solution of these problems? (If they see any problems.)

10) Which methods of employee motivation are used in your agency?

 - Are there any problems related to this issue? Please, elaborate.
 - Do you have any information regarding employees' motivation in other public agencies?
 - Can you elaborate on any changes in this regard that have taken place during the last year in public sector in general or in your agency in particular?
 - How do you see solution of these problems? (If they see any problems.)

11) How would you describe the performance evaluation system in your agency? Is there any formal evaluation system in your agency?

 - Are there any problems related to this issue? Please, elaborate.
 - Do you have any information regarding employees' motivation in other public agencies?
 - Can you elaborate on any changes in this regards that have taken part during the last year in public sector in general or in your agency in particular?
 - How do you see solution of these problems? (If they see any problems.)

12) What are the possibilities for professional development of public servants in your agencies?

 - Are there any problems related to this issue? Please, elaborate.
 - Do you have any information regarding employees' motivation in other public agencies?
 - Can you elaborate on any changes in this regard that have taken place during the last year in the public sector in general or in your agency in particular?
 - How do you see solution of these problems? (If they see any problems.)

13) What other problem can you name related to human resources management in the public sector in general and in your agency in particular?

# CHAPTER 2
# Tyranny of the Majority in Georgia: Can We Handle It?

**Tamar Koberidze**

## Introduction

One of the most prominent contributions of Alexis de Tocqueville is the claim that even a representative democracy can produce an "abuse" of power, which, in the absence of controlling independent associations, could turn a functioning of democracy into a "tyranny of the majority" (1835). According to de Tocqueville, even if all branches of the government seem democratic, underrepresented groups are still at risk of being subjected to "tyranny" (1835). Therefore, the presence of controlling independent organizations is key to avoiding the potential for oppression of those underrepresented groups.

The understanding of civil society as a "part of *society* that is distinct from the states and markets ... in which membership and activities are voluntary ... (is) the direct descendant of de Tocqueville's ideas" (Edwards 2004). Commonly referred to as the "third" or "non-profit" sector, civil society, by its essence, is a subset of democratic life.

It is widely accepted that, despite the fact that various forms of voluntary associations had existed in Central and Eastern Europe for hundreds of years, the intervening Soviet system hampered the establishment and development of civic society. After the collapse of the Soviet system, Georgia, like many post-Soviet countries, has seen a resurgence of associational life in the form of a community of non-governmental organizations (NGOs). These NGOs have been identified with and represent various facets of civil society. Despite its hiatus in the Soviet era, due to its deeper historical legacy, civic participation, in the form of civic activism, still plays a role in relations between government and society.

### *Georgian Civil Society's Influence on Government*

This research addresses the question of the degree of influence of civil society on government by analyzing the emergence, independence, and volunteer nature of Georgian civil society, as well as its role, through advocacy, in influencing government decisions to address community problems. This research describes the civic advocacy initiatives of approximately 30 civil society organizations, evaluating both the advocacy process and its outcomes. In addition, this research reveals various internal and external factors behind the success or failure of advocacy activities, and seeks to become a source for civil society organizations for analyzing advocacy challenges. Findings suggest that it is important to determine the state of civil society cooperation with the public sector, and identify flexible approaches and strategies that it is hoped will ultimately provide better tools for the establishment of democratic institutions.

## Methodology

### *Theoretical Basis*

Various global theoretical frameworks discuss the existence and maintenance of balance in society with regard to relations between citizens and the state. The most common theoretical analyses include the "tyranny of the majority," "open society," and "deliberative democracy" frameworks. The theoretical literature also elaborates on the origins of civil society, both in the West, and in post-Soviet environments, and on the differences that underline dissimilar actions of contemporary civil societies in different parts of the world. Special attention is given to inter-society relations, defined as Georgian social capital, and the outcomes of those relations with regard to public participation.

This research evaluates the importance of "localization" of public policies and analyzes the mechanisms and approaches used by society to influence them. The difference in behaviors of societies having different historical experiences is analyzed, highlighting a wide spectrum of civil society activism, such as street actions, civic monitoring, and participatory budgeting. Special focus is devoted to civic advocacy, as an active process through which citizens try to influence public policies or implement social change.

### *Technical Approach*

More than 20 sources of methodologies, guidance and tools (ORS 2007a, ORS 2007b, 2008; Sprechmann and Pelton 2011; ICNL 2013) for the evaluation and assessment of advocacy and political environment were examined and analyzed in the course of this research, resulting in one universal approach being developed to assess both, taking into consideration research needs. This review revealed that the process of civic advocacy and its outcomes are evaluated on four main dimensions: (1) advocacy capacity of the organization; (2) advocacy tactics; (3) funding sources of the campaign; and (4) advocacy campaign outcome (Figure 1). With regard to advocacy outcomes, in addition to specific changes in policy, contemporary sources underline a "shift in social norms", as part of social capital that is considered to be an imperative condition for a successful advocacy.

The main targets of the research are more than 20 Civil Society Organizations (CSOs) and initiative groups from the Tbilisi, Georgia region, selected based on formalized criteria. The research focuses on two CSOs operating within a defined mandate/public policy category, the first of which demonstrates how a CSO can struggle in reaching its intended outcome, and the second of which demonstrates how a CSO can succeed at enriching social capital. Information was collected through in-depth interviews, based on the above four-component framework.

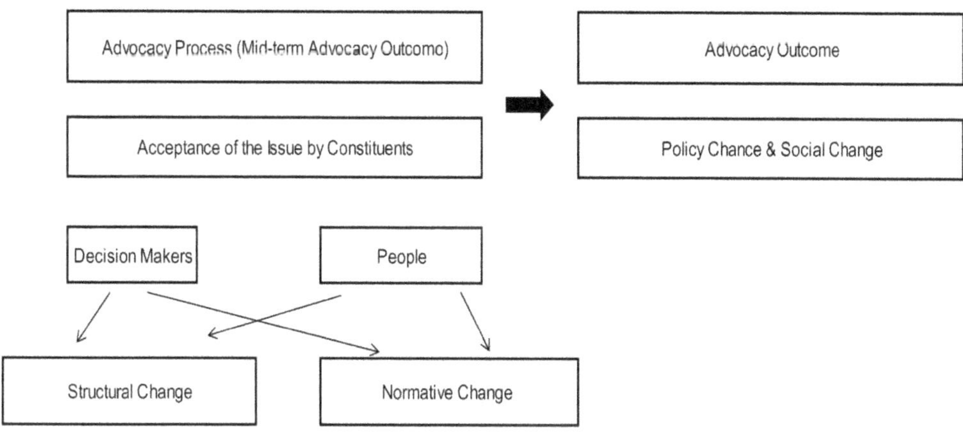


Figure 1. Dimensions for Assessing Civic Advocacy and Its Outcomes

## Institutionalized Associations Versus Oppositional Culture of Civic Life

In democratic countries, the widely accepted role and function of civil society is to maintain balance in the state, both on the national and local levels. The culture of volunteering and "active citizenry" has been in existence for centuries. The "active citizen," with a self-imposed sense of responsibility to contribute to public life, is considered to be an essential component of a well-functioning democratic system.

Various mechanisms of civic participation and engagement in governance have been widely practiced all over the world. Prevailing wisdom holds that some such mechanisms have long been an integral part of many nations' traditions and civic culture. Others have emerged in the post-Soviet context as a result of active promotion of the Western liberal model, through support for civil society development and pressures to liberalize the economy. After more than 20 years of Georgian independence, accompanied by general support from the international community, the question of whether civil society actually influences government decisions seems relevant.

Government–civil society relations are rather complex in Georgia, and perceptions of the sector are mixed. While publicly the importance of a civil society sector seems to be generally accepted, individual leaders active in civil society often become objects of criticism and accusation. There is an active distrust toward formal leaders and government officials among the population. Only 7% completely trusts the government, and 40% neither trusts nor distrusts it (CRRC 2013). According to an Asian Development Bank (ADB) report (2011), relations between CSOs and the government in Georgia are limited to information sharing, at most, and rarely extend further. A 2010 CIVICUS report, however, noted a more positive trend of broadening existing forms of dialogue between the government and citizens.

The majority of studies conclude that the enabling environment in Georgia for CSO's has remained generally favorable for years. Legislative procedures regulating the registration of CSOs are simple, and the political and institutional framework for enhancing the role for CSOs in public policy dialogue is, in general, supportive. No cases have been reported of CSOs being denied registration for arbitrary or political reasons. Equally, there are no direct administrative impediments to CSO operations in Georgia, and no controversial cases of state harassment were reported during the period of 1998–2015.

For the CSOs' financial sustainability, Georgian legislation allows for carrying out commercial activity, but it is subject to taxation, similar to any other business. Perhaps because the legal incentives for philanthropy are insufficient, the private sector has shown no interest in supporting CSO initiatives, and direct donations from businesses remain rare. In addition, a "membership fee" mechanism does not work. Charity from individuals and corporations has not yet become an important source of CSO revenue. Overall, the CSOs hardly depend on donor assistance.

It seems that despite the minor shortcomings with the legislation, mainly with regard to state initiatives facilitating business contributions, there are no impediments to public participation. Taking into consideration that some donors do offer multi-year assistance to the civil society sector, the question of what is challenging their success remains unanswered.

The classical Tocquevillian theory of the "active citizen," who demands and protects his or her own interests, for the most part, has been developed in Europe and the United States. Therefore, a series of assumptions is made about the rights, responsibilities, roles, and characteristics of active citizens, as a composite of civil society, who are supposed to act collectively, form well-institutionalized associations, and make change in a mode that has been "approved" by the Westernized neo-Tocquevillian actors (Seligman 1992).

To understand the norms, nature, and outcomes of participation, however, requires a closer look into the historical prerequisites and traditions of civic action for a particular community. Different cultures think differently about belonging, solidarity and citizenship, and therefore act in accordance to their long-held beliefs.

Georgia, like many other post-Communist countries, has only begun using the term 'civil society' relatively recently. Prevailing wisdom holds that communism wiped out traditional civil societies and turned them into populations that can neither contribute to democracy and markets, nor block authoritarian decisions (Ekiert and Kubik 2014). The locally registered CSOs, with financial and technical backing from the West for civil society development, have become synonymous with civil society themselves. This de facto monopolization of the civil society discourse has left wider society and other non-institutional forms of citizen engagement behind (Ekiert and Kubik 2014). In between the "active citizens" protesting on the streets and Western-supported local CSOs are media, political parties, faith-based organizations, trade unions, and other segments of civil society, which have been attributed to the sector by the academics or civil society experts, at most. Some authors also outline that the Westernized top-down approach, initiated in 1990s to make CSOs active in influencing the state, is reflected in the fact that the activities of the former do not connect with citizens' demands.

Criticism of CSOs is widespread. International polls and cross-national surveys, such as USAID's NGO Sustainability Index, the World Values Survey, and other cross-European attitude polls, characterize Georgian civil society as weak and fragmented, lacking cooperation, and poorly known by the beneficiary communities. Reports state that only a few CSOs "have the capacity to conduct professional, rigorous policy analysis of complex issues and to advocate for change based on research" (ADB 2011). Many authors argue that despite continuous financial and institutional support of international donors, civil society cannot carry out its duties. Such reports also outline that despite institutional strengthening and improved public image, as well as certain successes in affecting public policies, the sector has developed an "elite" segment, which is distanced from the real problems and needs of the people. Trust in the sector is low and, therefore, CSOs cannot provide a platform for large-scale public participation (CIVICUS, CIPPD & CSI 2010; USAID 2014, WVS 2002, 2014). It has also been noted that advocacy initiatives are most often successful when backed by international donors, and they tend to be more effective at the local government level.

While not putting under question the professionalism or intentions of those assessments, the current work challenges a number of issues, such as the essence of civil society and its participation, ability to conduct policy analyses, and the nature or inevitability of donor backing for advocacy success.

The term "advocacy" itself, as a broad definition for actions undertaken by civil society to influence a country's political processes or social change, has also been introduced in Georgia only relatively recently, since the beginning of the twenty-first century. Meanwhile, development assistance has gradually transferred into advocacy projects, broadening the scope of the former and upgrading it to the public policy influence level (donor–civil society–government–people).

According to USAID data, a total of 18,733 non-profit organizations were registered in Georgia as of mid-December 2013. The Civil Registry data as of June 2015 shows that the number increased to 21,097, but according to various assessments, only 10%–15% of the registered organizations were operational. The number of Tbilisi-based CSOs was twice as big as that in the Georgian regions (Tbilisi makes up about 30% of the country's whole population, excluding the autonomous Region of Abkhazia and South Ossetia Region) (Nodia 2005). The majority of CSOs claim to have a broad scope of activities, identified by their charters. Grants from foreign foundations are the main source of funding, while charitable contributions from Georgian businesses are scarce and rather sporadic. Until recently, both Tbilisi-based and regional organizations would address nation-wide issues, such as awareness raising, democratization, human rights, and social security, and the only difference between them was the geographical location of the particular project's beneficiaries. Organizational capacity and experience has been carefully analyzed, and funding almost certainly goes to the best/strongest organizations, which most of the time are located in the Tbilisi capital or other bigger cities. Donors' attention has gradually shifted from nation-wide initiatives to activities of a lower scale, targeting smaller communities and/or local governments. Therefore, the funding of Tbilisi-based CSOs has drastically decreased in favor of those operating in the regions, having in mind that the leading aim of civil society is to support and encourage the formation of strong public demand at the local level.

An exact list of donor organizations that provide funding to Georgian CSOs is not available. Nor is there accurate information on the amount of funding that goes directly to local CSOs. One can make only approximate calculations, such as with USAID's substantial civil society development initiative of 2010–2014. USAID's USD 13 million, 4-year *Policy, Advocacy, and Civil Society Development* project in Georgia was charged with the task of providing grants and technical assistance to think tanks and advocacy organizations in Georgia, with almost 90% of the assistance going to CSOs targeting local needs. (The next 5-year USAID Civil Society Development project started at the end of 2014 and was worth USD 5 million.)

It has been widely discussed that an excess amount of funding and other benefits enjoyed by CSOs causes: (a) the establishment of a so-called non-governmental elite; and (b) the alienation of CSOs from the real problems of society. This might mean that CSOs do not actually represent civil society, or that "non-profitable, non-commercial legal entities" (the official legal status of NGO/CSOs in Georgia) are, in fact, not civil society at all. Alternatively, multi-year investments, education, activation, and assessments of citizen activities should have paid some dividends, which might urge us to get out of the frame and look into the "unity of active citizens" in Georgia, as an integral part of the civil society and its work.

CIVICUS: World Alliance for Civic Participation defines civil society as "the arena, outside of the family, the state, and the market, which is created by individual and collective actions, organizations and institutions to advance shared interests" (2010). Therefore, while elaborating on concepts such as democracy, participation, freedom of speech, rule of law, and, most importantly, policy influence, why not look into civic activism, which has its reasons, and roots in Georgia.

It should be noted, however, that civil society in Georgia was not built from scratch. Some authors trace the existence of some rudimentary form of civil society back to the medieval period, to the activities of artisan and merchant guilds in Tbilisi, which facilitated a relatively high level of public participation as late as the nineteenth century (Tevzadze, cited in Nodia 2005). The initial modern civil society organizations, emerging at the end of the nineteenth century, were mainly cultural and educational, and had strong potential for development. Unfortunately, after the invasion of Georgia by Soviet Russia in 1921, the subsequent totalitarian system left little room for the development of private initiatives for the common good. Various so-called "civil" organizations in existence during Soviet times in reality represented only imitations of civil society organizations and were completely controlled by the state. During the last years of the Soviet era, from 1960 and through the Georgian declaration of independence in 1991, the country experienced multiple forms of civic activism, such as dissident movements inspired by national independence ideas, and a number of public protest campaigns targeting political/public policy issues. The core motivation for all of these was mobilizing mass opposition against the Soviet regime. Therefore, initiatives were "local" by their nature, targeting "local issues," but the decision-makers were far removed from the political process. The legacy of street actions, such as massive calls in 1978 for retaining Georgian as the state language in the Constitution of the Soviet Union, or environmental protection protests against the construction of the Khudoni power station at the end of 1980, has affected behavioral models of Georgian society. Notwithstanding 25 years of institutionalized assistance from the West for civil society development, and the accompanying resources available to the Georgian population for their initiatives, such street protests still clearly played a critical role in influencing policies.

## Civil Activism and Social Capital

As in many countries of the "Soviet Bloc," civic activism in Georgia was often associated with burning tires and blocking streets. Nevertheless, the concept also encompasses creative and sarcastic activities designed to draw attention to issues. Even when having no desire of achieving consensus, creative activities still convince and/or inform the public, garner popular support, and put pressure on particular stakeholders. Therefore, civic activism can be illegal or violent, but also positive, legal and non-violent. Despite the fact that civic activism in Georgia is often confrontational, violence tends to be absent. Recent history, of massive protest during the Rose Revolution in 2013, or against violations of human rights in 2007–2012, has demonstrated that while protesting, Georgian citizens do not break shop windows, ruin neighborhoods, or burn buildings or cars, and do not maraud. Furthermore, street protests often represent a public platform, where people meet, socialize, and have fun.

Despite the fact that civil activism in the form of street action might not be considered the most effective way of promoting liberal ideas (except perhaps in the case of women's or LGBT rights), Georgia's civil society sector has consistently increased using civic activism as a mechanism for involving the population in policy advocacy efforts.

### *Can we attribute the peculiarities of civic activism in Georgia to cultural factors, like social capital?*

It is widely accepted that in the process of development, social capital acts as a critical support for successful democracy. It is also known that collaboration among individuals across society brings mutual benefits, which are linked to economic prosperity, better education, safer neighborhoods, and overall, to better democracy.

Nevertheless, when it comes to the definition of social capital, there is no general agreement as to what it is. Sociologist James Colman defines it as "people's ability to work together in groups" (cited in Fukuyama 2002), while Francis Fukuyama refers to "shared norms or values that promote social cooperation, instantiated in actual social relationships." Some authors also note that social capital is still present, even if a collective identity of people is absent, if there are ties, based on mutual trust and mutual recognition among the actors involved in the relationship (Diani 1997). Many argue that pre-existing social networks, also known as developed social capital, facilitates collective action, such as social movements.

Commentators often characterize Georgian social capital as bonding. According to the Caucasus Research Resource Center's (CRRC, a non-governmental, non-profit research organization that collects, analyzes and publishes policy relevant data on social, economic, and political trends in the South Caucasus) assessment of social capital, the country exhibits strong in-group social networks, which, however, rarely formalize and institutionalize their collaboration. At the same time, the assessment highlights Georgians' generosity in their solidarity with each other, often putting the needs of others before their own. According to a 2011 survey, 27% of Georgians trust their neighborhood completely, while a further 65% trust it a little; a mere 1% of Georgians has no trust in their local community. At the same time, the 2008 World Values Survey found that only 18% of Georgians said that most people can be trusted, while 82% said that "you cannot be too careful" when dealing with other people (in contrast to countries like Switzerland, where 54% felt that most people could be trusted, or Norway and Sweden, where it is more than 65%). The CRRC assessment stated, however, that there were clear signs that some formal or informal associations, such as business lobbying groups or professional unions, were beginning to collaborate effectively. Also, the Caucasus Barometer of 2013 shows that 50% of the total population helped a neighbor or friend with household chores during the last 6 months.

In evaluating linkages between social movements and social capital, Mario Diani, a professor of Sociology at the University of Trento, reverses the condition-impact approach of "social network-social movement" and develops a new paradigm, according to which "social movements create new linkages to prospective supporters, the general public, and elites"(Diani 1997), thereby producing social capital.

Social movements, as a type of group action by "individuals, groups and/or organizations, engaged in a political or cultural conflict" (Diani 1992) can be equated with civic activism, as an intentional action to bring about social, political, economic, or environmental change (TACSO 2011).

Despite the fact that the direct effect of civic activism on social change is quite difficult to assess, it seems clear that it influences individuals by informing, educating, and affecting their decisions. Civic activists influence their micro-networks, and their individual decisions return back to a wider network of citizens, who make further efforts to influence policies.

Of the 3.7 million people in the Georgian population, half are ready to provide help in case of a "crisis" (CRRC 2011). This predisposition, in combination with historical traditions of street (civic) activism, could well outweigh a low level of trust in society. In the case of Georgia, it seems the classic definition of undeveloped social capital being directly linked to an inability to make change is not borne out. The missing link could be a participation mechanism that is more "acceptable" for this particular culture and society, creating a unique version of social capital that motivates the drive for participation.

Bearing in mind the historical and cultural characteristics of Georgia, the following two cases illustrate different approaches to and results of civic advocacy. The first example represents the donor-funded advocacy initiative of the CSOs outside the Tbilisi capital, while the second focuses on the activities of an initiative group in Tbilisi. Though having limited capacity for generalization, the two cases represent true stories and provide illustrative examples of Georgian civil society.

## Case 1: Advocacy for Social Change

The Georgian CSO, Association for Civic Culture (ACC – a pseudonym to protect the organization's confidentiality), operating in a municipality of the Kahketi region of Georgia (population 409,551) was established in 1998 as one of the first independent, nonprofit, and nongovernmental organizations of the municipalities of the Kakheti Region. The goal of CSOs in general is to improve transparency and accountability of local government bodies in the Georgian regions, with the aim of insuring social protection of the local population. ACC serves as a mediator between the local government and population; promotes the public interest; facilitates the process of promoting civic culture; and implements civic initiatives, based on local demand. ACC is a membership-based organization of 17 members, governed by a board, and employs seven full-time and two part time staff members, and three volunteers. One hundred percent of its funding is provided by international donors, such as The Netherlands Organisation for International Assistance (NOVIB), European Endowment for Democracy (EED), European Union (EU), Eurasia Partnership Foundation (EPF), and United States Agency for International Development (USAID). Therefore, it is considered to be a trusted and "low risk grantee" by the donors.

The projects implemented in 2008–2014 included various activities aimed at social protection of vulnerable populations in Georgian regions, through advocating for policies and maintaining rule of law. The CSO often partnered with other civil society organizations operating in different Georgian municipalities and villages. The total budget for 2008–2012 was about USD 160,000.

In 2012, with financial assistance provided by USAID's implementing partner, ACC undertook a 10-month civic advocacy project aimed at development and adoption of social programs for three (out of eight) Khakheti Municipalities with a population of about 200,000 people. By the time of the project implementation, more than three million Georgian Lari (About USD 2 million, as of 2012) had been allocated in the local budgets of the eight Khaketi municipalities to provide social assistance to vulnerable populations of the region. None of the municipalities, however, had developed or adopted any social assistance program, or set criteria for selection of vulnerable populations.

During the project, ACC carried out a survey to identify and select 30 socially vulnerable people throughout the three targeted municipalities, and provided human rights and advocacy training to them to involve beneficiaries in the process of developing social policy and advocacy campaigns. The developed action plan for policy influence included mapping of decision-makers, consultations, and meetings with various stakeholders, and a media campaign though local media outlets. ACC participated in the local Sakrebulo (Municipality Council) meetings and advocated for the development of social protection programs. As a result of the successful advocacy campaign, the local governments of the three municipalities developed and adopted social programs reflecting public opinion and expert suggestions. The campaign also enabled the CSO to participate in the development of criteria for identifying vulnerable individuals and detailed instructions for enforcement of regulations. One of the main achievements of the campaign was the regulation that enabled inclusion of two representatives from the beneficiary community into the commissions that were responsible for allocation of one-time social assistance.

**Evaluation 1** (undertaken through the support provided by the USAID G-PAC Project, implemented by the East West Management Institute (EWMI):

In 2013, with the participation of local community representatives, a focus group was invited to consider the project's impact on advocacy and the activities of the CSO, beyond its immediate results. The focus group included 11 local community representatives from the 3 Kahketi municipalities where the project was implemented. Variation sampling involved diverse citizens groups, representative of individuals of various genders, ages, and professions. Group members were given 1 hour to read the reports/proposals and fill in the evaluation form before starting the discussion.

The evaluation revealed that the majority of the focus group members were aware of the simplified process of applying for and getting one-time social assistance, but they had little or no knowledge of the targeted activities of ACC and would have credited local governments for the new policy before they had read the proposal during the meeting.

The majority of respondents, however, recalled that the time period when information on the availability of one-time social assistance became available had coincided with the project time-line. They also admitted that the process of selecting social assistance beneficiaries had become transparent and efficient, and that, to the best of their knowledge, all the recipients had really deserved the assistance.

Four out of 11 focus group members (3 from Lagodekhi, the director's home municipality, and 1 student from Telavi) were familiar with both the CSO, and its director. An additional six were familiar with and/or had heard about the director only. Only one focus group member had not heard anything about either the CSO or its director. Therefore, the capacity of the organization was not possible to assess.

The three focus group members from the Director's home city had better knowledge of the project, as did one student from Telavi, who was apparently involved in networking activities implemented by the CSO. The majority of the focus group members from the two other municipalities had heard about the activities described in the proposal, but did not know that they were implemented by that particular CSO. Two had heard about the training component only. Only one member (from Lagodekhi municipality, the home city) was able to name a particular organization with which GCDA had cooperated, and had seen the project publications.

Overall, after reading the project documents, the majority of the focus group members assessed the project as survey-based activities that provided a unique opportunity to socially vulnerable populations to become aware of their rights and mechanisms to get social assistance, as well as to improve the transparency of local government; they also expressed the view that the organization had a qualified staff to implement projects of concern.

What could be done better? The focus group members unanimously stated that projects like this have to involve more people with regard to information sharing, awareness, and beneficiaries.

## Case 2: A Local Initiative to Protect Cultural Heritage

A group of Tbilisi-based activists united in 2005 under the title Tfilisi Hamkari to protect and preserve Tbilisi's unique, authentic urban environment and cultural heritage. Their mission goes beyond just protecting cultural heritage and aims at development and modernization with respect to historical and cultural values, in accordance with enacted legislation based on European standards.

The organization united Tbilisi residents by their love for the city. Despite the fact that the first international funding did not come until 2010, Tfilisi Hamkari managed to successfully implement cultural education programs aimed at raising awareness of the city's history and cultural heritage among the broader public, including the library program, a series of multimedia publications about events, people, and buildings throughout Tbilisi history. Though various approaches of the campaign, such as face-to-face meetings and negotiations with the authorities, and even cases filed against the Ministry of Culture of Georgia, the population of Tbilisi became aware of the activities of the organization through street protests, open air exhibitions, rallies, street artistic expressions and other entertaining events. In 2010–2014 the total budget, accumulated through donors' support, was about USD 100,000. Today, the organization continues to operate largely on local donations of time, labor, and money.

The primary goal of the Public Monitoring and Advocacy Program, implemented by the organization in 2011–2014, was to make municipal authorities of Tbilisi more accountable and the decision-making process concerning urban development and heritage management more transparent. The major component of the program was street protests against the destruction of Gudiashvili Square, as a part of the Tbilisi government's campaign to "clean up" the city to attract investors. The "victims" of the modernization plan had already become many architecturally important buildings of Tbilisi. Gudiashvili square and its neighboring street are one of the most vivid examples of the cultural heritage assemblages of buildings in the historic Sololaki district of Tbilisi. It completely maintains its Old Tbilisi appearance. Around the square there are 11 buildings, 9 of which have historical monument status.

Hamraki publicly criticized the Tbilisi Development Fund and its management's activities, and implemented a wide-range advocacy campaign, urging the government to stop the destruction of the buildings and start reinforcing and restoring them. Advocacy activities included about 50 peaceful protests and public rallies under the slogans "Manifest as Manifest" and "Occupy Gudiashvili," street exhibitions, art actions, a short documentary about the importance of cultural heritage and civic advocacy efforts, and various one-on-one and public meetings with City government officials. Word of the campaign and its goals spread widely in the city, and gathered considerable media attention. Initiative group representatives became frequent guests of the major Georgian media sources.

Finally, in May 2012, Hamkari's efforts resulted in the denying of approval of the controversial construction plan by city officials and the construction permit was not issued. The square's radical redevelopment had stopped, thanks to public pressure and the exposure of alleged corruption within the Tbilisi Development Fund. The rehabilitation work necessary for maintenance of the square, was delayed, however.

In its continuous efforts, the CSO developed policy recommendations, which reflected the gaps in the relevant legislation and concrete advice for institutionalizing the rehabilitation/restoration process for all the responsible parties of the City and the National Government. Also, in anticipation of the Local Government elections of 2013, the CSO held meetings with political parties, and signed Memoranda of Cooperation to protect the square and implement the policy with the Tbilisi mayoral candidates.

After the elections and shift in the Municipal Development Fund management, the square development process became a priority. The City government took into consideration the policy proposal by Hamraki and acted in compliance with the legislation. As of this writing in 2016, the square and its surrounding area's conservation and development planning process is in an active phase, in cooperation with the Hamkari, professional architects and other specialists in the field.

**Evaluation 2** (Conducted through the support provided by Shota Rustaveli National Science Foundation within the framework of the PHD grant):

In the spring of 2016, a focus group with the participation of 13 Tbilisi citizens was organized to evaluate Gudiashvili project awareness and attitudes toward cultural heritage protection versus economic growth, and to get a better understanding of general advocacy activities of Hamkari. The participants, from nine (central and remote) Tbilisi districts, were selected through variation sampling, involving various gender, age, profession, employment, and sector of activities.

The evaluation revealed that more than half of the focus group members had a general awareness of the problems associated with Gudiashvili Square, and the majority had heard about the "concerts" and "exhibitions" organized in the square. In fact, three people from the focus group had actually taken part. One of those who had participated admitted that he had not known what the event was about, but had just joined friends for the visiting exhibition, and become aware of advocacy only upon arrival. The "Gudiashvii" participants were able to name all three of the leaders of Hamkari and identified "cultural heritage protection" as a major focus of the organization. Only two participants, however, were aware of the new target of Hamkari—the Panorama project, and just one out of those two could recall Hamkari's mainstream Old City Tours.

Overall capacity of the organization was assessed positively, mainly due to the fact that Hamkari managed to gather crowds of people, host creative and interesting events, and had the ability to mobilize media.

In response to the question of what was more important, to protect the old city of Tbilisi and cultural heritage, or to support construction investments, the majority of the respondents chose protection. One women living in the old town, however, noted that while she understood what cultural heritage stands for, she would nonetheless appreciate investors' help in achieving decent living conditions. All respondents confirm that the state has to have a policy and strategy on both—cultural heritage preservation and social benefits for improving living conditions of old city residents. In addition, they expressed the view that none of the construction should satisfy investors' interest only, but should be part of the common development strategy. The majority of respondents also negatively linked construction projects with the deterioration of greenery in the Tbilisi capital.

None of the participants were aware on the policy achievements of Hamkari, but assumed that Hamkari had won, because street actions to protect Gudiashvili Square have stopped. Also, two participants had heard about preservation/rehabilitation works announced by the Tbilisi Municipality.

The focus group members unanimously stated that in the advocacy process it is important to act creatively, widely disseminate information, and utilize various media sources in order to mobilize and gather people. They also stressed the importance of organizing open-air events for attracting attention.

## Can We Handle It?

The answer to the question of whether independent associations in Georgia can prevent or eliminate an "abuse" of power by the majority is complex and multi-dimensional.

Discussions on CSO-Government relations and the level of CSO influence on policies often underline the role of the government in supporting and facilitating public participation. At the same time, many commentators discuss the idea that weak governmental institutions are unable to empower populations, which is known to be true for the developing democracies. As Fukuyama outlines, not every society is capable of building state bureaucracies that are "equal in terms of efficiency, transparency, and professionalism". According to Fukuyama, it is the relationship between culture and institutions that is critical, since institution building itself requires social capital (Fukuyama 2002).

Many believe that strengthening civil society in Georgia will strengthen influence on the government and, therefore, democracy. These *strengthening efforts* often mean *donors supporting CSOs institutionally and providing funding for implementing projects*. This approach is a commonly accepted, westernized way of influencing society. The same Westernized theories imply that strong civil society will contribute to improving social capital.

The degree of access that civil society has to the policy-making process, defined as the "constitution of public space," is an important factor for differentiation of civil societies in different countries (Ekiert and Kubik 2014). States are responsible for defining this public space through making, or failing to create, relevant laws, institutions, and policies that empower civil society organizations.

This Georgian example of a relatively friendly and supportive enabling environment for

CSOs, with agreed upon mechanisms for civil society participation in the absence of institutionalized pressure from government authorities, raises the question of why the expected influence is not tangible. The answer shifts toward the people, in whose interest it is to participate for making change. Perhaps it is fair to say, however, that the problem resides on both sides of the equation, as the government represents the people and their history, attitudes and values, which also make up society as a whole.

Again, Fukuyama admits the possibility of institutions being changed, but outlines that cultural values are much more difficult to manage, manipulate, or direct through policies. Therefore, appeal to cultural factors often seems hopeless.

The context of westernized CSOs implies intervening for positive change at every level of Georgian society. This also relates to policy advocacy, which has been considered a duty of CSOs and requires utilization of advocacy leverage to affect three main areas: (a) policy change, (b) social change, and (c) shifts in social norms. Such leverage is variously defined in analytical papers and practical evaluations, which qualify policy advocacy as "lobbying" (Labonte and Hancock, cited in DeSantis 2010), an "attempt to affect institutional elites" (Jenkins, cited in Kimberlin 2010), or "informational exchange" (Rektor, cited in DeSantis 2010). In the twenty-first century, these and other theories for civic participation can be summed up in one "theory of change." Therefore, donor-suggested (through training and grant application forms) leverage for advocacy involves a wide spectrum of civic participation activities and includes many activities aimed at affecting decisions within political, economic, and social systems.

Mentioned activities include policy issue identification and analyses, development of advocacy strategy, surveys, mapping of and cooperation with decision-makers, development of alternative policies, beneficiary identification, and lobbying. All these mechanisms aim at improvement of policy or social conditions to be implemented solely by CSOs, without qualified involvement of the beneficiaries. Nevertheless, the contemporary concept of advocacy implies that advocacy, as a political process, shall primarily be oriented at changing attitudes toward particular issues (i.e. changing cultural and social norms) and activating structural (networks of collective action) and cognitive (trust and values) elements of society (i.e. social capital).

The above examples of civic participation demonstrate the difficulties associated with manipulation of cultural values, but nevertheless highlight the importance of appealing to cultural factors, replacing evaluation mechanisms, or finding different approaches for community development tailored to particular cultures.

The advocacy examples provided here have a lot of similarities: both illustrate civic advocacy initiatives aimed at a policy change at the local level; both were funded by international donors; and both affected local policies, and are therefore considered to be examples of successful policy advocacy.

Nevertheless, they are different by their nature. Though ACC achieved its stated goal, the evaluation shows that neither beneficiaries, nor wider constituents were part of an advocacy process. In addition, neither the CSO (established in 1998), nor its activities were known by target community representatives. That might not be that important for social change, as it is, but definitely does not contribute to the building of trust toward CSOs (aka civil society) nor, therefore, to improved social capital.

In contract to ACC, and despite the fact that the Tiflisis Hamkari is based in Georgia's capital, it does not represent typical elite-type, non-governmental organizations. Hamraki, as an initiative group (established in 2005) was working without any donor funding for 4 years. Nevertheless, the group had become known through its street rallies and thus gained notoriety, demonstrated by donor support, which such institutionally weak organizations almost never receive. It is also worth mentioning that donors targeting civil society development almost never support cultural heritage protection mandates.

In addition, Hamkari permanently monitors the status of cultural heritage in Tbilisi; its initiatives are not limited to one particular project and are not finished at the date of project completion. Therefore, it can be said that their advocacy activities achieve better results, not only in terms of policies, but also in terms of shifting social norms, as an imperative condition for successful advocacy. The activities of the organization are considered to be successful both by the donors and the wider community. The project is included in the donor's "success stories" booklet and, at the same time, a shift in the social norms of the targeted community is obvious. According to International Republican Institute (IRI) polls (2015), 41% of Tbilisi residents disapprove (as opposed to 32% who approve) of implementation of the Panorama Tbilisi project, another contentious construction initiative for the Old City of Tbilisi, which is a new advocacy target for Hamkari. This USD 7 million investment project is widely promoted by the Tbilisi Local Government as an "economic driver" for the city.

The two cases outlined in this study enable an in-depth look at Georgian civil society. They also show that political environment, donor support, institutional attributes, the significance of the issue to wider constituents, exhaustive knowledge of policies, and a rigorous approach to analyses, are all significant variables in terms of advocacy impact.

Policy advocacy, as a tool, provides various opportunities for the engagement of wider society. It also supports "open air" activities, despite the fact that it requires some knowledge of existing legal rules and regulations, facts and figures, and awareness of the interests of opposing parties. It is clear that certain ways of expression of Georgians, such as civic activism in the form of writing "protest letters" to politicians, political campaigns, boycotts, street rallies, creative actions, and other street-as public space utilizations, have much overlap with the forms and approaches of defined civic advocacy.

Despite the low level of trust in society in general, the Georgian neighborhood often serves as a proper ground for local initiatives, which means utilizing existing social capital, based on the society's traditions and values. During a "crisis" Georgians pull together and naturally collaborate, while various attempts by donors to support such collaboration have yielded uneven success. Therefore, national and local level protest-event analyses and case studies provide a more precise picture of successful advocacy, and subsequent policy impacts and shifts in social norms.

In addition to participation mechanisms tailored to cultural traditions, motivation is an important factor, which (probably intuitively) urges united individuals to utilize more "acceptable" and "people-friendly" initiatives to affect policies. Motive for involvement in civic advocacy is closely related to the identification of needs, gaps, and shortages within society, and awareness of "prospective better". Many civil society organizations in Georgia admit that the initial desire to form the organization or implement civic advocacy was closely linked to donors' development strategy or particular calls. Many were established by professionals who knew of policy deficits within certain sectors of concern, but did not have any particular knowledge or plan on how to influence them.

The above examples show that in Georgia, successful policy change by CSOs is possible through expert involvement and lobbying, and that such change does not necessarily require education, capacity improvement or the involvement of beneficiaries, public mobilization, or encouragement of collective action. Nevertheless, there are positive examples of civic advocacy initiatives that bring both policy change and shifts in social norms being implemented by citizens as the primary motivator. The networks might be ties in the community, where strongly motivated individuals "call" everyone they know, which also contributes to increased knowledge, information, trust, and, therefore, better actions to improve policies.

Therefore, evaluating the strength of civil society in Georgia and the level of government control requires more than just assessment of donor-facilitated initiatives in terms of sustainable social change or shifting social norms. It requires more than counting the number of organizations per capita or recording what people say in response to survey questions. Evaluation of independent associations requires paying attention to all forms of civic initiatives and actions by active individuals, who may hardly fit the Westernized definition of civil society, to understand their motives for involvement in political and public life.

## Implications for Future Research and Practice

Strengthening influence on the government requires supporting and strengthening civic activism. Importantly, the Georgian case reveals it is important to get the fundamentals right in the early stages of CSO formation. Scholars and aid organizations have suggested CSO activity is hindered by weak communication, working in isolation, limited cultural understanding, and, most importantly, an incentive structure and motivation that benefits the CSO's leadership more than the local community (WVS 2004; Nodia 2005; CIVICUS, CIPPD & CSI 2010; USAID 2014).

This study revealed that overcoming these obstacles requires assessing the cultural context, engaging policymakers early in the process, working with community partners, and communicating with interested parties. Importantly, when the CSO acts alone, does not have consensus, or has an incentive structure supporting ulterior motives, its initiatives can end up being counterproductive. Yet, when the fundamentals of communication, community involvement, and incentives are structured properly in the formative stages, the CSOs can contribute to enriching social capital, and ultimately, strengthening democracy.

While this study showed communication and motives are two of the most important variables in this process, future research on the topic may require broadening the definition of Georgian civil society. If civil society is defined by CSOs only, then their potential for impact is questionable. But if civil society includes active individuals and devoted initiative groups whose activities encompass popular traditions, the results may be much more promising. There is no doubt that the issues faced by the Georgian people can not be resolved without society's active engagement, namely civic activism. Despite the mediator role of CSOs between the public and government being legitimate, their statements and admonitions for change will hardly bring any tangible and sustainable results without the raised voices of the wider society.

When the term "advocacy" was introduced by international organizations back in 2003, donor-supported projects mainly addressed civic education, community mobilization, and civic monitoring issues, and to a certain extent, aimed at public policy for making positive social change. Over the years, donor assistance shifted toward supporting the civil society sector's role in policy advocacy. The more civil society organizations get involved in advocacy initiatives, the more it is possible to evaluate the outcomes and effects of their work. A shift in social norms is perhaps even more important than policy change, as such norms are critical in creating the context for sustainable policies, and overall democratic growth. The research results discussed here should be of interest to international donors operating in Georgia from the perspective of evaluating the sustainability and success of multi-year interventions. Future researchers should look at the impacts of civil society on the public sector and the development of social capital for positive political and social change.

## References

Asian Development Bank. 2011. *Civil Society Briefs; Georgia*. http://www.adb.org/sites/default/files/publication/29305/csb-geo.pdf (accessed December 14, 2016).

Caucasus Research Resource Center (CRRC). 2013. *Caucasus Barometer 2013 Georgia*. http://caucasusbarometer.org/en/cb2013ge/codebook/ (accessed December 14, 2016).

Caucasus Research Resource Centers (CRRC). 2011. *Assessment of Social Capital in Georgia*. http://www.crrccenters.org/20547/Assessment-of-Social-Capital-in-Georgia (accessed December 14, 2016).

CIVICUS, CIPDD & CSI. 2010. *An Assessment of Georgian Civil Society; Report of the CIVICUS Civil Society Index*. http://www.civicus.org/downloads/CSI/Georgia.pdf (accessed August 3, 2015).

DeSantis, Gloria. 2010. "Voices from the Margins: Policy and Marginalized Communities." *Canadian Journal of Nonprofit and Social Economy Research* Fall 1 (1): 23–45.

De Tocqueville, Alexis. 2010. *Democracy in America: Historical-Critical Edition of De la Démocratie en Amérique,* Eduardo Nola, Editor, translated from the French by James T. Schleifer. Indianapolis: Liberty Fund. http://oll.libertyfund.org/titles/tocqueville-democracy-in-america-historical-critical-edition-4-vols-lf-ed-2010 (accessed May 1, 2015).

Diani, Mario. 1992. "The Concept of Social Movement." *The Sociological Review* 40 (1): 1-25. http://onlinelibrary.wiley.com/wol1/doi/10.1111/j.1467-954X.1992.tb02943.x/abstract (accessed August 2, 2015).

Diani, Mario. 1997. "Social Movements and Social Capital: A Network Perspective on Movement Outcomes." *Mobilization: An International Quarterly* 2 (2): 129–147.

Edwards, Michael. 2004. *Civil Society*. Cambridge: Polity Press.

Ekiert, Grzegorz, and Jan Kubik. 2014. "Myths and Realities of Civil Society." *Journal of Democracy*, January 25 (1): 46-58.

Fukuyama, Francis. 2002. "Social Capital and Development. The Coming Agenda." *SAIS Review of International Affairs* 22 (1): 23–37.

International Center for Non-for-Profit Law (ICNL). 2013. "Assessment Tools for Measuring Civil Society's Enabling Environment." *Global Trends in NGO Law: A Quarterly Review of NGO Legal Trends around the World* 4 (3). http://www.icnl.org/research/trends/trends5-1.pdf (accessed August 3, 2015).

International Republican Institute (IRI). 2015. *Public Opinion Survey of Residents of Georgia: February 3-28, 2015*. http://www.iri.org/sites/default/files/wysiwyg/iri_georgia_

public_2015_final_0.pdf (accessed December 14, 2016).

Kimberlin, Sara E. 2010. "Advocacy by Nonprofits: Roles and Practices of Core Advocacy Organizations and Direct Service Agencies." *Journal of Policy Practice* 9: 164–182. DOI: 10.1080/15588742.2010.487249

Nodia, Ghia. 2005. *Civil Society Development in Georgia: Achievements and Challenges*. Policy Paper. Tblisi: CIPDD Citizens Advocate! Program. http://georgica.tsu.edu.ge/files/01-Politics/Civil%20Society/Nodia-2005a.pdf (accessed July 15, 2015).

Organizational Research Services (ORS). 2007a. *A Guide to Measuring Advocacy and Policy*, prepared for the Annie E. Casey Foundation. http://www.aecf.org/resources/a-guide-to-measuring-advocacy-and-policy (accessed June 16, 2015).

Organizational Research Services (ORS). 2007b. *A Handbook of Data Collection Tool: Companion to "A Guide to Measuring Advocacy and Policy"*, prepared for the Annie E. Casey Foundation. http://orsimpact.com/wp-content/uploads/2013/08/a_handbook_of_data_collection_tools.pdf (accessed June 15, 2015).

Organizational Research Services (ORS). 2008. *Theory of Change*. Seattle, Washington. http://orsimpact.com/wp-content/uploads/2015/08/TOC-Primer-web-friendly-version.pdf (accessed June 15, 2015).

Seligman, Adam. 1992. *The Idea of Civil Society*. Princeton, New Jersey: Princeton University Press.

Sprechmann, Sofia, and Emily Pelton. 2001. *Advocacy Tools and Guidelines, Promoting Policy Change*. A Resource Manual for CARE Program Managers. Atlanta, Georgia: CARE. http://www.careclimatechange.org/files/toolkit/CARE_Advocacy_Guidelines.pdf (accessed June 20, 2015).

Technical Assistance for Civil Society Organizations (TACSO). 2011. "Advocacy and Policy Influencing for Social Change." The Swedish Institute for Public Administration–SIPU International. http://www.tacso.org/doc/doc_manual_5.pdf (accessed June 16, 2015).

USAID. 2014. *The 2014 CSO Sustainability Index for Central and Eastern Europe and Eurasia*. https://www.usaid.gov/sites/default/files/documents/1863/EuropeEurasia_FY2014_CSOSI_Report.pdf (accessed December 14, 2016).

World Values Survey. 2004, http://www.worldvaluessurvey.org/WVSDocumentationWV4.jsp (accessed December 14, 2016).

World Values Survey. 2014. http://www.worldvaluessurvey.org/wvs.jsp (accessed December 14, 2016).

# CHAPTER 3
# Fighting Favoritism in the Georgian Public Sector

**Levan Samadashvili and Raja M. Ali Saleem**

## Introduction

Corruption occurs in a variety of forms, and societies do not always agree on how to define it. Favoritism, the practice of giving preferential treatment in employment and other matters to friends, relatives, or associates by high officials, also known as nepotism, is one common type. Although corruption and the fight against it are ancient pursuits, calls to eliminate corruption have become a mantra for many in the first two decades of the twenty-first century. There are many reasons for this eventuality. First, along with domestic pressures to decrease corruption, there are now international pressures for governments to take action. Second, corruption is no longer considered an issue just for criminologists and lawyers. Economists have come up with a variety of methods to measure the impact and costs of corruption. According to World Economic Forum, the costs of corruption run into the equivalent of trillions of dollars worldwide (World Economic Forum 2012). Research on its systemic nature has also led to focus on economic incentives that lead many to corruption. Third, gradually, the cultural explanations that used to portray corruption as innate part of some societies have been discredited. Even people in the developing world are no longer ready to accept these justifications of corrupt practices. Fourth, the focus of anti-corruption efforts has been shifting from state to society. Previously, the state was considered the bulwark against corruption. Now, civil society, the press, and social media are considered major anti-corruption institutions (Larmour and Wolanin 2013). Furthermore, global economic slowdown has been one factor resulting in a reduction of public services and an increase in unemployment across economies. People suffering under austerity policies want to make their governments more accountable (Streeck and Schafer 2013). This desire can help strengthen anti-corruption regimes.

Despite a generation of rising awareness, diverse legal instruments and codes of ethics, and concerted effort, both by national governments/agencies and their external multilateral partners, success in vanquishing corruption has been elusive. Success stories can be counted on the fingers of one hand, and may not be generalizable. Singapore and Hong Kong were authoritarian city-states when they defeated the menace of corruption. Botswana, which also found some success in the fight, is a small country, with a population of only two million. Japan and Belgium are also notable examples of progress, but they had strong public institutions before they started their fight against corruption, a luxury not available to most. While other countries have made progress, it has been limited (Johnston 2014, 1–3).

Due to widespread changes in their societies, governments, and legal systems since the fall of the Berlin Wall, many Eastern European countries have had a hard time controlling corruption during subsequent decades. In a 2015 report on combating corruption in five South Eastern European countries (Armenia, Azerbaijan, Georgia, Moldova, and Ukraine), Transparency International (TI) reported the following key findings. First, there are limited checks on executive power in these countries, where weak Parliaments have been unable to constrain it. Second, judiciaries have been politicized and themselves embroiled in corrupt practices. Finally, external watchdogs, such as civil society and mass media, are also not independent. Media companies and civil society organizations work in an increasingly restrictive environment, with threats and intimidation from the executive, which is not an unheard of phenomenon (McDevitt 2015).

Georgia has been regularly acknowledged as the star performer in the South Eastern European region. In October 2015, Georgia won the first the Open Government Partnership (OGP) Government Champions Award (IDFI 2015a). Georgia was ranked 24th (out of 183 countries) in 2015 for ease of doing business by the World Bank (World Bank 2015). Georgia has also managed to achieve good results in fighting corruption. According to TI's Global Corruption Barometer results, only 12% of the respondents thought corruption in Georgia was one of the three biggest problems facing their country, a percentage lower than that of Netherlands and Britain (Pring 2016). Furthermore, according to Democracy and Freedom Watch in 2014, Georgia ranked "second after Turkey among 18 Eastern European and Central Asian countries, and scored higher than a number of European Union (EU) member states, such as the Czech Republic, Slovakia, Bulgaria, Greece, Italy, and Romania" (DFWatch 2014). Major, successful anti-corruption initiatives identified by TI in Georgia are the introduction of a general code of ethics for civil servants, criminalization of active and passive bribery, augmented asset disclosure and whistleblower protection provision, reform of law enforcement agencies, strengthening of money laundering legislation, downsizing and raising of salaries in the public sector and strong enforcement (McDevitt 2015). Furthermore, the World Bank published an extensive report, "Fighting Corruption in Public Services: Chronicling Georgia's Reforms," which outlined achieved success in multiple areas such as tax administration, police reform, education, customs, energy, and business deregulation (World Bank 2012).

The success of Georgia in controlling corruption has led to the development of a relatively efficient public service. However, many problems remain, and favoritism is one of them. Georgia does not have a long tradition of unbiased, politics-free and merit-based decision-making. Favoritism has been a continuing problem affecting decision-making, and in many areas can be said to undermine civil service efficiency.

## Research Question and Literature Review

The research question that this chapter seeks to answer is why anti-favoritism policies have not been successfully instituted in Georgia. This question will be explored using Kingdon's Multiple Stream Framework (MSF).

Favoritism is a problem with serious repercussions for overall public service performance. It affects the public service's efficiency and effectiveness in a number of ways:

- *Efficiency and productivity*: public service becomes less competitive, less capable, and less attractive in the face of favoritism. More specifically, it is rendered unable to yield required products and tangible results, as qualified and professional staff become demotivated and unproductive;
- *Human rights dimension*: politically motivated, biased dismissal and recruitment, criminal prosecution, etc. establish selective justice and unfair treatment of individuals and cases; highly qualified employees become discriminated against in favor of biased, obedient candidates;
- *Democracy*: a politicized environment puts affiliated groups and individuals in more favorable positions. It constrains the activities of opposition parties and interest groups and limits the freedom of expression. Therefore, politicization encourages undemocratic processes and undermines Georgia's chances of Euro-Atlantic integration as recognized by the current Prime Minister of Georgia (The Messenger 2016);
- *Undermining public image and becoming a less attractive workplace for qualified personnel:* 90.4% of students surveyed with a public administration background reported that they feel that the public service is characterized by favoritism, and 88.5% thinks this could be a factor for them to consider different careers (survey conducted by the Georgian Institute of Public Affairs (GIPA) in April, 2016).

Due to the threat of favoritism, various countries have different instruments in place that aim to directly or indirectly prevent favoritism in the public service workplace. However, having formally good schemes and frameworks does not necessarily prevent favoritism in practice. Therefore, it is crucial, on the one hand, to analyze existing instruments and actors that facilitate limiting favoritism, and on the other hand, to diagnose whether and to what extent the problem still persists.

This chapter first presents existing evidence of how the current instruments are not effective enough to tackle favoritism in Georgia's public service. A number of reports indicate that far too many decisions and judgments in the public service have been based on favoritism. Unfair dismissals, recruitment, and career development cases are reflected in the reports of the TI, Institute for Development of Freedom of Information (IDFI), and many other local non-governmental organizations and there is need of urgent reform (TI Georgia 2013a, 2013b, and 2015c; IDFI 2015b and 2015d). The chapter then employs Kingdon's MSF to explore why these instruments have not improved outcomes.

Before discussing nepotism in Georgia, it could be useful to have a broad overview of corruption so that it is clear that nepotism is just one of the many ways to illegally benefit from one's position or power. Phillip O'Hara (2014) identifies six types of corruption: bribery (corporate to public), fraud (corporate to corporate), embezzlement (nonprofit to corporate), nepotism (elite to family), state capture (business elite to public), and extortion (mafia-boss to legitimate business). The focus here is on nepotism. O'Hara differentiates between two approaches to corruption, the "standard" approach, and the political–economy approach. The standard approach looks at corruption as mainly an economic problem to be solved by incentivizing honesty, reducing monopolies/discretionary powers, and increasing transparency. The political economy or institutional-evolutionary approach takes a more historical and holistic view of corruption. The focus here is on the standard approach, which may not eliminate corruption and nepotism, but could reduce them.

For at least two centuries, nation-states around the world have tried to eliminate corruption. Though the choice of anti-corruption instruments varies in almost every case, Yahong Zhang (2015) lists three categories of anti-corruption instruments that have been used often, whether individually or in combination with others:

- Stringent anti-corruption laws/rules;
- Empowered anti-corruption organizations;
- E-government and increased participation of the citizenry (Zhang 2015, 247–259).

Different types of instruments have been used to counter nepotism. Legislation is one of the most important instruments to fight favoritism, since it declares the practice illegal and penalizes it by fines or incarceration. However, legislation declaring favoritism illegal is rare. While legislation against financial corruption can be found in almost all countries, nepotism is generally not clearly defined or sanctioned by law, and may only be covered indirectly as part of anti-corruption legislation.

In those cases when it is addressed legally, the criminal or penal code is generally the place where favoritism is criminalized. For example, Division 142 of the Australian Criminal Code Act defines different types of corruption, including favoritism, and their corresponding punishments (Government of Australia 1995). Beside criminal codes, which are a direct instrument for prevention, favoritism may be regulated by civil service laws. These laws can proscribe favoritism directly or indirectly. Even when they do not mention favoritism explicitly, such laws, many believe, are important for the motivation that they provide within the public service. For example, leaving more or less discretion for the managers, and regulating pay scales and recruitment policies, can influence the environment in which government officials operate and choose between favoritism and merit. The Pendleton Act in the United States (US) is one such example.

Legislation related to freedom of information also helps to prevent favoritism. The freedom of information principle, including the obligation of proactive disclosure of public information, allows civil society organizations and interested individuals to request public information from government entities and monitor their workings and decisions. The US Freedom of Information Act can be viewed as an example of such legislation. Finally, legislation related to improving efficiency and performance can also indirectly encourage better policies and less favoritism. The US Government Performance and Results and Act is one such example.

Anti-corruption legislation has become common in the developing world, and even those countries considered to be the most corrupt, it seems, have anti-corruption laws. Afghanistan, which was declared the third most corrupt country in the world by TI in 2015, promulgated an anti-corruption law in 2004 after signing the United Nations Convention against Corruption. Furthermore, in July 2008, the High Office for Oversight and Anti-Corruption (HOOAC) was established by a presidential decree to coordinate, monitor, and oversee the implementation of the anti-corruption efforts (HOOAC 2015). Research in India has shown that anti-corruption laws will only be effective if the enforcement machinery is effective and there is a rule of law culture in the society (Kumar 2015).

In terms of institutions, courts and ombudsmen play a critical role in enforcing anti-corruption/favoritism legislation. Although they get involved post facto, the existence of efficient judiciary practices is considered to be vital as a preventive mechanism. Besides courts, the role of Civil Service Bureau-type organizations is also significant. If such agencies are independent of the executive branch, they can play a crucial role in terms of defining career development, recruitment policies, pay scales, etc. Finally, the role of oversight agencies, such as supreme audit agencies or performance monitoring organizations like the US Government Accountability Office, is also important.

After anti-corruption agencies' success in Singapore (the Corrupt Practices Investigation Bureau was established in 1952 but only became effective in 1959 under Prime Minister Lee Kuan Yew's control) and Hong Kong (where the Independent Commission Against Corruption was established in 1974) in the 1960s and 1970s, such agencies have been established in many countries (Quah 2008, 85-109). These agencies are different from general government departments fighting against corruption and favoritism, as they usually have more power and independence. Patrick Meagher (2005) defines them as "separate, permanent agencies whose primary function is to provide centralized leadership in core areas of anti-corruption activity" and contends that such agencies have not been universally successful. Studying 10 anti-corruption agencies in countries on 4 different continents, Meagher contends that these agencies are more effective when their independence and powers are ensured from the start. They should be able to take action against corrupt officials, collect information, freeze assets, protect informants, monitor assets, and seize travel documents. They should also have adequate human and financial resources. An enabling environment is crucial for success, as without an independent judiciary, the support of civil society, a free and active media, and other complementary institutions, anti-corruption agencies would fail. An environment where all institutions are infested with corruption and without a semblance of the rule of law cannot have an effective anti-corruption agency.

The role of civil society organizations (CSOs) is also important, since legislation on public information could be ineffective without them, as they are thought to be an important preventive instrument against favoritism. Media is, of course, another entity that can put pressure on the government and facilitate public scrutiny.

Global efforts to reduce corruption have nonetheless been largely unsuccessful. Despite the variety of instruments outlined above, corruption and nepotism have not been eliminated. Michael Johnston (2008) is of the opinion that the reason these efforts have failed is the mismatch between anti-corruption reform and the type of corruption evident in each country. He distinguishes among four different syndromes of corruption based on different levels of social, political, and economic development, and contrasting institutional settings. According to him, Georgia, like its neighbors Turkey and Russia, falls into the "oligarchs and clans" category (Johnston 2005, 120-54), making nepotism one of the most important types of corruption in Georgia.

Steven Sampson (2010) notes that a whole anti-corruption industry sprang up during the first decade of the twenty-first century, consisting of both international organizations, such as the World Bank, TI, and the EU, as well as local organizations. Sampson asks whether this is due to a more connected and more moral world, or is it a result of the extended reach of Western capitalism, which is using anti-corruption crusades to destroy the last barriers to its domination of the rest of the world? Whatever the reason for their institution, it seems clear that anti-corruption measures and organizations have not resulted in a significant decrease in the menace of corruption.

Another issue that Sampson highlights is the international dimension of the anti-corruption fight. International organizations, such as the World Bank, the International Monetary Fund, the United Nations, the Organisation for Economic Cooperation and Development, the Council of Europe, the Asian Development Bank, the Inter-American Development Bank, and the EU have all made corruption a primary target. Since these organizations transfer millions of dollars to poor countries, they are concerned about wastage and siphoning off of funds. Unwilling governments in the developing world, and transition countries that are indebted to these organizations, are sometimes forced to take action against corruption. Anti-corruption efforts in these countries, therefore, cannot be understood without bringing in the above-mentioned international organizations.

Since the focus of this article is Georgia, EU policies and assistance are particularly important for our analysis. The EU has been one of most influential players in the anti-corruption fight in the Central and Eastern European countries due to its ability to use the carrot of accession. During the last two decades, it has encouraged reforms in candidate and neighboring countries and supported non-discriminatory but strict anti-corruption policies. The results varied from successful, to acceptable, to disagreeable, but in all cases seem to have resulted in conditions better than those in the past (Moroff and Schmidt-Pfister 2010). The EU efforts in Bulgaria and Romania have been largely unsuccessful, with corruption still a major issue. The failure can be attributed to the entrenched corruption as well as to the lack of a powerful anti-corruption constituency within these countries (Ivanov 2010). In 2004, the EU launched its European neighborhood policy (ENP). The primary objective of the ENP was "avoiding the emergence of new dividing lines between the enlarged EU and its neighbors and instead strengthening the prosperity, stability, and security of all concerned" (European Commission 2013). The focus of the ENP was on countries that were not (yet) on a path to accession, such as Georgia. So, there was no promise of EU membership, but cooperation was incentivized by (i) financial assistance; (ii) technical assistance; (iii) positive conditionality; (iv) civil society strengthening; (v) political dialogue; and (vi) regional cooperation. Anti-corruption was one of the key areas on which the ENP focused (Chene 2008). The ENP is believed to have played a crucial role in controlling and decreasing corruption in Georgia. The EU-Georgia Action Plan under the ENP identified anti-corruption as one of the key priority areas and enumerated several actions required from the Georgian government (Government of Georgia 2006). Georgia was successful in implementing most of the anti-corruption agenda and this was recognized by international organizations, as discussed above (TI 2011; WB 2012).

The following section defines important terms used to analyze the anti-corruption and nepotism issues in Georgia in this chapter.

## Favoritism, Politicization, and Nepotism

One of the main problems scholars face while analyzing corruption is the lack of precision in definitional distinctions describing different but related concepts. For example, the terms "favoritism," "politicization," and "nepotism" have all been used interchangeably in the academic literature. All three terms describe illegally favoring someone because of some emotional attachment. However, in order to better understand the underlying reasons for and the consequences of this phenomenon, it is helpful to give proper definitions to each of these terms.

For a start, favoritism is a much broader term than nepotism. According to the US Merit Systems Protection Board (MSPB) report "Preserving the Integrity of the Federal Merit Systems: Understanding and Addressing Perceptions of Favoritism" (MSPB 2013, 2):

> Favoritism occurs when supervisors or managers base decisions regarding current or prospective employees on personal feelings and/or relationships and not on objective criteria, such as assessments of ability, knowledge, and skills. Since the MSPs do not define the term favoritism, we base our definition on the corollary prohibited personnel practice in 5 U.S.C. § 2302(b) (6), which forbids the granting of "any preference or advantage not authorized by law, rule, or regulation to any employee or applicant for employment (including defining the scope or manner of competition for any position) for the purpose of improving or injuring the prospects of any particular person for employment."

Favoritism, for the purposes of this chapter, entails politicization and nepotism. Politicization is a complex phenomenon and, therefore, defining it is not easy. B. Guy Peters and Jon Pierre, in their book on politicization, define it as 'the substitution of political criteria for merit-based criteria in the selection, retention, promotion, rewards, and disciplining of members of public service' (Peters and Pierre 2004, 2). Their definition casts politicization of bureaucracy as an unwelcome development that likely leads to subpar performance and results. Almendares (2011), however, contends that all types of politicization are not deleterious and a priori normative evaluation of politicization is not correct. He argues that there are two types of politicization, institutional politicization and behavioral politicization. Institutional politicization is the use of budgetary controls, administrative procedures, oversight mechanisms, and prior review of agency action to influence and monitor the bureaucracy. The motivations of institutional politicization can be patronage or policy-oriented. For example, more political appointments in the bureaucracy could be either for handing out jobs to party loyalists, or for better-implementing a policy agenda. Behavioral politicization is the responsiveness of bureaucracy to its political masters. This form of politicization might be an internal norm or a result of institutional politicization or a threat of institutional politicization. Edoardo Ongaro (2009, 224–227) examines politicization while focusing on levels of bureaucracy. He argues that top-level politicization has increased in France, Spain, Italy, Greece and Portugal, so that bureaucracy is more responsive to politicians. At the lower level of bureaucracy, the politicization is more for patronage purposes (clientelism). It is different from corruption, as money is not directly involved, but its effects on efficiency and effectiveness are equally harmful. In this chapter, we are focusing on institutional politicization that is motivated by patronage.

Defining nepotism is comparatively easier, as it refers to the act of aiding someone because (s)he is a relative. However, although the concept is easier to grasp, it is defined in at least three different ways by varying entities. Some laws, regulations or codes define nepotism by actually listing the specific relationships that would trigger a charge of nepotism. For example, the US federal government currently forbids nepotism under prohibited personnel practice number 7 of US Code No. 2302(b). Nepotism, in the code, is defined by naming all the relationships that would constitute nepotism:

> (7) appoint, employ, promote, advance, or advocate for appointment, employment, promotion, or advancement, in or to a civilian position any individual who is a relative [father, mother, son, daughter, brother, sister, uncle, aunt, first cousin, nephew, niece, husband, wife, father-in-law, mother-in-law, son-in-law, daughter-in-law, brother-in-law, sister-in-law, stepfather, stepmother, stepson, stepdaughter, stepbrother, stepsister, half-brother, or half-sister] of such employee if such position is in the agency in which such employee is serving as a public official [an officer (including the President and a Member of Congress), a member of the uniformed service, an employee and any other individual, in whom is vested the authority by law, rule, or regulation, or to whom the authority has been delegated, to appoint, employ, promote, or advance individuals, or to recommend individuals for appointment, employment, promotion, or advancement in connection with employment in an agency] or over which such employee exercises jurisdiction or control as such an official. (MSPB 2012)

The problem with these types of definitions is that they can be too long or restrictive. To deal with this problem, some governments have defined nepotism by mentioning the degrees of consanguinity and affinity. For example, the Philippines Civil Service Act of 1959 (section 30) defines nepotism, as follows:

> Nepotism. (a) All appointments in the National, provincial, city and municipal governments or in any branch or instrumentality thereof, including government-owned or non-competitive service, made in favor of a relative of the ap-

> pointing recommending authority, or of the chief of the bureau or office, or of the persons exercising immediately supervision over him, are hereby prohibited.
>
> As used in this section, the word "relative" and members of the family referred to are those related within the third degree either of consanguinity or affinity. (Government of Philippines 1959)

Employing degrees of consanguinity or affinity to define nepotism is more straightforward but it ignores modern-age relationships (e.g. cohabitation) that are "family" relationships but without any linkage of blood or marriage. The state of California has come up with a definition in its 'Statewide Guidance on Nepotism' memorandum that takes this issue into consideration:

> Nepotism is defined as the practice of an employee using his or her influence or power to aid or hinder another in the employment setting because of a personal relationship. Personal relationships for this purpose include but are not limited to, association by blood, adoption, marriage and/or cohabitation. In addition, there may be personal relationships beyond this general definition that could be subject to these policies ... (California Department of Human Resources 2015)

While California's definition is comprehensive, it makes one wonder whether the Californian government is trying to eliminate nepotism or favoritism, as this definition erases any difference between the two (see the definition of favoritism above).

As for the Georgian legislation, neither favoritism nor nepotism is defined as a legal term. In 2015, TI suggested the criminalization of nepotism; however, the ruling party did not support this initiative, arguing that the criminal code and the anti-corruption legislation had already covered this aspect (TI Georgia 2015a).

## Methodology—Multiple Streams Theory

Numerous models and frameworks have been developed that assist in understanding policy-making processes. Kingdon's multiple streams framework (MSF) has been one of the most prominent of these frameworks. It envisages three different but overlapping streams—the problem, policy, and political streams—coming together to open a policy window, which allows a particular policy to be put on the political agenda—a necessary first step toward eventual implementation. The role of policy entrepreneurs is also important as identified by this framework. These individuals spend their time, effort and money to get a policy implemented. Although Kingdon initially used the MSF to explain and analyze agenda-setting in the policy-making environment, it was later extensively used by scholars to explore success or failure in instituting, implementing, and changing public policies.

Some such applications of the MSF have been employed in diverse geographic and policy domains. Hadii Mamudu et al. (2014), for example, used the MSF to explain how the state of Tennessee, the third largest tobacco producer in the US, passed the Non-Smoker Protection

Act in 2007. The authors used interviews with prominent players, legislative debates, and archival documents to explore the change in policy. Hakon Normann (2015) later used MSF to analyze the rise and fall of policy related to the development of offshore wind resources for electricity generation in Norway. Nadine Lehrer (2010) used the MSF and discourse analysis to explain the ascendancy of biofuels in the early-2000s in US policy discourse, and the passage of the 2008 farm bill. Rachel Carey et al. (2016) explained how policy to develop a National Food Plan in Australia failed, despite the government's commitment and interest. And, using Congressional documents, Edieser Dela Santa and Jed Saporsantos (2016) explored the passage of the Philippine Tourism Act of 2009. They contend that the policy window opened in 2008–2009 due to the merging of the three streams and the work of policy entrepreneurs.

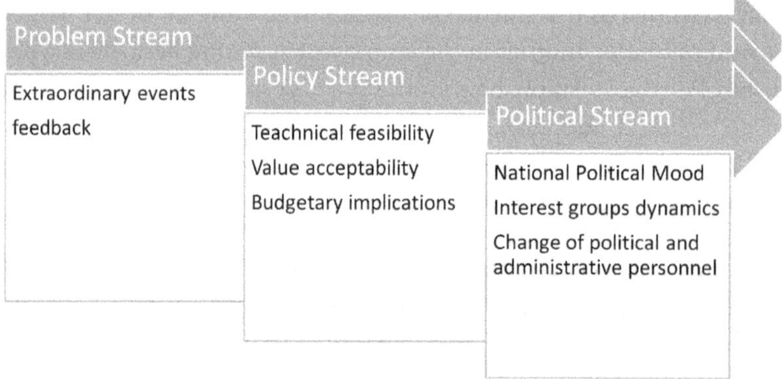


Figure 1: Kingdon's Multiple Streams Framework

### *Anti-favoritism Policies and Kingdon's Three Streams*

The problem of politicization is manifested in different ways and its intensity greatly depends upon current political arrangements. In Georgia, pre-election periods are particularly characterized by charges of politicization. However, the issue becomes especially acute in the periods of government turnover or in situations of political crisis. The change of government in Georgia in October 2012 again reminded many of this long-lasting issue. Increased staff turnover and structural reorganization with vague goals and unclear results raised suspicions of favoritism, which threatens the public service's efficiency and effectiveness, not to mention its credibility. The following section uses Kingdon's MSF to unpack why anti-favoritism policies have not been successfully instituted in Georgia. The focus is on policy institution, not merely on agenda setting. Unless favoritism is eliminated, it is feared that Georgia's public service and the overall system of public administration will remain less than optimal, and thus threaten the development of genuine democracy in Georgia.

## Problem Stream

According to Kingdon, recognition of a problem is crucial in terms of stimulating the policy process. Kingdon suggests that crisis, focusing events, and symbols are important in capturing the attention of policy makers and politicians (Kingdon 2003, 94–100). Examples of such focusing events could be high-profile cases of favoritism within the public sector that result in media attention and public outrage. Opposition parties' allegations that the ruling party is discriminating based on political views can also assist in highlighting such events, and such accusations become especially intense during election periods. For example, favoritism in Georgia is often in the news. The media has revealed that relatives of Prime Minister Irakli Garibashvili occupy certain public sector positions, and there have been a number of allegations that his relatives have been influencing decision-making, particularly in the Kakheti region. It has also been confirmed that the relations of numerous cabinet members hold formal positions in different government departments. Such events commonly capture media attention, causing public scrutiny and discussion (Kakheti Information Center 2013).

However, as Kingdon suggests, "crises, disasters, symbols and other focusing events only rarely carry a subject to policy agenda prominence by themselves...they need to reinforce some preexisting perception of a problem, focus attention on a problem that was already 'in the back of people's minds'" (Kingdon 2003, 98). Kingdon points out that sporadic occurrence of focusing events does not consolidate enough attention, and that systemic occurrence or continuous data is necessary—a dimension that Kingdon describes as feedback. In Georgia, reports of major civil society organizations (CSO) have been providing this feedback. For instance, TI Georgia recently published a research report on "staffing changes in the civil service." The study was conducted from October 2012 (when the parliamentary elections were held) to March 2013 and was based on requests for public information and media monitoring. The report documents that, in the central and local governments, 5,149 employees had left the service. While 45% of them had left of their own volition, considering the unemployment rates in Georgia, TI suspects that these people may be victims of politicization and might have been forced to leave by coercion or "friendly advice." According to the TI report, this suspicion was confirmed by several employees. As for recruitment, the same report suggests that out of 6,557 new employees recruited, only 4% has been selected based on open competition. Many of them were appointed using loopholes in an old law on civil service. Furthermore, the report also revealed outright illegal appointments as well. TI provided free legal services to many dismissed government officials and, according to their statistics, over 60 cases were won and 40 officials have been re-appointed based on the court decision (TI Georgia 2013b).

The IDFI, another active CSO, analyzed dismissals during 2014. The study revealed the dismissal of 8,388 government employees throughout Georgia, while a total number of 63,394 were employed. Similar to the data of the TI Georgia, 80.7% of total central government employees reportedly left service of their own accord, raising suspicions about coercion. Concerning local governments, the primary reason for laying the workers off has been reported as reorganization (IDFI 2015b).

Other interesting data can be found in the reports of the Innovations and Reforms Center (IRC), which revealed that public officials use various instruments to dismiss unwilling employees and then recruit staff based on favoritism. Besides coercion and reorganization, IRC reported many cases of multi-year contracts of key staff being discontinued. IRC emphasized that the discontinuation of contracts was one of the instruments used for "gradually cleaning the public sector from the pre-election staff." Suspicions are raised due to the fact that those positions have remained, and dismissed employees who had good working records were in many cases replaced with less competent staff. Also, certain employees noted that they learned of the discontinuation of their contract only one or two days before the end date, and since they had not received any negative feedback, they had expected to continue their work (Giorgi Gabrielashvili 2016).

Finally, the GYLA has made publicly available a Supreme Court decision that points out that "there is a massive tendency for employees writing dismissal letters on their own initiative… large numbers of dismissed personnel said that they wrote dismissal letters based on advice, coercion, and false promises of being appointed in other positions, etc." The decision acknowledged that nepotism and corruption in the Georgian bureaucracy remain an unresolved problem (Tabula 2014).

## Policy Stream

The policy stream, according to Kingdon, is comprised of a large number of competing solutions searching for problems, and can be characterized as a "primeval soup." Policy solutions rise to the top of this soup based on their technical feasibility, value acceptability, and budget implications.

As mentioned earlier, there are various mechanisms that countries employ as preventive measures against favoritism, and laws to reduce favoritism have been successful in various countries. In Georgia, a new Civil Service law was adopted in 2014 and will become fully effective in 2017. The express purpose of the law is to establish a merit-based civil service on the principles of political neutrality, and to ensure proper separation of administration and politics. To this end, the law lays down new regulations for recruitment, dismissal, and career development of civil servants. However, it should be noted that the law has been criticized by several organizations, and its effectiveness remains to be observed in practice as it enters into force. This law, and its predecessor, enables public officials to appeal to the court against their dismissals, and if the court rules the dismissal illegal, the dismissed official would be reinstated. The new law also specifies that the employee will be given 6 months compensation (based on the last paycheck) and be enrolled in the reserve if the position previously held is occupied. Another important piece of legislation regarding favoritism is the Georgian Criminal Code. Since 2013, "Forcing an employee to write a letter of dismissal is punishable by fines or a jail sentence of up to 2 years, and possibly also with the deprivation of the right to take on the job for up to three years." This clause is valid for both public as well as the private sector employees.

Although the above-mentioned legislation is in place, it is important to note that nepotism is not defined as a legal term. In the legislation, political neutrality and politicization are mentioned, but not nepotism or favoritism. While different countries have come up with various solutions, the evidence from Georgia suggests that the criminalization of nepotism should be the next logical initiative. However, such an initiative, when proposed by the TI in 2013, did not win enough support to be discussed in the parliamentary committees, as explained during an interview with the representative of TI Georgia (Lika Sajaia 2016). If we analyze underlying reasons according to Kingdon's terms, one might deduce that the reasons have to be primarily related to value acceptability, because the initiative was apparently otherwise feasible, both technically and financially. The explanation provided by relevant parliamentary committees for the lack of support for criminalization of nepotism was that the criminal code already prohibited preferential treatment and discrimination. However, as a representative of TI pointed out, there were no known cases when anyone had been punished for favoritism based on those particular clauses (Lika Sajaia 2016). Moreover, direct regulation with regard to nepotism is considered crucial not only in terms of its criminalization and resulting legal consequences, but also in terms of a governmental declaration to identify nepotism/favoritism as a particular category of crime and commit itself to fighting against it. Such practice already exists in the other legal realms, such as in the field of domestic violence. Although violence was always prohibited by the criminal code, separate clauses have been added to specifically address domestic violence and define specific penalties.

Another policy solution, currently being implemented in Georgia, for decreasing favoritism is more transparency in the public service. The principle of freedom of information is guaranteed by law in the General Administrative Code of Georgia, which is crucial for proper public oversight and monitoring. Public information can be requested in-person or electronically. Public sector organizations are obliged to respond to inquiries within ten business days. In the case of their inability to provide the required information, the applicant must receive, within three business days, a written explanation. The law provides a limitation on the provision of information, if it contains personal data or is classified as a state or commercial secret.

In 2011, Georgia also joined the Open Government Partnership (OGP) and a number of successful initiatives have been implemented to achieve greater transparency since. The standards for information requests have been introduced, and the proactive disclosure of public information has been put in place. Georgia was named as one of the most successful countries in terms of implementing the OGP Action Plan since joining (IDFI 2015a) and has been given the privilege of being a member of the OGP steering committee in 2016, and a co-chair of the same committee in 2017 represented by the Minister of Justice of Georgia (Agenda.ge 2016).

The problem of value acceptability becomes apparent if we compare favoritism and financial corruption. Since 2004, the parliament and politicians would not have dared to ignore anti-corruption initiatives, as they were high on the political agenda. So, they forced bureaucrats to change their acceptance of financial corruption as legitimate by instituting pertinent policies to combat it. As Kingdon distinguishes between the governmental and decision agenda, it can be noted that issues of favoritism periodically seem to be reaching the governmental agenda, but so far not a decision agenda. The discussion on value acceptability can be further justified by the fact that ministries and other government organizations have yet to mention favoritism in their codes of ethics, codes of conduct or other relevant documentation (according to IRC). Additionally, the only institution in charge of performance audit and control has so far performed not a single study on a favoritism-related case in the public sector, despite conventional wisdom indicating that such instances clearly exist.

As for budgetary feasibility, suggested policy initiatives ought not necessarily require additional resources. As was seen in the case of the fight against financial corruption, there could not be observed significant budgetary implications. When the previous government started to fight financial corruption during Saakashvili's administration, instead of creating additional administrative functions, some existing ones were actually abolished. In fact, Georgia was able to achieve progress in eliminating financial corruption without having either national or regional anti-monopoly and anti-corruption agencies, which are very popular in other countries, as discussed in the previous section. Similarly, the technical feasibility of anti-favoritism policies ought not be an issue, as the problem does not need to be addressed by sophisticated software or expensive equipment. Many countries, including Spain, have criminalized nepotism and international practices suggest that technically there are no issues of significant concern in policy implementation.

## Political Stream

For the political stream, Kingdon focuses on the national mood, the role and power of various interest groups, and the change of administrative and political personnel.

The national political mood is a major factor significantly affecting the governmental policy agenda. As mentioned in the policy stream section, Georgia has made drastic improvements in the fight against financial corruption, which is recognized by various international organizations. This success has to be ascribed substantially to the fact that there was a consolidation of the societal views against financial corruption. Maintaining status quo on financial corruption had electoral consequences. Since 2004, people were no longer willing to accept the need to pay bribes to police officers, doctors, and teachers, as had been accepted practice. However, favoritism does not appear to be gaining as much attention from the wider public and the national mood does not seem to be as unanimous on this issue. As Sikk and Koeker (2015) hypothesize, in the Central and Eastern European countries, the lack of political will to tackle corruption might be related to the lack of electoral consequences for governing parties.

In this context, it is important to note that every sixth employed individual in Georgia serves in the public service according to IDFI (2015d). This fact could also be influencing national mood, although a considerable portion of the people now employed by government have come through a merit-based process.

According to Kingdon, a change of administrative and political personnel also affects policymaking. In the context of favoritism, certain changes seemed apparent in the wake of the new government coming to power in 2012. A new law on civil service was adopted in 2014 replacing the law promulgated in 1997. There had been extensive discussions to adopt the new legislation during the previous government tenure but the law could not be passed so new law was a big achievement for the current government. The quality and practical application of certain aspects of the new law, however, have been challenged by many experts and organizations (TI Georgia 2015b). Although the law will become fully effective in 2017 and is a bit early to judge, it is important to note that it recognizes the problem of favoritism indirectly by specifying its goal of establishing a merit-based civil service on the principles of political neutrality and the separation of administration and politics.

Interest groups are an important component of Kingdon's political stream. Several watchdog organizations are monitoring the field and reporting on favoritism and corruption in Georgia (for instance, Georgia's Young Lawyer's Association (GYLA), IDFI, TI Georgia, Civil Development Agency (CIDA), and Georgia's Reforms Associates (GRASS)). However, they lack coordinated effort, as there is a lack of a consolidated campaign. For instance, the initiative of TI about the criminalization of nepotism has remained the initiative of one organization only, making it easier for parliamentary committees to turn it down. It is also noteworthy that when journalists asked the political parties about their support for the initiative, one of the leaders of a popular opposition party could say no more than "every initiative that comes from a civil society organization is worth discussing and considering." While examining the role of various interest groups, the role of media has to be mentioned separately. Georgian media has been highlighting favoritism scandals. Particularly, such scandals have related to the Prime Minister Irakli Garibashvili as well as the Vice Prime Minister Kakha Kaladze, both of whom were forced to explain themselves publicly. These cases have been covered by various media channels, including Rustavi 2 and Imedi TV. Furthermore, regional nongovernmental organizations, such as Kakheti Information Center, often report about such violations within municipalities. However, sustained coverage of the issue is not there. There is a need for coordination among the CSOs to help change the national mood on favoritism and to sustain pressure on the government.

## Policy Entrepreneurs

Finally, MSF discusses the importance of policy entrepreneurs in the policy process. The lack of policy entrepreneurs is one of the biggest problems in the fight against favoritism in Georgia. Few local agents are pushing for radical changes, and spending their time, effort, and resources for this cause.

Policy entrepreneurs can be grouped into the following three categories: politician, CSOs and media. (1) Politicians: these are primarily the opposition parties, such as the United National Movement, Free Democrats, and others who reveal and report about the cases of favoritism, and, specifically, nepotism, in order to discredit the ruling party and win certain political support. Due to the mentioned motivation, their effort is not consistent, and is mostly of a reactive rather than a proactive character. Consequently, their involvement and interest increases if favoritism relates to political level positions; however, there is not enough political support and unity around the issues; (2) CSOs: as mentioned TI, IDFI, GRASS, and other CSOs are relatively active in this area, however, limited resources and uncoordinated efforts decrease the impact of civil society entrepreneurs; and (3) Media is another important actor. Specifically, several investigative journalism programs have devoted their time to revealing facts of favoritism. Although, as mentioned earlier, these attempts have been sporadic, and are not coherent; therefore they are not significantly influencing the national mood or political agenda.

## Conclusions and Recommendations

The research has demonstrated that many of the instruments to check favoritism in the public sector are already present in Georgia, such as legislation and institutions, as well as a relatively active third sector. However, it is also the case that existing mechanisms do not seem to be effective enough in practice. There is, therefore, an apparent need for additional and more focused changes. For example, although the criminal code, which envisages punishment for preferential treatment, is in place, there has never been a case when someone has been penalized by this law for nepotism or politicization. Moreover, the legal and the human rights committees of the Parliament have refused to criminalize nepotism, since they have noted that it is already covered in the criminal code, despite the lack of charges or convictions.

Similarly, Georgia has freedom of information-related legislation. Georgia is also a member of the OGP ruling committee, represented by the Minister of Justice, and everything seems to be working. In reality, though, the Ministry of Justice has the worst response rate in terms of public information requests according to an IDFI report. The same report also points out that responses to public information requests have improved but there was a danger of relapse. In 2010, almost 50% of information requests were not fulfilled, and many of those that received responses had insufficient or irrelevant information. The period from July 2012 and June 2013 was the best year, with a 90% response rate to queries. After 2013, however, there was slight decline in the response rate (IDFI 2015c).

Why has policy change to mitigate favoritism yet to be successfully instituted in Georgia? This analysis, in its application of Kingdon's MSF, suggests that there is something missing in all three streams that contributes to getting a policy issue on the agenda and eventually implemented. There have been some scandals, but no particularly high-profile case specifically related to favoritism that could cause public outrage (problem stream). Anti-favoritism as a value is not very popular in the bureaucracy (policy stream). And the national mood is not critical and consolidated as it was during the early 2000s on issues of financial corruption (political stream). Therefore, the ruling party feels no pressure and fears no severe legislative/electoral consequences if favoritism in the public sector continues. Finally, policy entrepreneurs, another key ingredient to successful agenda-setting and implementation, appear to be inadequate in number and power to bring about change in terms of the elimination of favoritism in Georgia.

## References

Agenda.ge. 2016. "Georgia Becomes Co-Chair of Open Government Partnership." May 5. http://agenda.ge/news/57345/eng.

Almendares, Nicholas. 2011. "Politicization of Bureaucracy." SSRN Scholarly Paper ID 2641351. Rochester, NY: Social Science Research Network. http://papers.ssrn.com/abstract=2641351.

California Department of Human Resources. 2015. "Statewide Guidance on Nepotism Policies." http://www.calhr.ca.gov/PML%20Library/2015014.pdf.

Carey, Rachel, Martin Caraher, Mark Lawrence, and Sharon Friel. 2016. "Opportunities and Challenges in Developing a Whole-of-Government National Food and Nutrition Policy: Lessons from Australia's National Food Plan." *Public Health Nutrition* 19 (1): 3–14.

Chene, Marie. 2008. "European Union Strategies to Support Anti-Corruption Measures in Neighbouring Countries." *U4*. April 3. http://www.u4.no/publications/european-union-strategies-to-support-anti-corruption-measures-in-neighbouring-countries/.

DFWatch. 2014. "Georgia Ranked 50th on Corruption Index." *Democracy & Freedom Watch*. December 3. http://dfwatch.net/georgia-ranked-50th-on-corruption-index-62801-32511.

European Commission. 2013. "European Neighbourhood Policy (ENP) - Fact Sheet." March 19. http://europa.eu/rapid/press-release_MEMO-13-236_en.htm.

Giorgi Gabrielashvili. 2016. Board Member of IRC. Favoritism in the Georgian Public Sector. July 23. Interview by Levan Samadashvili.

Government of Australia. 1995. *Australian Criminal Code Act*. http://www.austlii.edu.au/au/legis/cth/consol_act/cca1995115/sch1.html (accessed March 20).

Government of Georgia. 2006. "EU-Georgia Action Plan | EU Neighbourhood Library." http://www.enpi-info.eu/library/content/eu-georgia-action-plan.

Government of Philippines. 1959. *Civil Service Act of 1959*. http://www.lawphil.net/statutes/repacts/ra1959/ra_2260_1959.html.

High Office of Oversight and Anti-Corruption (HOOAC). 2015. "History of HOOAC." http://anti-corruption.gov.af/en/page/8463.

IDFI. 2015a. "Georgia wins the first OGP Government Champions Award." October 28. https://idfi.ge/en/georgia-wins-the-first-ogp-government-champions-award.

IDFI. 2015b. "Statistical Analysis of Dismissal of Employees from Various Public Institutions in 2014." November 25. https://idfi.ge:443/en/statistical-analysis-of-dismissal-of-employees-from-various-public-institutions-in-2014.

IDFI. 2015c. "Access to Public Information in Georgia—Report Summarizing 2010–2015." December 11. https://idfi.ge/en/access-to-public-information-in-georgia-report-summarizing-2010%E2%80%932015.

IDFI. 2015d. "Increase of Bureaucracy." December 16. https://idfi.ge/ge/rise-of-bureaucracy-georgia.

Ivanov, Kalin. 2010. "The 2007 Accession of Bulgaria and Romania: Ritual and Reality." *Global Crime* 11 (2): 210–219. doi:10.1080/17440571003669217.

Johnston, Michael. 2005. *Syndromes of Corruption: Wealth, Power, and Democracy.* New York: Cambridge University Press.

Johnston, Michael. 2008. "Japan, Korea, the Philippines, China: Four Syndromes of Corruption." *Crime, Law and Social Change* 49 (3): 205–223. doi:10.1007/s10611-007-9095-z.

Johnston, Michael. 2014. *Corruption, Contention and Reform: The Power of Deep Democratization.* New York: Cambridge University Press.

Kakheti Information Center. 2013. "Tamazashvili Clan in Kakheti." http://ick.ge/articles/15413-i.html.

Kingdon, John W. 2003. *Agendas, Alternatives, and Public Policies.* Longman Classics in Political Science. New York: Longman.

Kumar, C. Raj. 2015. "Corruption in India: A Violation of Human Rights Promoting Transparency and the Right to Good Governance." *UC Davis Law Review* 49: 741–792.

Larmour, Peter, and Nick Wolanin. 2013. "Introduction." In *Corruption and Anti-Corruption,* eds. Peter Larmour and Nick Wolanin. Canberra: ANU E Press, xi–xxiv.

Lehrer, Nadine. 2010. "(Bio)fueling Farm Policy: The Biofuels Boom and the 2008 Farm Bill." *Agriculture and Human Values* 27 (4): 427–44.

Lika Sajaia. 2016. TI. Favoritism in the Georgian Public Sector. March 2. Interview by Levan Samadashvili.

Mamudu, Hadii M., Sumati Dadkar, Sreenivas P. Veeranki, Yi He, Richard Barnes, and Stanton A. Glantz. 2014. "Multiple Streams Approach to Tobacco Control Policymaking in a Tobacco-Growing State." *Journal of Community Health* 39 (4): 633–45.

McDevitt, Andrew. 2015. *State of Corruption: Armenia, Azerbaijan, Georgia, Moldova, and Ukraine.* Berlin: Transparency International.

Meagher, Patrick. 2005. "Anti-corruption Agencies: Rhetoric Versus Reality." *The Journal of Policy Reform* 8 (1): 69–103. doi:10.1080/1384128042000328950.

Moroff, Holger, and Diana Schmidt-Pfister. 2010. "Anti-Corruption Movements, Mechanisms, and Machines—An Introduction." *Global Crime* 11 (2): 89–98. doi: 10.1080/17440571003669118.

MSPB. 2012. "Nepotism." May. http://www.mspb.gov/ppp/mayppp.htm.

MSPB. 2013. "Preserving the Integrity of the Federal Merit Systems: Understanding and Addressing Perceptions of Favoritism." MSPB. http://www.mspb.gov/netsearch/viewdocs.aspx?docnumber=945850&version=949626&application=ACROBAT.

Normann, Hakon E. 2015. "The Role of Politics in Sustainable Transitions: The Rise and Decline of Offshore Wind in Norway." *Environmental Innovation and Societal Transitions* 15 (June): 180–93.

O'Hara, Phillip Anthony. 2014. "Political Economy of Systemic and Micro-Corruption Throughout the World." *Journal of Economic Issues* 48 (2): 279–308. doi:10.2753/JEI0021-3624480203.

Ongaro, Edoardo. 2009. *Public Management Reform and Modernization: Trajectories of Administrative Change in Italy, France, Greece, Portugal and Spain*. Cheltenham, UK: Edward Elgar Publishing.

Peters, B. Guy, and Jon Pierre. 2004. "Politicization of the Civil Service: Concepts, Causes, Consequences." In *The Politicization of the Civil Service in Comparative Perspective: A Quest for Control*, eds. B. Guy Peters and Jon Pierre. London: Routledge.

Pring, Coralie. 2016. *People and Corruption: Europe and Central Asia*. Berlin: Transparency International.

Quah, Jon S.T. 2008. "Anti-Corruption Agencies in Four Asian Countries: A Comparative Analysis." In *Comparative Governance Reform in Asia: Democracy, Corruption, and Government Trust* 17. Research in Public Policy Analysis and Management 17. Bingley, UK: Emerald Group Publishing Limited.

Sampson, Steven. 2010. "The Anti-Corruption Industry: From Movement to Institution." *Global Crime* 11 (2): 261–278. doi:10.1080/17440571003669258.

Santa, Edieser Dela, and Jed Saporsantos. 2016. "Philippine Tourism Act of 2009: Tourism Policy Formulation Analysis from Multiple Streams." *Journal of Policy Research in Tourism, Leisure and Events* 8 (1): 53–70.

Sikk, A., and P. Koeker. 2015. "Replacing the Rascals? Corruption and Candidate Turnover in Central and Eastern Europe." In *Presented at: ECPR Joint Sessions of Workshops, Warsaw. (2015)*. Warsaw. http://discovery.ucl.ac.uk/1469053/.

Streeck, Wolfgang, and Armin Schafer. 2013. *Politics in the Age of Austerity*. Cambridge, UK: Polity Press.

Tabula. 2014. "Supreme Court: Nepotism in the Public Service Remains an Unresolved Problem." November 19. http://www.tabula.ge/ge/story/89967-uzenaesi-sasamartlosajaro-samsaxurshi-nepotizmi-gadauchrel-problemad-rcheba.

The Messenger. 2016. Announcement of the Prime Minister of Georgia at Business Forum in Berlin. http://www.messenger.com.ge/issues/3651_june_16_2016/3651_tea.html.

TI Georgia. 2011. "National Integrity System." http://transparency.ge/sites/transparency.ge.nis/files/TIGeorgia_NISReport_en.pdf.

TI Georgia. 2013a. "Announcement after the Parliamentary Elections of 2012 about the Dismal of Employees." January 17. http://www.transparency.ge/post/general-announcement/sajaro-samsakhurebidan-tanamshromlebis-gatavisuplebis-shesakheb.

TI Georgia. 2013b. "Staffing Changes in the Civil Service." August 12. http://www.transparency.ge/sites/default/files/post_attachments/Staffing%20Changes%20in%20the%20Civil%20Service%20after%20the%202012%20Parliamentary%20Elections%2C%20AUGUST%202013_0.pdf.

TI Georgia. 2015a. "TI Georgia Proposes Criminalization of Nepotism in the Civil Service." *TI Georgia.* March 10. http://www.transparency.ge/en/post/press-release/ti-georgia-proposes-criminalization-nepotism-civil-service.

TI Georgia. 2015b. "Strengths and Weaknesses of a New Draft Law on Civil Service." 2015. *TI Georgia.* September 22. http://www.transparency.ge/en/blog/strengths-and-weaknesses-new-draft-law-public-service.

TI Georgia. 2015c. "Nepotism, Abuse of Power, and Bribery: Public Opinion Survey Outcomes." *TI Georgia.* September 25. http://www.transparency.ge/en/blog/nepotism-abuse-power-and-bribery-public-opinion-survey-outcomes.

TI Georgia. 2015d. "TI Georgia Assesses Certain Aspect of Civil Service Reform." *TI Georgia.* December 9. https://www.scribd.com/embeds/300132733/content?start_page=1&view_mode=scroll&show_recommendations=true.

World Bank. 2012. "Fighting Corruption in Public Services: Chronicling Georgia's Reforms." 66449. The World Bank. http://documents.worldbank.org/curated/en/518301468256183463/Fighting-corruption-in-public-services-chronicling-Georgias-reforms.

World Bank. 2015. "Ease of Doing Business." http://www.doingbusiness.org/rankings.

World Economic Forum. 2012. "Global Agenda Council Report 2011–12." *Network of Global Agenda Councils Reports 2011–2012.* http://reports.weforum.org/global-agenda-council-2012/councils/anti-corruption/.

Zhang, Yahong. 2015. "What Can We Learn from Worldwide Anti-Corruption Policies?" In *Government Anti-Corruption Strategies: A Cross-Cultural Perspective,* eds. Yahong Zhang and Cecilia Lavena. Boca Raton, FL: CRC Press.

# CHAPTER 4
# Local Governance and Citizen Engagement: Determining Municipal Budgetary Priorities through Georgian Civic Engagement

**Liza Sopromadze, Nino Loladze and Jessica N. Terman**

## PROBLEM IDENTIFICATION

Self-governance is fundamental to the health of modern democracies. However, self-governance is dependent on the willingness of citizens to meaningfully engage in the governance process, and on governments to facilitate and mobilize this engagement. Municipalities are one of the most meaningful levels of government with which citizens can engage (European Charter of Local Self-Governance 1985). As stated by the European Charter of Local Self-Governance, "Local authorities are one of the main foundations of any democratic regime .... Local authorities with real responsibilities can provide an administration which is both effective and close to the citizen" (1985, 2). Thus, it is incumbent on researchers and policymakers alike to maximize citizens' ability to civically engage.

The Republic of Georgia, however, faces significant challenges in relation to civic engagement. Recent research on Georgian democratic participatory processes indicates that, although national legislation on local self-governance exists, citizen participation remains quite low (Gamsakhurdia 2009; Swianiewicz 2010). In fact, numerous researchers have suggested that low citizen involvement represents the greatest challenge to effective collaboration and self-governance in local governments. The researchers identified the following reasons for citizen passivity (Center of Training and Consultancy 2014):

- Citizens have low awareness of their democratic rights and responsibilities.
- Local citizen populations do not have realized goals, nor do they understand their collaborative role in the process of self-governance.
- Citizens do not view their opinions as important in the local decision-making process.
- Local citizen populations do not see the connection between civic participation and their own prosperity.
- Local governance bodies (mayoral offices and city assemblies) are unprepared to collaborate with their communities.

Other, more comprehensive research suggests similar reasons for low participation. BCG Research (2008) conducted 3,000 citizen interviews across the Republic of Georgia, in addition to interviewing members of four different municipal assemblies and executives' offices.[1] Researchers reported that only 1.5% of the respondents attended self-government meetings. In Tbilisi, the capital city of Georgia, 47% of respondents, and 57% of respondents in other regions, reported being unwilling to even engage with the local municipal assemblies. However, 25% of Tbilisi respondents declared that they did not attend self-government meetings because they did not have information about them. The researchers also highlighted that many study respondents discussed the importance of transparency and accountability in government. Of particular importance was the finding that most respondents expressed the belief that the development of budgetary priorities was an effective way to incorporate the principle of self-governance. Thus, while few citizens participate, they appear to recognize the importance of self-governance.

Later research focused on citizen perceptions of the effectiveness of self-governance and participation. According to the results of Research of Rural Communities that was conducted by CIDA within the framework of the "Regional Network of Civic Society" (the project was implemented by support of G-PAC program of East-West Management Institution and financial assistance of USAID in January–February 2013), self-governance did not influence everyday life of local populations (34.6% of respondents) or had a minimal impact on it (24.8% of respondents). Only 7.7% of respondents thought that local self-governance affected their lives. Interestingly enough, however, 78.7% of the respondents stated that their communities should be involved in self-governance. The results of this research suggest that, despite the passivity of the population, they are willing, at lease in theory, to participate in local self-governance.

These results have strong support from later research conducted by NDI and its partner organization Caucasus Research Resource Center (CRRC). Of those interviewed, 60% indicated that they do not have any information on activities of self-government organizations and 83% of respondents were unable to identify the name of their representative on the municipal assembly (their majoritarian) (CRRC 2014). At the same time, communication between local municipal representatives and citizens is minimal: Only 6% of the respondents noted that they were contacted by one of their city representatives while only 3% report being contacted by their elected executive. Nonetheless, of those respondents who met with their majoritarian (municipal assembly representative), 69% said that these representatives were competent and 88% reported that they were respectful. This suggests that there is room for additional citizen engagement activity.

All of this is to say that Georgian citizens face challenges both within themselves and in relation to the institutions with which they civically engage. The purpose of this study is to identify effective and sustainable forms of collaboration between citizens and Georgian local governance institutions. We study this by looking at techniques for citizens to become involved in the development of local budgetary priorities.

---

1 Municipal governments that were studied include: Tbilisi, Kutaisi, Dusheti, and Akhaltsikhe.

## Chapter 4

## Research Design

### *Context*

One of the most significant processes through which citizens might engage with local governments is in the creation of the document of budgetary priorities. This document is a 3-year development plan for each municipality. It outlines local preferences, such as economic development activities and local services, in addition to defining various self-governance activities (i.e. local town halls and other forums for civic participation). Thus, citizen involvement in the development of budgetary priorities is important to ensuring local self-governance. As it stands, participation of the local population is not mandated by legislation. However, national legislation dictates that, "the citizens of Georgia have the right and capability to decide on local issues through their elected local authorities" (Organic Law of Georgia 2013, 1). As such, our investigation and inquiries surrounding local citizen participation are centered on determining the best method for sustainable collaboration between municipal assembly members and their local populations in the development of budgetary priorities.

The research was conducted in five Georgian municipalities with varying regional and geographic characteristics, governance structures, and founding ages: Rustavi, Mtskheta, Gori, Ozurgeti, and Kharagauli. The following selection criteria were used: self-governing city (Rustavi—Kvemo Kartli), newly established self-governing communities (Mtskheta—Mtskheta-Mtianeti, Ozurgeti—Guria, Gori—Shida Kartli) and (Kharagauli municipality—Imereti).

Before moving forward, it is important to discuss the governance structure and context of Georgian local governments. Municipalities are considered self-governing units, which are headed by gamgebelis. However, many of these municipalities have cities, villages, and towns, which are headed by mayors. Mayors often report to the gamgebeli, who is considered the head of the self-governing unit. This is particularly the case in geographically large, self-governing units where citizens struggle to attend public meetings that are located in the administrative center of the unit. The gamgebeli also have representatives in the smaller towns, villages, and cities that make up the municipality. These representatives are known as public servants. City hall—the location of the gamgebeli and central administration—is referred to as the gamgeoba. Council assembly members are referred to as majoritarians. The majoritarian is elected by the local community.

## Methodology

A qualitative research design, similar to those in the previously discussed literature, was developed to investigate local citizen participation (OSGF 2015). Two focus groups were conducted in each self-governing unit: one focus group of citizens and one focus group of local elected officials. Eight to 12 people participated in each focus group.

Nonprobability sampling was used for selection of assembly members. The head of the Assembly was asked to invite assembly members for participation in focus groups. The gender balance of the assembly member focus groups was statistically proportional to those in the Assembly. For the citizen focus groups, gender and age representativeness were the primary selection criteria. Local nonprofits and community organizations helped to identify potential participants. Table 1 shows the gender and age break down of the focus groups.

The duration of each focus group meeting was between 1.5 and 2 hours, depending on the size of the group. At the beginning of each focus group session, the moderator outlined the rules of discussion. Moderators were trained in interviewing and participant engagement. Participants expressed considerable enthusiasm toward participation. This was supported by the fact that all participants who expressed interest in the focus groups attended them in their entirety.

Table 1: Focus Group Sample Breakdown

| Municipality | Target group | Number of participants | Gender | | Age groups | | |
|---|---|---|---|---|---|---|---|
| | | | Male | Female | 18–24 | 24–49 | 49+ |
| Mrskheta | Government officials | 9 | 7 | 2 | 0 | 3 | 4 |
| | Citizen population | 8 | 5 | 3 | 2 | 3 | 3 |
| Gori | Government officials | 11 | 10 | 1 | 0 | 4 | 7 |
| | Citizen population | 8 | 5 | 3 | 1 | 3 | 4 |
| Ozurgeti | Government officials | 8 | 8 | 0 | 0 | 2 | 6 |
| | Citizen population | 12 | 3 | 9 | 1 | 6 | 5 |
| Rustavi | Government officials | 9 | 7 | 2 | 0 | 4 | 5 |
| | Citizen population | 8 | 4 | 4 | 1 | 4 | 3 |
| Kharagauli | Government officials | 12 | 8 | 4 | | 5 | 7 |
| | Citizen population | 10 | 6 | 4 | 2 | 3 | 5 |

Ten in-depth interviews with high-level officials (gamgebeli, mayors, public servants, heads of financial departments, majoritarians) in each unit were also conducted. All gamgebelis, mayors and public servants that were contacted for interviews agreed to participate. Only men hold these positions; thus, all of our interviewees were men. The average age was 45. Data from the focus group meetings was used to develop open-ended interview questions. We also conducted extensive content analyses of national and local legislation to guide both our interview questions and inform the research overall. Our interview and focus group questions centered on the development of the budgetary priority document, which is currently submitted by the municipal assembly to the gamgebeli's office in October–November with minimal input from citizens. Based on our analysis of the interview, focus group and secondary data (i.e. legislation and policy documents), there are five core areas that were frequently discussed by respondents. We have created subsections below to explore these areas and the introduce data to support assertions made in each subsection.

# Results

## Observation 1: Citizen Participation in Development of the Budgetary Priorities Document

The results of the research indicate that citizens are not involved in the process of development of the document of priorities and the budget and that only a small group of citizens attend public discussion of the actual budget. This is largely because the budgetary priorities document is provided to the gamgebeli of the self-governing unit in November and, only after this, will the gamgebeli hold public hearings for development of the final budget.

The majority of the respondents felt that the municipality budget was not "theirs" and expressed that their participation in the development of the budget was not important. Moreover, many citizens described not knowing what the document of budgetary priorities was, or that they could potentially play a role in the development of this document. The respondents indicated that they were never asked to express their opinion on priorities of the municipality.

A few citizen respondents in Ozurgeto, Kharagauli, and Mtskheta described that the municipal budget is not their business and that they elected the gamgebeli and municipal council to plan the budget. One Ozurgeti focus-group member noted that, "Nobody needs to involve us in development of the budget. Specialists take care of it. There is an economic team in city hall that works on the budget." Similarly, focus group members in the Mtskheta Assembly explained that, "citizens cannot be involved in budget development, as they do not have the skills nor do they have the information."

The majority of municipal assembly members of Kharagauli suggested that low interest in the municipal budget is caused by low citizen awareness. As one assembly member stated:

> The local population is not interested in the municipal budget because they were not involved in meetings and discussions that created it. Their awareness is improved at present and therefore, they are more interested in budget development now.

At the time that this research was conducted, the Gori Municipal Assembly had just started the process of local involvement in the development of budgetary priorities. All of the elected officials interviewed for the research noted, one way or another, that the local population has been heavily active in identifying municipal priorities. The Gori gamgebeli noted the following:

> We actively collaborate with the local population. We meet citizens residing in villages in order to learn about their needs and problems for the document of the priorities. We work in two directions; we meet adults as well as youth to ensure that everyone's opinion is taken into consideration.

Furthermore, public servants—representatives of the Gori gamgebeli—explained that the new government encourages citizen participation in the process of budget planning. Thus, the heightened participation in Gori may be explained by the newness of the municipality.

One of the authorities of Mtskheta stated that the village mayors provide the majority of communication between village preferences and the municipal government administration. Specifically, an authority in Mtskheta made the following comment:

> We have 2–3 representatives in each village who are aware of the problem. We actively collaborate with the local population. If the village population visits me or I go there, we will not need these representatives and will be able to save money on the salaries of these 2–3 persons and will visit villages more times than I do it now. We have these representatives to collect and distribute information in villages as well as provide us with information on problems and priorities of the local population; so that the village population does not need to travel back and forward. We work this way.

Additionally, Mtskheta gamgebeli representatives stated that the budgetary priorities are identified based on letters from the local population. The mayor develops a list of village priorities that is forwarded to the Mtskheta gamgebeli.

To the extent that citizens are directly involved in the identification of priorities, they do so through the "Rural Assistance Program." These respondents stated that citizen participation in the development of the municipal budget is essential, and that it is extremely important that the population's needs are reflected in the budget. But, they argued that this is the responsibility of the municipal government. "The Gamgeoba should ask the local population what do we need and plan the budget accordingly."

### Observation 2:<br>General Citizen Readiness for Collaboration

The majority of citizen and assembly member focus group members revealed that the passivity of the local population is due primarily to the perceived disconnect between citizen participation and real results. Furthermore, this is not unique to the budgetary process. One Mtskheta interviewee stated: "There are few active people in the villages. People are tired of government's unmet promises. Meetings should not be carried out just for reporting; the populace would like to see results." One Khragauli citizen noted the following:

> Citizens are not active at present because they think that their opinion will not be taken into consideration. If we see that our opinion is heard, we'll start to collaborate with the local-government.

Similarly, Ozurgeti assembly members stated that the population's passivity is the result of their disappointment with the lack of results in the political process. The vast majority of assembly members across the five counties were concerned with the difficulty of mobilizing the whole population. This disappointment is likely compounded by the fact that only small groups of citizens are willing to participate in municipal activities.

Citizen focus-groups did reveal that the village populations currently collaborate with the gamgebeli representatives. However, interviewees expressed the importance of having assembly members engaged in the budgetary priorities decision-making process actually visit villages and discuss the problems and priorities of the populace. This is largely because gamgebeli representatives have no independent authority. The following observation was made in the Gori focus group:

> Authorities are responsible for visiting citizens. Local populations will also visit authorities, but the first steps should be taken by elected officials. We do go to our gamgebeli representatives [the public servant] when we have a problem. We wish that it was possible to solve our problems in the village because some elected officials will not visit the villages.

This is to say that the villages contained by each municipality are interested in self-government but recognize the difficulty in independently solving many of their own problems. Therefore, they want to actually talk to decision makers. As Rustavi focus group members explained:

> Citizens should actively collaborate with local-government bodies, competencies and resources of authorities are limited and therefore, we are often not able to solve our problems.

**Observation 3:**
**General Collaboration between the Local Population and Assembly**

Focus group members frequently mentioned that collaboration between the gamgebeli representative in the village and the local majoritarian is essential—regardless of whether it is for the budget. "The village population informs the representative about their problems first of all and, after this, they go to the municipal assembly" noted members of the Gori focus group. It was obvious that the village population was more active and mobilized in those villages where the gamgebeli representative and local majoritarian collaborate. In other words, where citizens felt that their issues were heard and that their government was working for them, they were more likely to civically participate.

In Gori citizen focus groups, respondents frequently referred to the majoritarian as the most important person for the village. As one person stated, "The majoritarian should express the people's opinion and take their problems to the assembly; we believe that the majoritarian is willing to take care of our problems, but he does not have an authority." An Ozurgeto focus group member explained that, "The gamgebeli representatives—the public servant—should be responsible for taking our problems to the municipal assembly and gamgebeli in order to assist us in solving these problems."

Most citizen focus group members mentioned that majoritarians needed to have leadership skills and personal knowledge of the village in order to effectively communicate with citizens. Moreover, comments were made that the village mayor should "be able to carry out planned activities with the local population as well as solve their problems." However, the villages, town and cities are not given the same level of authority as municipalities.

Nonetheless, citizens commented that, while there is some collaboration between the local population and the majoritarian, it is neither consistent nor results-oriented. For example, many citizens could not identify the name of their majoritarian. Even fewer citizens could identify their majoritarian or noted that they have communication with their majoritarian. As a citizen focus group explained it:

> I voted in local elections [for the majoritarian], but do not remember who was the candidate. I did not see this person after the elections. They should meet citizens. Unfortunately, they are not active and do not meet population.

Members of the Rustavi Assembly stated that they are responsible for providing the population with needed information in a timely manner. One Rustavi assembly member noted the following:

> A goal of gamgebeli representatives and the assembly should be to inform the population about their decisions, identify priorities and ways of solving problems. An informed population will collaborate with authorities.

### Observation 4: Feedback, Form, and Long-term Collaboration

The core problem of citizen participation at the local level is centered on the lack of communication between the municipal assembly and the citizenry. Almost all citizen respondents explained that meetings between their majoritarian and citizens should be target-oriented and organized regardless of whether they are formal or informal. Both parties should realize the needs and results of such meetings. Citizens described fairly high expectations of assembly members while assembly members expressed that it was difficult to fulfill current obligations with existing municipal competencies and resources. One of the core problems of the current meeting structure is that the government holds one-off meetings with the population but does not provide any follow-up. Citizens do not receive communication on either decisions made or results following the meetings.

To be informed about current projects as well as have communication between the population and members of local-government bodies is essential for citizens. The results of the research revealed that members of local-government bodies should realize the importance of feedback. As one Kharagauli respondent explained:

> Feedback with the local population is important. The village population is capable of getting mobilized in the process of problem solving, but they do not have experience and therefore do not take initiative. Some changes may take place in this direction if meetings are conducted on a regular basis.

A Mtskheta focus group member made the following suggestion: "It does not matter how often meetings are conducted. It is necessary, that these meetings are conducted on a regular basis and collaboration is established."

Similarly, Ozurgeti focus group respondents explained, "We would like to see reports of majoritarians, feedback is also very important. When they report to the population we feel that they respect us." Yet another citizen focus group member—from Gori—described that, "The population would like to have regular meetings with specific goals and results. Also, we would like to hear about current projects and receive information on problems that were solved as well as hear the reasons why some problems were not solved." When asked, none of the citizen focus group members could recall a single instance of long-term collaboration with their local government.

Results of the research indicate that communication between the population and the authorities is currently spontaneous and fragmented. Citizens do not see prospects of long-term collaboration. Rustavi respondents mentioned that "citizens do not have dialogue skills. Local government authorities do not take an initiative to communicate with population. Due to these reasons, there is no collaboration between these two parties." Thus, the lack of communication seems to go both ways. However, one Ozurgeti citizen did note that, "The village population will participate in meetings if we see that there are resources that will be provided to us." As a Gori majoritarian explained, "Mainly we meet with the more active groups of the population. We meet citizens through them and define priorities based on the problems that are identified at these meetings." Thus, the natural assumption in this is that, if government educates the citizens, they will be capable of participating in the development of budgetary priorities documents.

However, there were important observations made about the form and frequency of civic participation. Members of the Kharagauli focus-group noted the following:

> The majoritarian should meet citizens on a regular basis. Probably he or she will not be able to collect the opinions of the whole population. But, it will be possible to distribute information in the village if there are 5–6 contact persons in each district of the village.

Discussions with government officials and citizens revealed some consensus that meetings with majoritarians should take place at least every 2 months. A few citizen focus group members even asserted that it would be good to conduct weekly meetings. Citizens prefer face-to-face meetings, in order to get direct answers from their elected officials. Ozurgeti citizens explained that it is very important to have a schedule of formal meetings with the majoritarian in addition to informal meetings. The focus group respondents noted that, "People prefer face-to-face meetings. It is very important that officials, who have authority to make decisions, see problems on site. Decisions will be more effective when this happens." However, most respondents agreed that the majority of the village population would not be able to attend meetings held in the administrative center of the self-governing unit. Seasonal prevalence of farming in villages limits the availability of the population to participate in public activities. Therefore, it would be more effective if gamgebeli representatives and majoritarians travelled to the villages and rural communities in the unit.

However, it is notable that, in all of the focus groups, respondents expressed considerable willingness to attend formal and informal local village meetings for which they do not travel a great distance (meetings with authorities, sending letters, collecting signatures, etc.). Ozurgeti respondents explained that:

> When 28 villages have one budget it is extremely hard to identify priorities. So multiple public meetings should be carried out and priorities should be identified based on the results of the information collected at the meetings. Then, citizens should be informed about the information that was collected.

However, citizen focus group members made clear that not everyone can attend planned meetings. Thus, some mentioned that surveys may be the best way to learn about the preferences of the population. Both focus groups asserted that it would be good if a form of citizen surveying was established.

It is clear that citizens and local government authorities are ready to work together on the development of the document of budgetary priorities. However, there are important processes and mechanisms that need to be put in place to train citizens in self-governance and make government open to citizen involvement.

## Recommendations

### *A Plan to Increase Civic Engagement*

The research shows that there is not a one-size fits all form of collaboration to increase Georgian civic participation. However, it is necessary to follow some principles for ensuring the effectiveness of the process to engage citizens. As such, we have developed some recommendations aimed at improving civic participation in the creation of the document of the budgetary priorities.

As it stands, citizen input is often not sought until after the assembly has submitted the document of budgetary priorities to the gamgebeli of the self-governing unit. Thus, citizens have traditionally been given very modest opportunities for participation. We advance a model for citizen participation based on our data collection efforts and the observations made above. We intentionally formulate this model so that it may be implemented by majoritarians and mayors, and will not require special skills or education. Of particular importance are our suggestions for a survey questionnaire method and a timeline for gathering citizen preferences and opinions.

Thus, we recommend that local governments begin by developing (1) a questionnaire to determine citizen preferences and priorities, and (2) a schedule setting forums for public meetings. Such a timetable for Georgian citizen participation is laid out in Table 2. The timetable begins with informational meetings with local populations toward the beginning of

Table 2: Suggested Timetable of Civic Engagement*

| Period—date | Activity | Individuals responsible |
|---|---|---|
| February–March | **Informational meeting with the local population** Local government authorities and the village population work together to evaluate implemented projects and activities. The assembly will inform the village population by starting development of the document of budgetary priorities. Citizens will receive a schedule of meetings for the year. | Assembly members, Representatives of gamgebeli |
| March | **Develop a questionnaire** | Assembly members, Representatives of gamgebeli |
| April | **Distribute questionnaire** | Assembly members, Representatives of gamgebeli |
| May | **Village population completes questionnaires** | |
| June | **Questionnaires are collected and analyzed** | Assembly members, Representatives of gamgebeli |
| July | **Discuss results of the questionnaire** in collaboration with city hall administrators. Develop a draft of the document of priorities. | Assembly members, City hall administrators |
| August–September | **Conduct meetings with the village population and** inform them of results of the research and share a copy of the draft document of priorities. Collect notes and comments of citizens. | Assembly members, Gamgebeli representatives, City hall administrators |
| September | **Prepare a list of priorities based on discussions with citizens.** Prepare and conduct a presentation for City hall administrators. | Assembly members |
| October | **Assembly members and city hall administrators will collaborate and work on priorities.** Projects aimed at development of the municipality will be identified and a list of priorities will be finalized. | Assembly members, City hall administrators |
| September–October–November | **City hall administrators will review assembly member document of budgetary priorities** to generate budget. | Assembly members |
| November–December | **Organize meetings with local population** and present the document of priorities and the budget. | Assembly members, City hall administrators |
| December | **Document of priorities and the budget will be discussed in assembly** for later review by the gamgebeli | Assembly members, City hall administrators |

* This timetable is subject to change and conditional on the timetable of the budget and submission of the document of budgetary priorities.

the year. The meetings are to assess past and current projects and activities in addition to discussing potential projects for the future.

After these meetings, local majoritarians and gamgebeli representatives will have a sense of the important issues for their citizens. They will develop and distribute a questionnaire.

Questionnaires are particularly important since not everyone can attend the planned meetings. Information collected from these questionnaires will be used to conduct meetings with village populations and build a document of budgetary priorities. What is important—and different—about this process is that the majoritarian(s) for the villages are involved with the local population and the timeline is such that citizen input comes before the formation of the document of budgetary priorities. Only after this input is considered will a budget be developed. The previous model of participation, for the most part, only involved citizens in discussions of the actual budget, once it had already been devised.

Thus, this overall model, in essence, forces members of the municipal assembly to engage with their local populations. By doing so, they will likely be building trust among the local electorate, in addition to making them part of the total process. The survey questionnaire method allows for the collection of a greater number of citizen perspectives. The act of compiling questions based on citizen meetings also encourages municipal officials to take into account these various perspectives—even if they are not included in the final budget. Of greatest importance is the fact that the timeline ensures that government officials can include citizens in the process.

## Conclusion and Future Research

The results of this research indicate that local government authorities do not conduct meetings with their local populations on a regular basis. Thus, they are unable to exercise participatory forms of governance that are defined by national legislation on the implementation of self-governance. The results also highlight that, while citizen awareness is low, citizens *are* willing to participate in self-governance activities, and local government authorities are open to collaborating with them. Thus, it is crucial to identify administrative mechanisms to allow for this self-governance and essential partnership between citizens and their municipal representatives. We have provided a recommended timetable to this effect.

The results also revealed that the existence of legislation and regulations is insufficient to guarantee citizen participation. Rather, municipal authorities must have the appropriate skills and instruments to ensure the establishment of sustainable citizen participation. Officials should have a clear understanding of decision-making processes and the mechanisms that are established in their municipalities. This way they can recognize where it is possible to involve the local population in the decision-making process. Furthermore, local leaders need to identify what they want to learn from the population, which mechanisms should be used to hear citizen perspectives, how the information on these perspectives will be analyzed, and how the results will be reflected in the decision-making process.

In closing, we believe that the process is more important than the outcomes. Education, awareness raising and empowerment of citizens are goals of this process because they create social capital and reinforce the principles of self-governance. This expansion of individuals in the decision-making process is also crucial because it reinforces the legitimacy of local government decision-making.

## REFERENCES

Caucasus Research Resource Center. 2014. *Caucasus Barometer*. Tbilisi, Republic of Georgia. CRRC Centers. http://www.crrccenters.org/caucasusbarometer/ (accessed February 10, 2016).

Center of Training and Consultancy. 2014. *Research of Rural Population*. Tbilisi, Republic of Georgia: Regional Development Center Publications.

European Charter of Local Self-Government. 1985. "European Charter of Local Self-Government." http://www.coe.int/en/web/conventions/full-list/conventions/treaty/122 (accessed March 1, 2016).

Gamsakhurdia, Zviad. 2009. *Citizen Participation in Local Self-Governance*. Tbilsi, Republic of Georgia: Institute of Civic Opinion Publications.

Organic Law of Georgia. 2013. "Local Self-Government Code of Georgia, Section I." http://www.civil.ge/files/files/2013/LocalSelfGovernance-bill.pdf (accessed March 18, 2016).

OSGF. 2015. *Methodology of Citizen Participation*. Prague, Czech Republic: Regional Development Center and Agora-Central, Czech, NGO Publications.

Public Broadcasting (BCG). 2008. *Local Self-Government Reform—Awareness and Evaluation*. Tbilisi, Republic of Georgia: OSGF Publications.

Swianiewicz, Pawel. 2010. *Public Opinion about Local Government in Georgia*. Open Society–Georgia Foundation http://www.osgf.ge/files/publications/2011/Report_ENG_18 gverdi_Web.pdf (accessed March 18, 2016).

# CHAPTER 5
# Student Plagiarism in Georgia's Higher Education

**Vano Tsertsvadze, Lali Khurtsia and Yulia Krylova**

## Introduction

With the rapid spread of digital technologies, plagiarism has become a common problem in higher education institutions throughout the world. There have been an increasing number of studies related to student plagiarism in Western countries (e.g., Alschuler and Bliming 1995; Stearns 2001; Jensen et al. 2002; Landau, Druen, and Arcuri 2002; Zimitat 2008; Guo 2011). In Georgia, there have been no systematic studies of the problem of student plagiarism in the national context. This study is aimed at filling this gap in the literature by analyzing plagiarism and cheating in student academic writing in Georgia.

In 2014, there were 73 higher education institutions in Georgia, with 124,000 bachelors, masters, and doctoral students (National Statistics Office of Georgia 2015). Every year, more than 25,000 Georgian students defend their theses in different scientific areas as a final stage of their undergraduate and graduate studies in universities. Due to the lack of plagiarism detection systems in Georgia's universities, it is difficult to verify the authenticity of student theses. It is also very difficult to assess the scope of plagiarism in Georgia's higher education because of a lack of relevant studies and representative surveys.

In Georgia, plagiarism is also common in scholarly research. For example, many scientific articles published in Georgian scholarly journals do not contain original research, relying instead on paraphrasing already published studies and secondary sources. Situations of self-plagiarism, when scholars reuse their own published works in different journals, are also not rare in Georgia. The spread of instances of plagiarism among students and faculty members deteriorates the quality of higher education and academic research in the country.

The objective of this study is to define incentives and perceptions of Georgian students regarding plagiarism, as well as to analyze different methods of cheating used in academic writing. This chapter is organized as follows: first, we review the literature on student plagiarism, formulate our key hypotheses, and describe the methodology of our research. The next section presents an analysis of the results of our study, followed by a discussion of cultural, social, and historical factors that are responsible for the spread of plagiarism in Georgia's higher education. Based on the results of our analysis, we formulate recommendations to prevent student plagiarism and to increase academic integrity in Georgia's higher education.

## Literature Review

In a broad sense, plagiarism can be defined as the use of another author's words, opinions, or ideas without mentioning the author's name and acknowledging the original source. Studies of student plagiarism distinguish different types of dishonest behavior in academic writing. For example, Chris Park (2003) distinguishes four types of student plagiarism: (1) stealing materials from other sources, including buying pre-written or specifically written papers from a research service or specialized company, and copying a whole paper without proper acknowledgement, (2) submitting papers written by somebody else, (3) copying sections of papers from other sources, and (4) paraphrasing materials without proper references (2003, 475).

One of the challenges identified in the literature on student plagiarism is related to defining the seriousness of different types of cheating, because it ranges from "sloppy documentation and proof-reading to outright, premeditated fraud" (Wilhoit 1994, 162). In this respect, Roger Bennett (2005) distinguishes between minor and major plagiarism. Minor plagiarism represents copying a relatively small part of student papers from other sources without proper acknowledgements, while major plagiarism means that a substantial part or a whole work is plagiarized. In our study, we analyze both forms of plagiarism, exploring major cases when students buy their theses from specialized companies and minor cases where students copy several sentences or paragraphs from other sources without acknowledging the original sources.

Earlier research into student plagiarism was initiated by academics in English speaking countries, particularly the United States and United Kingdom. The pioneering large-scale research on cheating in education institutions was conducted by William J. Bowers as early as 1964. Based on a survey of 5,000 students in the United States, he found that 75% of them cheat at least once in their studies (Bowers 1964). Since 1964, an increasing number of studies of academic dishonesty have been published in different countries. The existing research focuses on different aspects of plagiarism, such as incentives and motivation of students, the impact of institutional factors on the frequency of cheating in academic studies, and perceptions and attitudes toward plagiarism.

One of the current streams of the research into student plagiarism explores incentives of students who cheat in their academic studies (e.g., Stevens and Stevens 1987; Davis et al. 1992; Love and Simmons 1998; Park 2003; Owens and White 2013). These studies distinguish between intentional and unintentional motives. For example, Caleb Owens and Fiona White indicate that student plagiarism can "result from a failure to understand how to acknowledge a source, carelessness in doing so, or a deliberate attempt to present another person's work as your own" (2013, 14). They define the latter as "dishonest plagiarism" and the former as "negligent plagiarism" (ibid.). Similarly, Chris Park (2003) distinguishes between unintentional motives, such as a lack of understanding of how to quote and reference sources, and intentional motives, such as efficiency gain, better grades, lack of interest in studies, peer or parental pressures, and defiance or disrespect of authorities.

Another stream of research explores the role of institutional factors in affecting plagiarism in higher education (e.g., McCabe 1992; McCabe and Trevino 1993, 1997; McCabe, Trevino, and Butterfield 2001). Institutional factors include honor codes, students' understanding of academic integrity policies, the perceived risk of plagiarism detection, and severity of punishment for cheating. For example, based on a survey of 6,000 students at 31 academic institutions, Donald McCabe and Linda Trevino (1993) find that university policies regarding plagiarism significantly affect the frequency of cheating in academic studies. In this respect, they suggest that "programs aimed at distributing, explaining, and gaining student and faculty acceptance of academic integrity policies may be particular useful" to curb plagiarism in higher education (McCabe and Trevino 1993, 534).

Since the 1990s, many studies have been conducted to explore perceptions and attitudes toward plagiarism among students in various countries (e.g., Davis et al. 1994; Waugh et al. 1995; Burns et al. 1998; Lim and See 2001). As Vivien Lim and Sean See indicate, "cross-cultural studies conducted to examine students' attitudes toward academic dishonesty have found evidence that students of different nationalities and of different cultures vary significantly in their perceptions of cheating" (2001, 262). In this context, the applicability of the Western studies of student plagiarism to Georgia's higher education is questionable due to substantial differences in their institutional and sociocultural environments. Therefore, the study of plagiarism in the Georgian context should necessarily include analysis from cultural and historical perspectives.

Georgia is located on the border of European and Islamic cultures. This location greatly influenced the formation and evolution of cultural norms among the people of Georgia, including their attitudes and perceptions about plagiarism. The Islamic perspective on plagiarism differs significantly from the Western tradition. For example, Abdul Rashid Moten describes the key difference between these perspectives in the following way (2014, 173):

> The rise in plagiarism allegations is associated with the developments in European-American history, which advanced the notion that since the human mind is the creator of all knowledge, it should be privately controlled and the creator should be entitled to benefit financially or otherwise from the knowledge so created (Stearns 1999) ... Muslim scholars, on the other hand, conceived knowledge as God-given and as common property, which needs to be shared rather than monopolized.

Culture does not completely predetermine individual choices, but it sets the context within which these individual choices are made. For example, in some Eastern collective cultures, borrowing ideas from friends and relatives is not considered plagiarism (Tayraukham 2009). Furthermore, throughout its history, Georgian literary works have borrowed ideas from their predecessors. Early literature of Georgia was greatly influenced by Greek myths and legends, which became the major source of its national folklore. For example, the Greek hero Prometheus served as a prototype for the Georgian hero Amirani in one of the oldest and most popular legends in the country (Gugunava 2012). Georgia's literary tradition was also greatly influenced by Persian writers. For example, the Georgian historian Ivane Javakhishvili notes that many poems written by Persian Muslim poets, such as *Shahnameh* by Abu Al-Qasim Ferdowsi, *Vis and Rāmin* by Asad Gorganiand, and *Layla and Majnun* by Nizami Ganjavi, served as a source of ideas for Georgian Christian poets who considered them a precious treasure of art (1985, 305–306). Cultural norms also have a significant impact on the use of other authors' opinions and ideas in academic works.

Plagiarism in student academic writing is not unique to Georgia. This problem is persistent in other ex-republics of the Soviet Union, from Russia and Ukraine to Kazakhstan and Uzbekistan. An increasing number of studies are devoted to corruption in higher education in the post-Soviet space (e.g., Taksanov 2003; Podolyan 2006; Antonovich and Merezhko 2006; Osipian 2009, 2010). The spread of corruption in universities in post-Soviet countries led to the formation of informal businesses that sell pre-written or specifically written term papers, bachelor's and master's theses, and doctoral dissertations.

In this informal market, graduate and undergraduate students who buy their theses and term papers represent the demand side. Different companies that offer their consulting services to students, including theses and term papers written by their employees, represent the supply side. For example, Ararat Osipian analyzes Russia's informal sector where "master's theses and term papers can be bought online or custom prepared for clients, and so can doctoral dissertations" (2009, 12). He refers to this informal sector as "the dissertations for sale market" (ibid.).

Georgia's education system has a similar informal market where students can buy their theses and term papers online or order them from specialized companies. The existing demand for such services explains a growing number of Internet sites that sell student theses. The increasing instances of plagiarized student papers in Georgia's higher education system suggest the need for research into the demand and supply sides of its informal market of academic writing.

## Hypotheses and Research Methodology

The identified gap in the Georgian literature on plagiarism allows for the formulation of hypotheses regarding students' incentives, motives, and perceptions about plagiarism. In this respect, this study explores how the frequency of plagiarism in Georgia's higher education institutions is related to students' intentional motives to cheat in academic writing, to university polices regarding academic integrity, and to students' attitudes toward plagiarism. These factors are hypothesized to influence the decisions of students to engage in minor and major plagiarism.

Drawing on Owens and White (2013) and studies about corruption in higher education in post-Soviet countries, we propose a hypothesis about the prevalence of "dishonest plagiarism" among Georgian students who have various intentional motives. Furthermore, drawing on the literature about the role of institutional factors, we hypothesize that decisions to cheat in academic writing are affected by Georgia's university policies regarding plagiarism. In particular, the frequency of students' cheating in academic writing is negatively related to the perceived risk of plagiarism detection by university staff and the related penalties.

Finally, we hypothesize that decisions to cheat in academic writing are motivated by positive attitudes and perceptions about plagiarism among Georgian students.

The data for this study come from in-depth interviews conducted with representatives of both the demand and supply side of the informal market for student thesis writing. In order to study incentives and attitudes of students toward plagiarized theses, we interviewed 120 bachelor and master's students at the Georgian Institute of Public Affairs and the Department of Economics and Business of Tbilisi State University. Our objective was to obtain information about incentives, attitudes, and sources of plagiarism used by students during their studies. The Georgian Institute of Public Affairs is a relatively small university, with about 1,000 undergraduate and graduate students. Tbilisi State University is one of the largest universities in Georgia. Tbilisi State University has about 5,000 students pursuing their bachelor's and master's degrees. The sampling was based on the probability technique. Every fifth student was randomly chosen from the registry of the Georgian Institute of Public Affairs and the Department of Economics and Business of Tbilisi State University.

Interviews with students were semi-structured in order to encourage them to express their personal opinions about ethical and moral aspects of plagiarism in their studies. As a possible disclosure of subjects' responses represented the primary source of potential harm, the data were collected anonymously. Since the term "plagiarism" has negative connotations, we decided to substitute it in our questions with "borrowing citations, opinions, and ideas from other authors without mentioning their names." This was done to encourage respondents to give more honest answers about their informal activities.

The consent discussion and consent forms were provided to the participants with all necessary information related to the research before interviews took place. All subjects were informed that their participation was voluntary, and that they could withdraw from the study at any time and for any reason. All procedures performed in the study involving human participants were in accordance with the ethical standards of the institutional research committee.

In order to collect data about the informal market for academic writing, we administered the questionnaire among Georgian companies that offer such services for students on the Internet. Since the survey was not enough to obtain in-depth information about specific characteristics of this market, it was followed by eight telephone interviews with representatives of these companies. The key objective of phone interviews was to collect information about scientific areas, academic degrees, approximate time, and costs of theses sold by these companies online.

The interviews did not provide enough information to explain the existence of the shadow sector of Georgia's education system. Taking this into account, we conducted a focus group devoted to an analysis of cultural, social, and historical roots of the problem of plagiarism in Georgia's higher education. Another reason for the combination of these methods is that anonymous interviews provide more honest answers to questions about informal activities, while a focus group is more useful for discussing factors responsible for the problem of plagiarism in Georgia's higher education system, and comparing different views of psychologists and professors who specialize in natural sciences, social sciences, and humanities.

## Research Findings

The interviews conducted with students at the Georgian Institute of Public Affairs and the Department of Economics and Business of Tbilisi State University included questions about how often students use plagiarized works, how they perceive the frequency of plagiarism among their classmates, how often cheating was detected in their academic writing, and what sanctions were set by universities in plagiarism incidents. Finally, to assess students' attitudes toward plagiarism, we also included questions about the ethics and justifiability of plagiarism and cheating in academic writing.

The results of the interviews supported our hypothesis about the prevalence of "dishonest plagiarism" among Georgian students. More than 60% of the respondents (72 students) admitted that they personally engaged in cheating on at least one occasion, by using works of other authors without mentioning their names and without acknowledging the original sources. Among them, 2.5% (three students) admitted that they asked another person to write theses for them. In addition to the question about their personal engagement in plagiarism, students were asked to indicate how they perceive the frequency of cheating in academic writing among their university classmates. The numbers related to perceived prevalence of cheating by peers were commensurate with, but a bit higher than, the reported plagiarism instances in students' personal experiences. Thus 62% of the interviewed respondents perceived that their university classmates plagiarized at least once in their studies, while 33% considered that students cheat systematically in most of their written works.

The interviews demonstrated that most cases of cheating in academic writing were deliberate attempts by Georgian students to present other authors' works as their own. The questions about incentives and motivations of students who deliberately cheated in their academic writing produced various responses. As their incentives, students indicated a desire to get high grades (14 out of those 72 students who acknowledged that they plagiarized in at least one instance), the ease of plagiarism (43 students), a lack of personal interest in the topic of their thesis (13 students), and parental pressures to perform well academically (2 students).

Furthermore, the results of the interviews seem to support our hypothesis about the role of the perceived risk of plagiarism detection and severity of penalties. All respondents assessed the detection risk as very low. Importantly, in practically all cases, university staff did not detect plagiarism. The only exception was a student who failed to defend his thesis due to plagiarism issues and, as a result, had to rewrite it.

A key reason for low detection rates is that universities do not install any plagiarism detection software. In most cases, university staff uses the Google search engine to check the originality of student theses written in Georgian. This method is ineffective in situations where students paraphrase already published works or translate materials from foreign sources. It was also found that in those rare cases when plagiarism is detected, the related penalties are too liberal for students. In most cases, students just have to rewrite their theses or retake their exams. According to the respondents, the lack of specialized detection software and inadequate penalties for plagiarism produce additional incentives for them to cheat in their academic writing.

The interviews with students also focused on defining their perceptions and attitudes toward plagiarism. In particular, we were interested in collecting personal opinions of students about moral and ethical aspects of plagiarism. About 20% of the respondents considered that selling and buying theses online are legal activities. At the same time, some of these students acknowledged that potentially, such activities might have negative consequences. For example, they expressed the opinion that they personally would not like to use the services of lawyers or doctors who had bought their student theses, instead of writing them themselves. Furthermore, two students suggested that buying theses from specialized companies is ethically justifiable in those cases when the students themselves write the conclusions. According to one respondent who expressed that there is nothing wrong in using the services of such specialized companies:

> They [companies that sell academic papers] only help because those students who are talented can write theses themselves, but those students who do not have sufficient time or possibilities can pay money for this work to be done by somebody else.

However, the majority of the students interviewed for this study disagreed with this opinion. About 80% of the respondents suggested that buying or selling pre-written and specifically written student theses is not ethical. One of the respondents put it in the following way:

> Freedom of doing business does not mean that you can sell everything. In particular, selling authorship does not make any sense because the author is always the person who wrote the work. Therefore, such activities are fraud. To say that selling theses is legal means that one can also pay somebody else to take his exams instead of himself.

The interviews with students produced rather controversial results about their attitudes and their use of plagiarized theses. Based on their responses, we identified that the key source of plagiarism in student theses is the Internet. Thus 57% of students used Internet websites to download and copy materials for their papers, or bought their theses online from specialized companies. Less popular sources of plagiarism included printed literature (10%) and TV and radio programs (5%). Interestingly, those students who can speak Russian often copy or buy theses from Russia's Internet sites. For example, one of the respondents confirmed that to write his thesis, he used the Russian search engine *yandex.ru* and a Russian website that specializes in academic papers known as *referat.ru,* and then asked one of his family members to translate the downloaded materials into Georgian. Another respondent noted that he and his friends often used the services of employees of public libraries to write their student papers for money.

Since the majority of students used the Internet as the key source of cheating in their academic writing, we conducted an analysis of companies that sell theses for students online.

To obtain information about their services, we conducted telephone interviews with eight service providers represented by Georgian companies that offer consulting services for students online. We introduced ourselves as a customer who wanted to buy a thesis. The results of our interviews show that service providers sell theses for both undergraduate and graduate students. They specialize in various scientific areas, such as business, economics, banking, public policy, literature, art studies, history, religion, and philosophy. They offer their services in three languages: Georgian, English, and Russian.

We were particularly interested in obtaining data on the originality of theses sold online and included a question about plagiarism in the products provided by these companies. All service providers guaranteed that their products are unique and customer-oriented. They excluded any possibility of plagiarism in their works, as they were said to have been written by highly qualified professionals. For example, a representative of one Georgian company described their services in the following way:

> Writing theses for students is a process that involves a group of creative, professional, and dynamic specialists who have scientific degrees in relevant academic areas, with several years of experience in scientific research and education practice. And they are mostly educated in Western universities.

Based on the interviews with representatives of these companies, we found that "theses for sale" do not represent novel research. Service providers do not conduct interviews, surveys, or use other methods that allow for the identification of new evidence or information. All respondents indicated that their services include mostly an analysis of current problems based on the already exiting evidence and secondary sources. Yet, several respondents mentioned that they would include original research materials in the final product if a customer provides such materials himself.

As for price policies, they vary depending on time and language requirements of theses ordered by students. For example, an average price for one page of a thesis written in English is estimated at $25, while the price of one page written in Georgian ranges from $2.5 to $5. The official website of one company that specializes in these services contains the following pricelist: 7 days—$2.5 per page in the Georgian language, 5 days—$3 per page, 3 days—$3.5 per page, and 24 hours—$5 per page. Based on the interviews, it was found that in most cases, these prices are fixed, and it is very difficult to negotiate any discounts. For example, one of the respondents asked $500 for a 100-page thesis. When asked for a discount, the respondent refused, indicating that the process of writing, editing, and printing a 100-page thesis, including a literature review, analysis, and discussion, requires substantial time and costs.

Although a consideration of companies that sell student theses provides useful information about this shadow sector of Georgia's education system, it did not allow us to explain the roots of the problem of plagiarism. At the final stage of our study, we conducted a focus group to discuss this phenomenon with experts from the Georgian Institute of Public Affairs and Tbilisi State University. To participate in this discussion, we invited psychologists and university staff who specialize in different disciplines. The results of this discussion are presented in the following section. The main aim of the discussion was to analyze cultural, social, and historical factors that contribute to the existence of the shadow sector of student academic writing in Georgia's education system.

## Discussion and Analysis of the Results

The results of our study demonstrate that Georgian students use various types of plagiarism in their academic writing, including downloading papers from the Internet, buying papers from specialized companies, paraphrasing the existing literature, and translating materials from foreign languages without acknowledging the original sources. This study supports the hypotheses that motivation and institutional factors, including the perceived risk of detection and severity of penalties, significantly affect the cheating behavior of Georgian students. To a large extent, the problem of plagiarism is likely facilitated by the fact that Georgian universities lack preventative and proactive policies to curb plagiarism in academic writing. However, contrary to our hypothesis about positive attitudes toward plagiarism among Georgian students, we found that most of them perceive such activities as unethical. Taking this into account, we focused on an analysis of historical, cultural, and social factors to explain the prevalence of plagiarism in Georgia's higher education.

One of the explanations is that the problem of plagiarism is not unique to universities, but is common at all levels of Georgia's education system. For example, participants in the focus group provided certain evidence that plagiarism begins not at the level of higher education, but much earlier. For instance, in schools, many students copy assignments from their classmates, often paraphrasing them in order to hide their cheating. In secondary education, it is also very common among students to cheat during tests and exams, often by using cheating notes ("shpargalka" in Georgian). University students often use the same types of plagiarism and cheating as students in schools.

To explain the spread of cheating in schools, a psychologist in the focus group suggested that deviant behavior in the academic process and failure to fulfill assignments honestly is the result of peer-group pressures. Many students consider violations of rules set by teachers as heroic deeds to be admired by classmates. Therefore, early in academic studies, peer pressures become an important influence on students' cheating. The academic process is often viewed by students (and sometimes by teachers) as a confrontation process between two opposing parties, where one party is represented by students and another by school administrators, who establish the rules of conduct. Though plagiarism is less sanctioned or stigmatized in Georgia than in more Western cultures, participating in it is still considered a form of rule breaking.

The roots of such rebellious attitudes toward education authorities might also have historical explanations. Throughout history, Georgia has suffered from external occupations that imposed foreign cultures on its people. To preserve their national identity and culture, the people of Georgia systematically resisted invaders and expressed their discontent with foreign authorities through revolts, strikes, and protests. Georgian history is full of exciting stories of heroic deeds and dramatic battles against foreign invaders. For a long period, these stories were passed down orally, before they were written down. Nowadays, Georgian children are brought up on these tales of rebellious heroes. This provides a possible explanation of why resistance to authorities is deeply embedded in Georgian national character beginning from childhood.

The prevalence of plagiarism in academic writing in all former republics of the Soviet Union also suggests the importance of historical factors. For example, one participant of the focus group traced the roots of the problem of plagiarized theses back to the communist era:

> In the neighborhood of our campus, booksellers served as mediators [between students and theses writers] and prices for their services were well known in the community. Later, employees of public libraries began offering the same services to students. During the communist era, this was an important source of income for many people.

Apart from plagiarism in academic writing, other forms of corruption in higher education were widespread in the Soviet time. The Soviet education system and teaching social sciences, in particular, were strongly based on communist ideology and Marxist–Leninist philosophy. Universities were used as a basis for the spread of Soviet propaganda. Students were obliged to take courses on Marxist–Leninist philosophy and to study works by communist leaders. This often provoked hidden resistance among students. For example, many of them paid bribes to pass exams on ideology-related disciplines.

Finally, the contemporary system of higher education in Georgia does not address the problem of plagiarism in an adequate way. The results of the interviews with Georgian students provide sufficient evidence that they generally perceive the risk of plagiarism detection in universities and the related penalties for cheating in academic writing to be minimal. As a result, such perceptions reinforce students' incentives to engage in cheating behaviors. This suggests that universities in Georgia should focus on the development and implementation of plagiarism preventative methods, such as honor codes, academic integrity policies, and software detection methods. Furthermore, universities should make their penalties for cheating in academic studies more severe, especially in cases of major plagiarism when students buy their theses from specialized companies in the shadow sector of the education system.

## Conclusion

The results of the interviews suggest that plagiarism constitutes a serious challenge for Georgia's higher education system. The findings of the study point to a growing need for universities to raise awareness among students about cheating in academic studies. One of the problems identified in our research is that faculty members do not provide clear guidelines to students on ethical academic behavior. As a result, students are often unaware of what constitutes academic integrity. The study of student plagiarism in Georgia suggests that universities should implement different approaches to promote more effective anti-plagiarism standards and academic integrity, including installing plagiarism detection software, adopting honor codes, and improving penalty policies.

This study is limited to the Georgian context within which the data about student plagiarism were collected. While the findings are indicative, they may not be generalizable to other countries. Even though there is evidence that corruption in higher education is pervasive in most former republics of the Soviet Union, the problem of plagiarism in Georgia has unique historical and cultural roots that might not be observed in other countries. In Georgia, students' perceptions and attitudes toward plagiarism were found to be rather contradictory. On the one hand, the majority of them admitted to engaging in instances of plagiarism; yet, on the other hand, most of them consider such activities unethical. In our opinion, this phenomenon can be explained by Georgia's specific historical, cultural, and social factors, including its national identity, that was formed under resistance to external occupations, mutual influence of Islamic and European cultures, and path-dependent factors in education inherited from the Soviet era. Therefore, further cross-country comparative research is needed to explore similarities and differences in student plagiarism between Georgia and other countries, particularly, in the post-Soviet space.

## References


Alschuler, Alfred S., and Gregory S. Blimling. 1995. "Curbing Epidemic Cheating Through Systemic Change." *College Teaching* 43 (4): 123–125.

Antonovich, Miroslava, and Oleksandr Merezhko. 2006. "Yak podolati koruptsiju" [in Ukrainian]. October 27. http://gazeta.dt.ua/EDUCATION/yak_podolati_koruptsiyu.html (accessed December 29, 2016).

Bennett, Roger. 2005. "Factors Associated with Student Plagiarism in a Post-1992 University." *Assessment and Evaluation in Higher Education* 30 (2): 137–162.

Bowers, William J. 1964. *Student Dishonesty and its Control in College.* New York: Columbia University.

Burns, Susan R., Stephen F. Davis, Janice Hoshino, and Richard L. Miller. 1998. "Academic Dishonesty: A Delineation of Cross-Cultural Patterns." *College Student Journal* 32: 590–596.

Davis, Stephen F., Cathy A. Grover, Angela H. Becker, and Loretta N. McGregor. 1992. "Academic Dishonesty: Prevalence, Determinants, Techniques, and Punishments." *Teaching of Psychology* 19 (1): 16–20.

Davis, Stephen F., Linda M. Noble, Elizabeth N. Zak, and Kristen K. Dreyer. 1994. "A Comparison of Cheating and Learning/Grade Orientation in American and Australian College Students." *College Student Journal* 28: 353–356.

Gugunava, Maya. 2012. "Translations from Georgian into Spanish, 1970–present" [in Georgian]. http://www.bookplatform.org/images/activities/364/georgiantospanishtranslationsstudy_ge1.pdf (accessed December 29, 2016).

Guo, Xin. 2011. "Understanding Student Plagiarism: An Empirical Study in Accounting Education." *Accounting Education* 20 (1): 17–37.

Javakhishvili, Ivane. 1985. *The History* [in Georgian]. T. II. Tbilisi: Tbilisi State University.

Jensen, Lene A., Jeffrey J. Arnett, S. Shirley Feldman, and Elizabeth Cauffman. 2002. "It's Wrong, but Everybody Does it: Academic Dishonesty Among High School and College Students." *Contemporary Educational Psychology* 27 (2): 209–228.

Landau, Joshua D., Perri B. Druen, and Jennifer A. Arcuri. 2002. "Methods for Helping Students Avoid Plagiarism." *Teaching of Psychology* 29 (2): 112–115.

Lim, Vivien K. G., and Sean K. B. See, 2001. "Attitudes Toward, and Intentions to Report, Academic Cheating Among Students in Singapore." *Ethics and Behavior* 11 (3): 261–274.

Love, Patrick G., and Janice Simmons. 1998. "Factors Influencing Cheating and Plagiarism Among Graduate Students in a College of Education." *College Student Journal* 32 (4): 539–550.

McCabe, Donald L. 1992. "The Influence of Situational Ethics on Cheating Among College Students." *Sociological Inquiry* 62 (3): 365–374.

McCabe, Donald L., and Linda K. Trevino. 1993. "Academic Dishonesty: Honor Codes and Other Contextual Influences." *The Journal of Higher Education* 64 (5): 522–538.

McCabe, Donald L., and Linda K. Trevino. 1997. "Individual and Contextual Influences on Academic Dishonesty: A Multicampus Investigation." *Research in Higher Education* 38 (3): 379–396.

McCabe, Donald L., Linda K. Trevino, and Kenneth D. Butterfield. 2001. "Cheating in Academic Institutions: A Decade of Research." *Ethics and Behavior* 11 (3): 219–232.

Moten, Abdul R. 2014. "Academic Dishonesty and Misconduct: Curbing Plagiarism in the Muslim World." *Intellectual Discourse* 22 (2): 167-189

National Statistics Office of Georgia (2015). Higher Education Institutions and Enrollment by Type of Study. http://www.geostat.ge/index.php?action=page&p_id=2105&lang=eng (accessed December 29, 2016).

Osipian, Ararat. 2009. "Corruption and Reform in Higher Education in Ukraine." *Canadian and International Education* 38 (2): 104–122.

Osipian, Ararat. 2010. "Dissertations for Sale: Corruption in Russia's Doctoral Education." Presented at the Annual Meeting of the American Economic Association, Atlanta. https://www.aeaweb.org/conference/2010/retrieve.php?pdfid=88 (accessed December 29, 2016).

Owens, Caleb, and Fiona A. White. 2013. "A 5-year Systematic Strategy to Reduce Plagiarism Among First-Year Psychology University Students." *Australian Journal of Psychology* 65 (1): 14–21.

Park, Chris. 2003. "In Other (People's) Words: Plagiarism by University Students—Literature and Lessons." *Assessment and Evaluation in Higher Education* 28 (5): 471–488.

Podolyan, Lidia. 2006. "Chi mozhlivij ukrains'kij ekvivalent PhD, abo yak unemozhliviti kupivlju disertatsii" [in Ukrainian]. Dzerkalo tyzhnya, October 19. http://www.osvita.org.ua/articles/138.html (accessed December 29, 2016).

Stearns, Samuel A. 2001. "The Student-Instructor Relationship's Effect on Academic Integrity." *Ethics and Behavior* 11 (3): 275–285.

Stearns, Laurie. (1999). "Copy Wrong: Plagiarism, Process, Property, and the Law." In *Perspectives on Plagiarism and Intellectual Property in a Postmodern World,* ed. Lise Buranen & Alice M. Roy, (pp. 5-17). Albany, NY: State University of New York Press.

Stevens, George E., and Faith W. Stevens. 1987. "Ethical Inclinations of Tomorrow's

Managers Revisited: How and Why Students Cheat." *Journal of Education for Business* 63 (1): 24–29.

Taksanov, Alisher. 2003. "Yavlenie korruptsii v Uzbekistane" [in Russian]. CentrAziya, May 3.

Tayraukham, Sombat. 2009. "Academic Ethics in Research Methodology." *The Social Sciences* 4 (6): 573–577.

Waugh, Russell. F., John R. Godfrey, Ellis D. Evans, and Delores Craig. 1995. "Measuring Students' Perceptions about Cheating in Six Countries." *Australian Journal of Psychology* 47: 73–80.

Wilhoit, Stephen. 1994. "Helping Students Avoid Plagiarism." *College Teaching* 42 (4): 161–164.

Zimitat, Craig. 2008. "A Student Perspective of Plagiarism." In *Student Plagiarism in an Online World: Problems and Solutions*, ed. Tim S. Roberts (pp. 10-22). New York: Information Science Reference.

# PART 2
# Economics and Finance

# CHAPTER 6
# Balance of Payments Shock and GEL Depreciation: Causes and Policy Response

**Giorgi Bakradze, Nino Rusieshvili and Kurt Birson**

## Introduction

### *Background*

In early 1990s, the Georgian economy was in disarray. A first attempt, in 1993, to create its own currency—Kuponi—ended in hyperinflation and, unsurprisingly, Georgians considered the US dollar (USD) as both a store of value and unit of account, using Kuponi only in everyday small-scale transactions. The creation of the full-fledged Georgian currency in 1995—the Lari (GEL)—was able to withstand the fallout from the Russian crisis of 1998 (when the Russian Federation was forced to devalue the Ruble and eventually defaulted on its debt) and GEL depreciated by more than 80% between September 1998 and February 1999 as the National Bank of Georgia (NBG) ran down its reserves trying to protect the peg. Despite it being otherwise well managed, this was not enough, at least initially, to persuade the general population to decrease their dependence on the USD, with the latter accounting for more than 50% of both bank loans and deposits even into 2016.

By December 2015 deposit dollarization was 66.8% and loan dollarization 64.8%. The loan dollarization is particularly problematic, since there is a significant currency mismatch between loans and revenues (Figure 1). Therefore, the balance of payments shock and subsequent depreciation of GEL versus USD was a particularly serious challenge for both the population and authorities alike.

A 10-month period from November 2014 to September 2015 was easily the most turbulent time for the GEL in the twenty-first century. Due to a number of reasons, which we will discuss below in more detail, Georgian currency depreciated by almost 40% at the peak and by around 35%–36% by the end of 2015 (Figure 2).

This depreciation was a result of a significant balance of payments shock that hit Georgia. The shock is well visible in the annual data, with the current account deficit widening almost twice in 2014 compared with 2013 and remaining dangerously high in 2015. (The data for 2015 cover only quarters I–III; discrepancies in the table are due to rounding.) The timeline of the shock is particularly evident once we move to the quarterly data. The first shock to the current account occurred in late 2013, however this shock was purely idiosyncratic, caused by the extremely uneven government spending when the budget was in surplus throughout October, and massive deficit spending occurred in the last 2 months of the year (Figure 4).

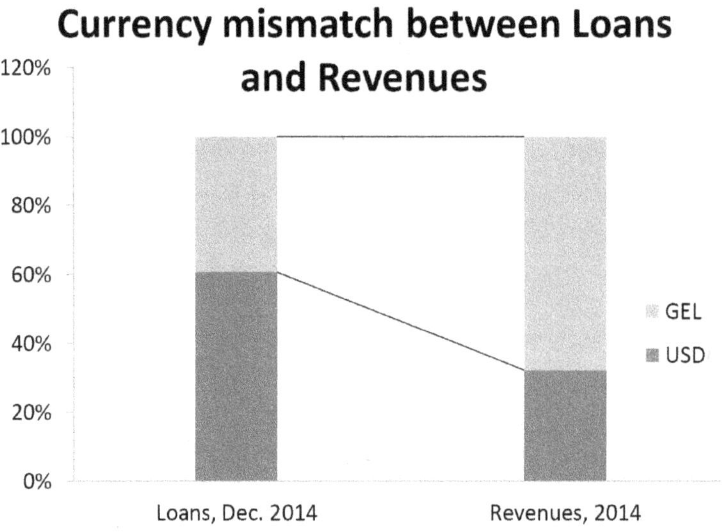


Figure 1: Currency Mismatch Between Loans and Revenues (Unless otherwise indicated, all Graphs and Tables are based on the data of the National Bank of Georgia. Authors would like to thank the Macroeconomics and Statistics Department for provided graphs.)

Figure 2: GEL/USD in Crisis Period

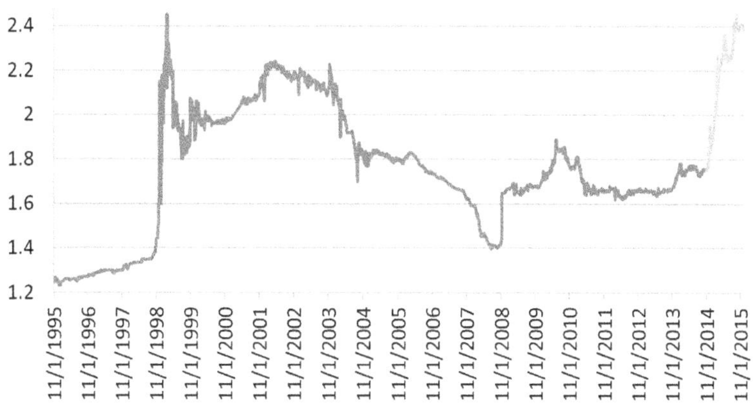


Figure 3: GEL/USD in 1995–2015

Table 1: Georgia Balance of Payments in 2013–2015

| *(Millions of USD)* | 2013 | 2014 | 2015 (Q1–Q3) |
|---|---|---|---|
| **Current account** | **−929.8** | **−1,745.0** | **−1,086.3** |
| A. Goods | −3,492.6 | −4,280.4 | −3,110.5 |
| B. Services | 1,405.5 | 1,297.8 | 1,160.1 |
| C. Income | −308.3 | −196.3 | −343.9 |
| D. Current transfers | 1,465.6 | 1,433.9 | 1,207.9 |
| **Capital and financial account** | **957.7** | **1,819.4** | **1,118.9** |
| **Capital account** | **134.1** | **109.7** | **47.9** |
| **Financial account** | **823.6** | **1,709.7** | **1,071.0** |
| A. Foreign direct investment (FDI) | 829.0 | 1,343.1 | 908.7 |
| B. Portfolio investment | −36.6 | 207.4 | −125.0 |
| C. Financial derivatives | −2.4 | 8.2 | −2.6 |
| D. Other investment | −11.6 | 117.6 | 129.2 |
| E. Reserve assets | 45.2 | 33.4 | 160.6 |
| **Net errors and omissions** | **−27.9** | **−74.4** | **−32.5** |

Table 2: Georgia Balance of Payments in 2013 (Quarterly Data)

| Millions of USD | I-2013 | II-2013 | III-2013 | IV-2013 |
|---|---|---|---|---|
| **Current account** | **−235.7** | **−198.3** | **−60.7** | **−435.2** |
| A. Goods | −745.3 | −876.1 | −861.3 | −1,009.9 |
| B. Services | 256.9 | 375.5 | 515.5 | 257.6 |
| C. Income | −105.0 | −-73.4 | −-70.7 | −59.2 |
| D. Current transfers | 357.8 | 375.8 | 355.9 | 376.2 |
| **Capital and financial account** | **250.2** | **192.8** | **56.4** | **458.3** |
| **Capital account** | **20.8** | **39.3** | **36.9** | **37.1** |
| **Financial account** | **229.4** | **153.5** | **19.5** | **421.2** |
| A. Foreign direct investment (FDI) | 236.9 | 170.7 | 253.9 | 167.5 |
| B. Portfolio investment | −31.1 | −94.6 | −73.8 | 162.9 |
| C. Financial derivatives | 0.0 | −1.4 | −0.2 | −0.7 |
| D. Other investment | 116.1 | 130.0 | −96.6 | −161.2 |
| E. Reserve assets | −92.5 | −51.2 | −63.8 | 252.7 |
| **Net errors and omissions** | **−14.5** | **5.5** | **4.3** | **−23.2** |

Table 3: Georgia Balance of Payments in 2014 (Quarterly Data)

| Millions of USD | I-2014 | II-2014 | III-2014 | IV-2014 |
|---|---|---|---|---|
| **Current account** | **−352.1** | **−423.4** | **−267.9** | **−701.6** |
| A. Goods | −848.0 | −1,065.7 | −1,094.3 | −1,272.4 |
| B. Services | 215.4 | 337.8 | 517.9 | 226.7 |
| C. Income | −74.5 | −62.7 | −62.5 | 3.3 |
| D. Current transfers | 355.0 | 367.2 | 370.9 | 340.8 |
| **Capital and financial account** | **363.6** | **410.6** | **292.3** | **752.9** |
| **Capital account** | **12.6** | **30.5** | **24.4** | **42.2** |
| **Financial account** | **351.0** | **380.0** | **268.0** | **710.7** |
| A. Foreign direct investment (FDI) | 251.3 | 142.1 | 484.9 | 464.8 |
| B. Portfolio investment | −16.6 | 206.9 | 4.9 | 12.2 |
| C. Financial derivatives | 3.0 | 0.3 | 1.0 | 3.9 |
| D. Other investment | −115.4 | −72.7 | 41.2 | 264.5 |
| E. Reserve assets | 228.8 | 103.4 | −264.0 | −34.9 |
| **Net errors and omissions** | **−11.5** | **12.8** | **−24.4** | **−51.3** |

Table 4: Georgia Balance of Payments in 2015 (Quarterly Data)

| Millions of USD | I-2015 | II-2015 | III-2015 |
|---|---|---|---|
| **Current account** | **−459.2** | **−346.8** | **−280.3** |
| A. Goods | −972.7 | −981.9 | −1,155.9 |
| B. Services | 216.7 | 334.9 | 608.6 |
| C. Income | −44.7 | −123.5 | −175.7 |
| D. Current Transfers | 341.4 | 423.6 | 442.8 |
| **Capital and Financial account** | **436.8** | **369.6** | **312.4** |
| **Capital account** | 17.0 | 17.2 | 13.6 |
| **Financial account** | **419.8** | **352.4** | **298.8** |
| A. Foreign direct investment (FDI) | 117.8 | 317.3 | 473.6 |
| B. Portfolio investment | −86.8 | 7.2 | −45.4 |
| C. Financial derivatives | 2.4 | −4.5 | −0.5 |
| D. Other investment | 201.6 | 52.6 | −125.0 |
| E. Reserve assets | 184.8 | −20.2 | −4.0 |
| **Net errors and omissions** | **22.4** | **−22.8** | **−32.2** |

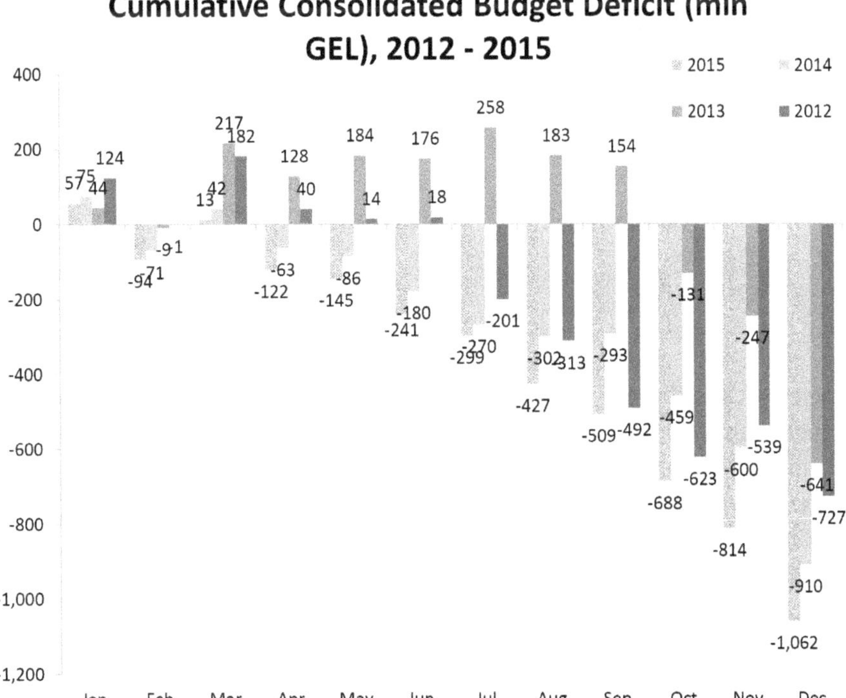


Figure 4: Cumulative Budget Deficit, 2012–2015 (Ministry of Finance, Georgia)

On the other hand, 2014 was completely different, with exogenous factors playing the main role. Despite the increase in the current account deficit obvious in the first three quarters of 2014, the shock only hit in the fourth quarter, when the current account (CA) deficit dropped to its lowest quarterly level since the second quarter of 2008. The result was almost immediate—the exchange rate versus the USD started to drop and in a matter of months GEL lost almost 40% of its dollar value. This balance of payments shock can be divided into global (Fed moving out of quantitative easing (QE), drop in oil prices), regional (e.g. Russia–Ukraine war), and ensuing idiosyncratic (e.g. drop in remittances' inflow) components.

### *Global Factors*

2014 was not a particularly successful year for the global economy. In the developed world only the US and UK showed some strength, whereas the Eurozone, despite being on the rise, still lagged behind.

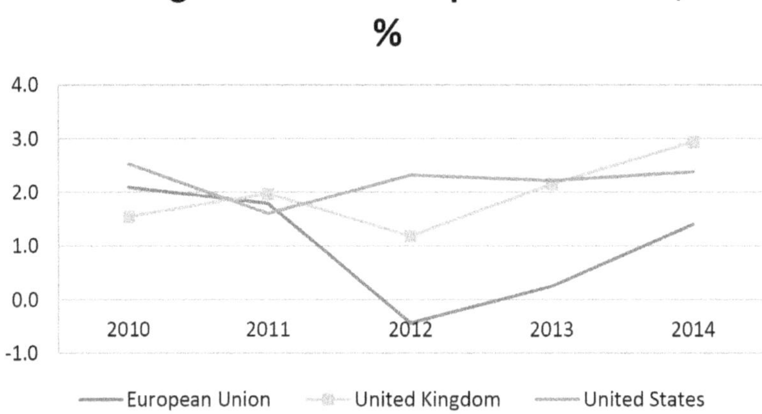


Figure 5: Growth in Developed Countries (IMF, World Economic Outlook, October 2015)

The strong growth in the US motivated the Fed to move out of quantitative easing (QE) policy, which allows the central banks to operate at the zero lower bound via large-scale assets purchase (Benford et al. 2009). Through QE the Fed increased its balance sheet "by close to $3 trillion from December 2007 to November 2013", thus significantly lowering the value of the USD relative to other currencies and causing substantial capital inflow to the developing countries (Park, Ramayandi, and Shin 2014; Ricketts and Waller 2014). Coupled with the "too low for too long" interest rates in the US; strong economic performance in Georgia in the mid-2000s (prior to 2008's double crisis, when the global financial crisis was "complemented" by the Russia–Georgia war in August); and a glut of foreign direct investment (FDI) pouring into Georgia (with a peak of $2 billion in 2007) the appreciation of GEL versus USD was a completely understandable and natural event. Hence, when the Fed first announced tapering of QE in June 2013 and halted asset purchases completely in

October 2014, it was clear that despite the FED keeping interest rates close to zero lower bound (ZLB), the era of the cheap dollar had come more or less to an end (Prial 2013). Of course, the effect of these events on the GEL/USD exchange rate had not been direct—despite the USD index starting to grow even before the complete halt in QE, the GEL depreciation started only a month later and was an indirect consequence of dollar strengthening and events that took place in the EU and Georgia's neighbors.

Figure 6: USD and USD/GEL Indices, 1999–2015
Source: National Bank of Georgia and St. Louis Federal Reserve (FRED database).

Moving out of large-scale asset purchases (LSAP) in the US almost coincided with the change in monetary policy in the Eurozone. Mario Draghi, President of the European Central Bank (ECB), in April 2014 admitted that the QE was being discussed as a possibility, given the low inflation, and in June, after another cut to the main refinancing rate, he announced that "The Governing Council is unanimous in its commitment to using unconventional instruments within its mandate should it become necessary to further address risks of too prolonged a period of low inflation" (Kitco News 2014; Wearden 2014). Growth in the Eurozone in 2014 remained unsatisfactory, with inflation steadily dropping, from 0.8% in January to −0.2% in December. Accordingly, in January 2015, Draghi announced an expanded asset purchase program, with combined monthly purchases to be equal to €60 billion, and plans for the program to last at least until September 2016 (Draghi 2015).

The markets reacted to the possibility of QE in the Eurozone well before the announcement itself; the mere possibility was enough to send the Euro onto the path of depreciation, with the currency dropping from almost 1.4 USD in May 2014 to 1.16 by January 22, 2015 (the QE announcement date; the Euro dropped an additional 0.042 points on this day alone) and remained below 1.15 throughout the year, occasionally dropping close to 1.05.

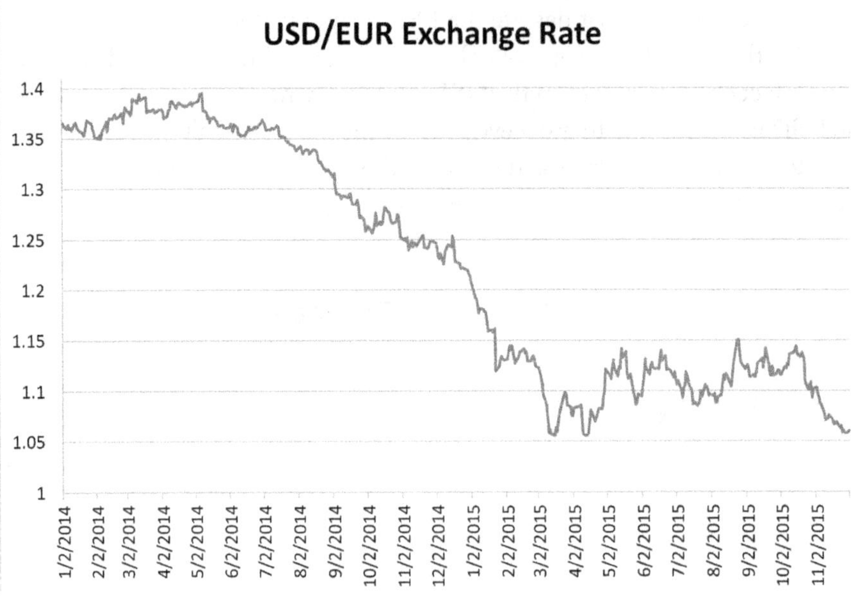


Figure 7: USD/EUR Exchange Rate, 2014–2015
Source: European Central Bank.

Not being necessarily a concern for the citizens of the EU, the depreciation affected the dollar income of Georgians living in the EU, and the level of remittance coming from therein. This drop in remittances was aggravated by the events in Greece, which traditionally has been the second largest source of remittances in the Georgian economy after Russia (averaging 12.8% of the total in 2011–2014). After the cash withdrawals were capped at €60 per day, and foreign money transfers banned altogether, the remittances from Greece dropped by more than 90% in the summer of 2015. On the whole, the remittances from the EU dropped in the first 11 months of 2015 by 23%—a reduction in foreign currency inflow on its own large enough to cause depreciation pressure. However, the pressure on the exchange rate was not limited to the shocks coming from the developed world.

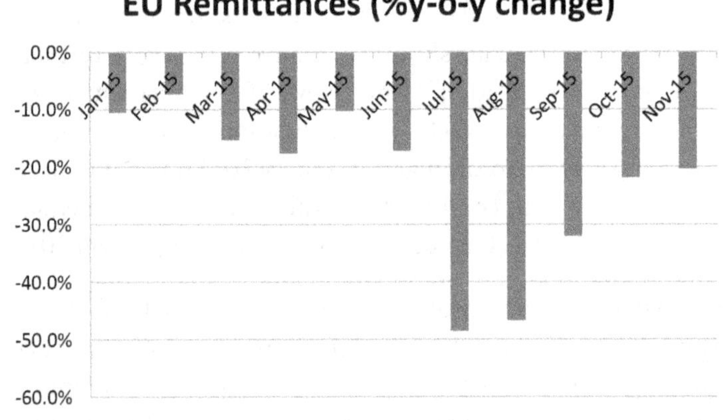


Figure 8: Annual Change in Remittances to Georgia from the EU

*Regional Factors*

Unlike in the US and UK, the growth in emerging markets in 2014 slowed down substantially, particularly in BRIC countries (apart from India). While the slowdown in Brazil and China should not have had a particularly significant effect on Georgia, problems in the Russian economy certainly did. The crisis in Ukraine and ensuing war between Russia and Ukraine affected Georgia in many ways, and the sanctions imposed on Russia by the West exacerbated the situation.

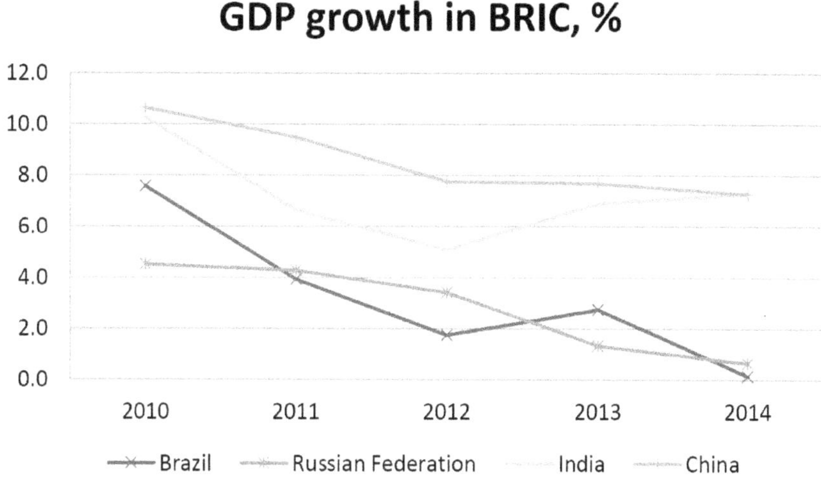


Figure 9: Growth in BRIC Countries. Source: IMF (2015).

The depreciation of the Ukrainian hryvnia, along with weakening demand in Ukraine due to war, decreased the competitiveness of Georgian exports, which dropped as a share of the total from 6.6% in 2013 to 4.9% in 2014 and 2.5% in the first 11 months of 2015.

The reopening of the Russian market for Georgian products in 2013 had an immediate effect, with the share of Georgian exports to Russia rising from below 2% in 2012 to 9.6% in 2014. However, the depreciation of the ruble and general economic slowdown in Russia caused this indicator to drop to 7% in the first 11 months of 2015.

Sanctions on Russia, coupled with the significant drop in oil prices in 2014 (e.g. the price of West Texas Intermediate oil (WTI) fell from $105.65 in June 2014 to $48.55 in January 2015), had a significant depreciation pressure on the ruble. While in the first 8 months of 2014 the ruble had been more or less stable, fluctuating in the range of 33–37 rubles per USD, in September it started to fall, reaching almost 60 by the end of the year, and, but for an appreciation period between February and May, depreciating more or less steadily throughout 2015. In total, depreciation in the 2 years since January 2014 reached almost 120%. Along with the shock to Georgian exports, this depreciation was particularly harmful for the remittances coming from Russia, which has always been the largest source of remittances (averaging 53.5% of total remittances in 2009–2013).

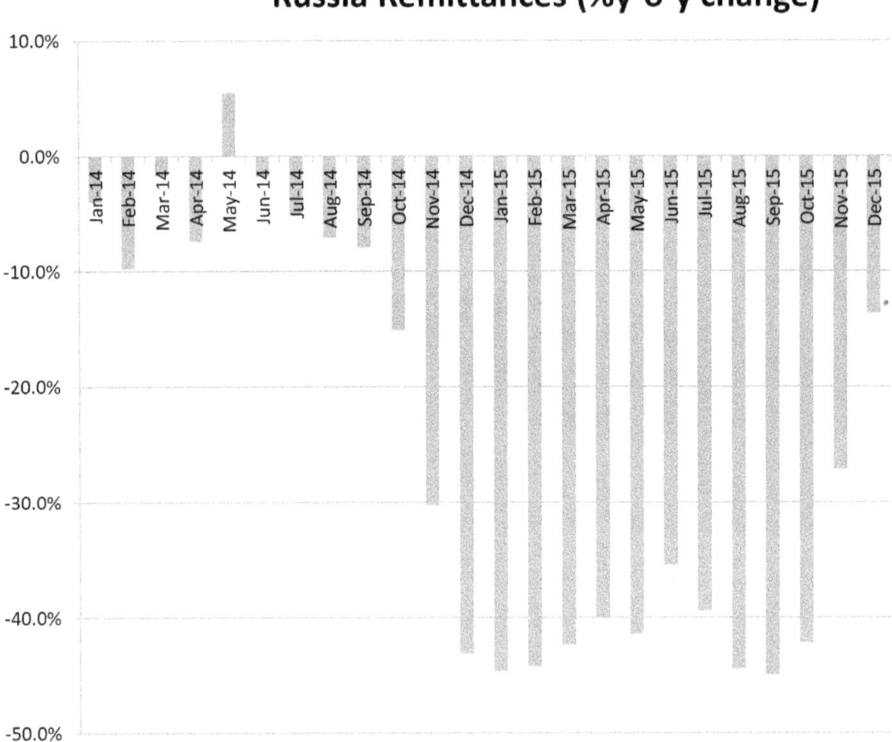


Figure 10: Annual Change in Remittances to Georgia from Russia

It should be noted that due to the depreciation of almost all the major trading partners' currencies versus GEL, the nominal effective exchange rate (NEER) of the Lari was appreciating throughout 2014 until the depreciation versus the USD started.

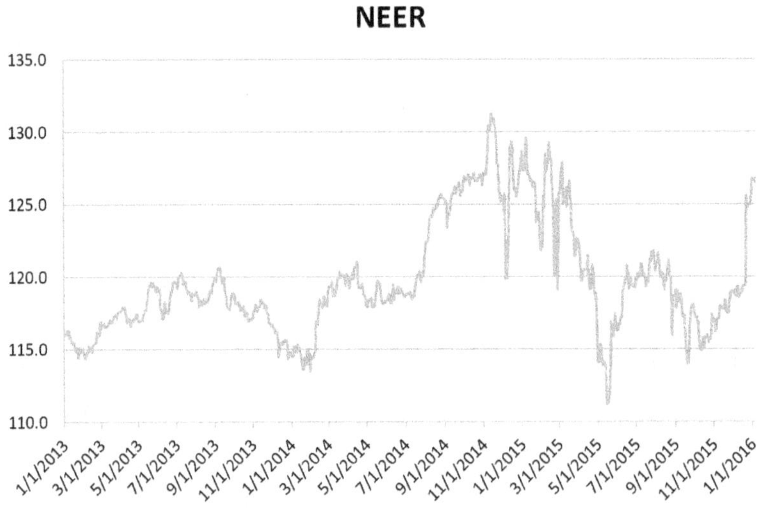


Figure 11: Nominal Effective Exchange Rate, 2013–2015

As a result, exports dropped (as well as total remittances), while imports did not adjust until mid-2015.

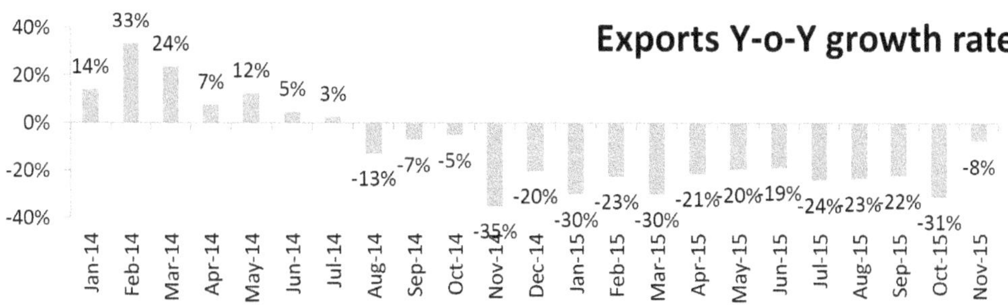


Figure 12: Exports y-o-y Growth Rate

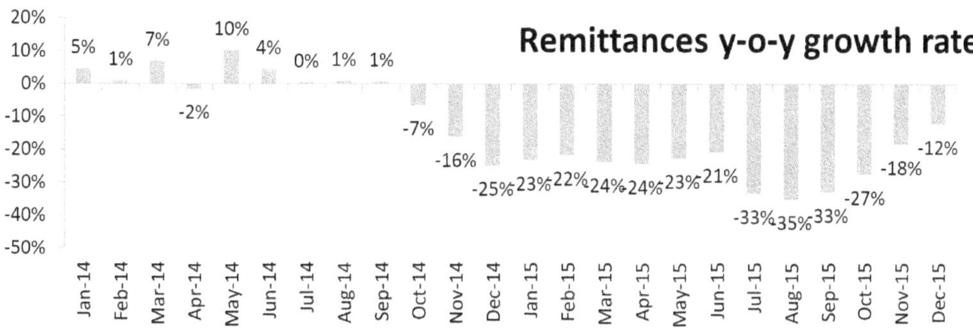


Figure 13: Remittances y-o-y Growth Rate

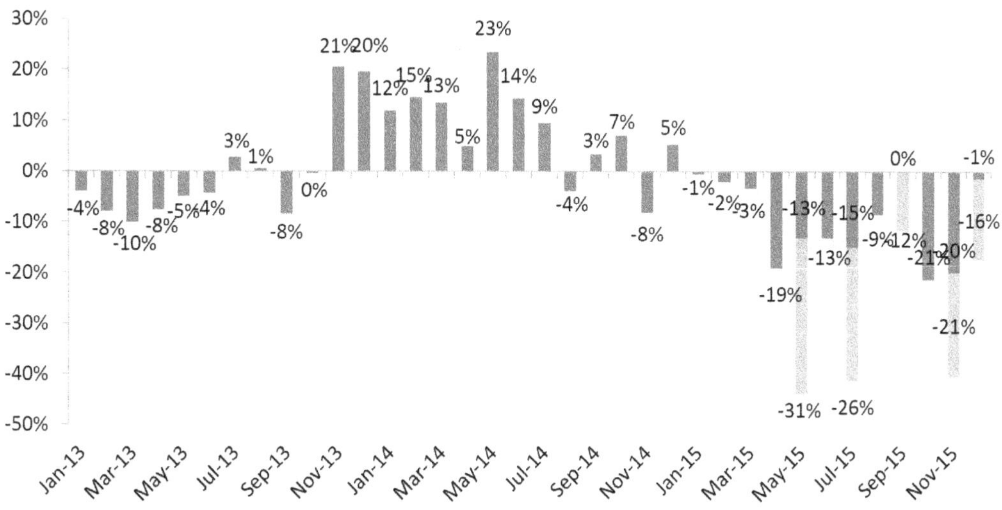


Figure 14: Imports y-o-y Growth Rate

Eventually, the depreciation caused a rebalancing of the balance of payments. The drop in exports, particularly significant in the first quarter of 2015, was eventually met by a commensurate drop in imports, and it is notable that exports increased in volume in the second and third quarters of 2015 (Figure 15).

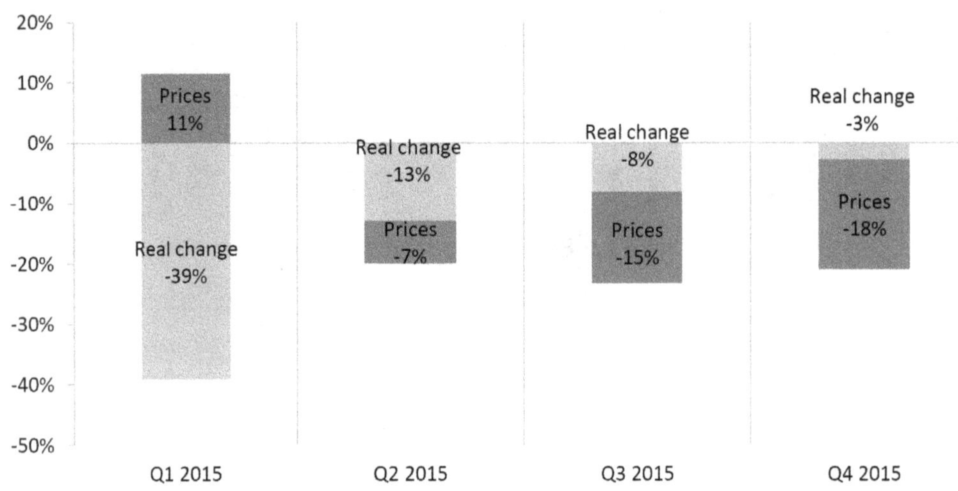


Figure 15: Change in Exports by Quarters (Calculation by the NBG Staff)

On the other hand, as mentioned above, due to the NEER appreciation, imports did not start dropping until the second quarter of 2015 (Figure 14). As expected, most of the decrease in imports was accounted for by low demand in consumption goods, with the import of investment/intermediate goods decreasing insignificantly (Figure 17).

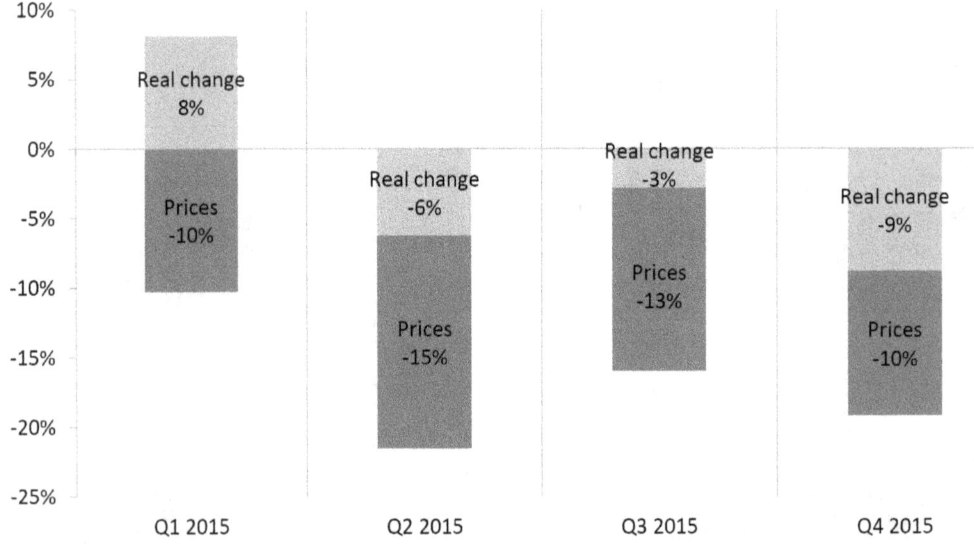


Figure 16: Change in Imports by Quarters (Calculation by the NBG Staff)

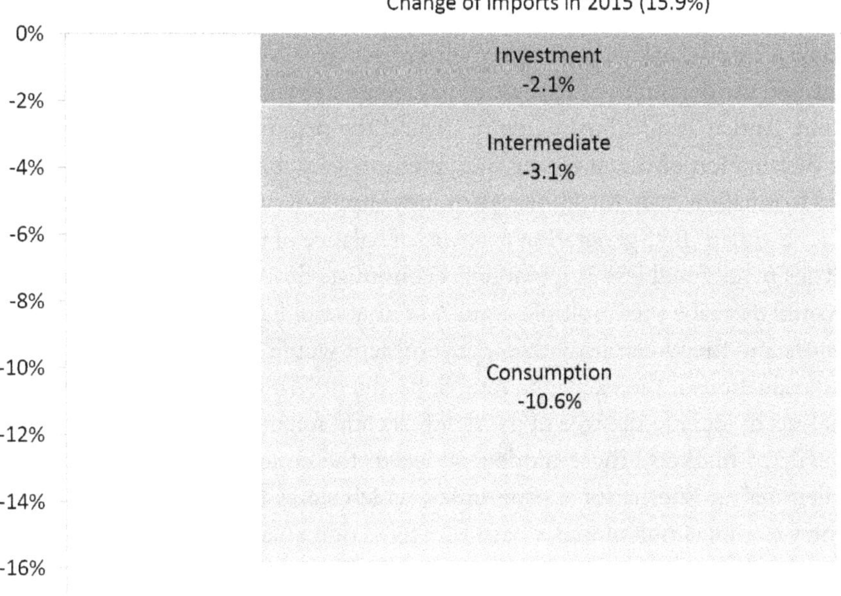


Figure 17: Imports' Decline Break-up (Calculation by the NBG Staff)

On the whole, the data show that Georgia lost around $1 billion in inflows in 2014/2015, a significant drop creating significant depreciation pressure, which was only alleviated once the outflows had lost a similar amount, and the current account rebalancing ended with the new equilibrium exchange rate of around 2.4 GEL/USD.

## Literature Review

Increased globalization and the liberalization of trade and financial markets have led to the growing attention paid to the balance of payments, and specifically the vulnerability of countries to balance of payments and currency crises. In certain circumstances, prolonged imbalances in accounts can lead to currency speculation and devaluation, which can cause significant stress on a country's domestic economy at several levels. This happened most prominently in the early 1990s in the European Monetary System, in Mexico in 1994, East Asia in 1997–1998, and Argentina in 2002–2003 (IMF 2005; Danniger 2008; Müller-Plantenberg 2010; Glick and Hutchinson 2011).

The balance of payments is of particular concern for relatively smaller or emerging market countries open to international trade and capital flows (Barbosa-Filho 2012). Moreover, the nature and impact of these crises differ depending on several factors identified through empirical studies, such as the domestic money supply, short-term debt ratios, net export growth, market openness and the overvaluation of the Real Effective Exchange Rate (Müller-Plantenberg 2010; Al-Assaf, Al-Tarawneh, and Alawin 2013; Chernyak, Khomiak, and Chernyak 2013; Kulkarni and Kamaiah 2015).

Krugman's article, "A model of balance-of-payments crises" (1979) was one of the pioneering works that analyzed the dynamics of balance of payment crises under a fixed-rate or pegged exchange system. Anticipating adjustments to defend the peg, financial speculation could then lead to a devaluation of the currency, and attempts to stabilize it through short-term debt could lead to inflation from the increased money supply. Krugman's paper would come to represent the so-called "first-generation models" of balance of payments crises. However, as more countries maintained less strict targets, economists developed "second-generation models" that could describe the "multiple equilibria" that could arise when uncertainty between speculators and the uncertainty that a government would defend a target rate could still lead to a devaluation of the exchange rate. Subsequent "Third generation" models extended the analysis to include the role of fiscal deficits and financial institutions within the context of liberalized markets. These models all led to the conclusion of the "impossible trinity" or "trilemma" in international economics, which states that when capital is freely mobile, a country cannot simultaneously have (i) a fixed or managed exchange rate, and (ii) an independent domestic monetary policy, i.e., control of domestic interest rates (Glick and Hutchinson 2011; Sen 2014).

Though many countries have since abandoned fixed rate regimes, some have imposed restrictions on capital movement through inflation targeting schemes. This has been shown to have detrimental effects on the balance of payments similar to those of fixed-rate currency regimes (Kumhof 2000; IMF 2005; Danninger and Jaumotte 2008; Glick and Hutchinson 2011). Kumhof, Li, and Yan (2007) demonstrates that given a government's commitment to inflation targeting, emerging market countries are vulnerable to short-term currency speculation rather than instantaneous speculation evident in fixed-rate systems.

A demand-side approach to balance of payments crises, called the Balance of Payments Constraint, suggests that in an open economy, the Balance of Payments represents a constraint on demand. Thus actual GDP growth can be approximated as a function of export growth divided by the elasticity of demand for imports. Such a model links the importance of exchange rate dynamics with next exports, reserves of foreign exchange and domestic income (Thirlwall 2014). Several studies have shown the model to be robust in predicting GDP growth, and its relevance to the understanding of balance of payments crises (Moreno-Brid 1998; Moreno-Brid and Pérez 1999; Pacheco-López 2005; Thirlwall 2011; Blecker and Ibarra 2013; Gökçe and Çankal 2013).

Balance of payments crises have been frequent in the last several decades, with a few well known cases mentioned above. Though criteria used to identify the incidence of such crises differs, Glick and Hutchinson (2011) of the San Francisco Federal Reserve Bank employ the definition used in Laeven and Valencia (2008), where a country is said to have undergone a balance of payments crisis if the domestic currency experiences a devaluation of at least 30%. Based on this criteria, there were 201 currency crises between 1975 and 2007, and in one 6-month period between August 2008 and February 2009 alone, 23 countries experienced currency crises (Glick and Hutchinson 2011). Danninger and Jaumotte (2008) identifies nearly 50 events or "prolonged episodes" of current account imbalances from 1970 to 2007, which were key triggers to balance of payment crises. Further study would have to determine whether these prolonged episodes of current account imbalances were concurrent with the balance of payments crises noted in Laeven and Valencia (2008).

Responses to balance of payments crises vary. Generally, Glick and Hutchinson (2011) observe that the degree of openness to trade and freely floating exchange rates help a country become more resistant to currency crises. Others identify currency devaluation as another potential solution to an impending speculative attack, where changes in net exports would smooth fluctuations in the current and capital accounts (Remolona, Mangahas, and Pante 1986; Ghartey 1987; Thanh and Kalirajan 2006). Fahrholz and Freytag (2012) argue that in order to resolve the persistence of balance of payments problems in Europe, the European Stability Mechanism (ESM) should reduce capital controls, and set limits on the intervention of government in the form of bailouts, which relates to concerns of the "third-generation" models of crisis, where governments create a de facto peg by raising the money supply.

## REGIONAL EXPERIENCE

**(Hereinafter "region" means former Soviet republics and Turkey.)**

The regional and global components of the shock have hit all countries in the region and there have been different policy responses, with different results. In the case of most post-Soviet countries, the main channel of the shock came through Russia, due to close social and economic contacts. Tables 5 and 6 list the dynamics of relevant variables in the countries of the region, including Turkey. Notably, most of the countries, apart from Armenia, experienced worse depreciation than Georgia, at the same time having sold significantly more international reserves and mostly having higher inflation. Below is a brief description of how four of these countries fared in the wake of the shock.

Table 5: Depreciation in the Region (Data Taken from Central Banks' Web Sites of Respective Countries)

| | Depreciation since beginning of 2014 (%) | Depreciation since beginning of 2015 (%) |
|---|---|---|
| Russia | 99.7 | 15.3 |
| Ukraine | 171.5 | 37.6 |
| Turkey | 33.9 | 23.2 |
| Azerbaijan | 103.8 | 103.8 |
| Kazakhstan | 62.7 | 37.1 |
| Armenia | 17.2 | 0.9 |
| Moldova | 44.4 | 20.6 |
| **Georgia** | **33.9** | **23.5** |

Table 6: Use of Policy Instruments in the Region (Data Taken from Central Banks' Web Sites of Respective Countries)

| | Selling reserves, 2014 (million USD) | Selling reserves, 2015 (million USD) | Inflation (%) | Policy rate (%) |
|---|---|---|---|---|
| Russia | 125,000 | 30,000 | 15.6 | 11.0 |
| Ukraine | 14,000 | | 55.3 | 30.0 |
| Turkey | 6,500 | 2,700 | 6.8 | 7.5 |
| Azerbaijan | 2,500 | 7,630 | 4.5 | 3.0 |
| Kazakhstan | 28,000 | | 3.9 | 5.5 |
| Armenia | 770 | 130 | 4.2 | 10.5 |
| Moldova | 660 | 400 | 8.3 | 17.5 |
| **Georgia** | **100** | **200** | **4.9** | **6.0** |

*Armenia*

Armenia is traditionally dependent on remittances from Russia, which constitute 16%–18% of GDP. The depreciation of the ruble against the Armenian Dram in 2014–2015 (the value of RUB in AMD dropped from 11.8 in January 2014 to 6.1 two years later) caused significant problems for the Armenian economy, which, coupled with the significant drop in remittances in 2015, resulted in the low growth of just 1% in 2015 (Amirkhanyan 2016). In response to 22% depreciation in December 2014, the Central Bank of Armenia (CBAr) raised the interest rate from 6.75% gradually to 10% in February 2015, in an attempt to curb inflation expectations, simultaneously raising other lending rates and increasing minimum reserve requirements for the commercial banks (Danielyan and Gabrielian 2014; Danielyan 2015). At the same time, Armenia attempted to curb the depreciation by active intervention in the foreign exchange market, mostly in 2014, by selling around $770 million, and continued this practice occasionally in 2015 (however also buying dollars, when the market allowed) (Sahakian 2015).

As a result of an interest rate hike, the aggregate demand in Armenia was weakened and growth decreased to 3% in 2015 from 3.5% a year before. Overall, it could be said that Armenia withstood the balance of payments shock, however it remains to be seen whether the exchange rate stability achieved over the 2015 is sustainable.

*Azerbaijan*

The dramatic decline in oil prices which saw oil prices to drop from levels above 100 USD per barrel in the first half of 2014 to below 50 USD in the second half of 2015 (and below 30 USD in January 2016) hits oil-rich countries harder than oil importers, who had an additional cushion in lower fuel prices, pulling inflation down. This decline can be compared with a similar sharp drop in oil prices that occurred in 1985–1986, and, if the analogy is correct, it might take quite a long time until oil prices reach at least the levels of the mid-2000s. Under such circumstances, oil exporters would face challenges different from those that were prevalent during previous oil price declines, when the world was in recession. If, for other countries in the region, a balance of payments shock were the only (if very dire) problem, energy exporting countries would face an increased budget deficit as well. Azerbaijan, similar to other oil exporters, heavily used its sovereign wealth fund—State Oil Fund of Azerbaijan (SOFAZ) to replenish declining budget revenues, thus adding to the pressure on the Azeri Manat (AZN).

The Central Bank of Azerbaijan Republic (CBAR) has maintained the peg to USD since 2001, at 0.78 AZN/USD. When the oil prices started declining and the balance of payments started deteriorating, piling pressure on AZN, the CBAR started intervening heavily in the foreign exchange market, selling USD in order to keep the peg. In December 2014 through January 2015 alone, defending AZN cost $2.2 billion, however an almost 60% decline in oil prices caused the CBAR to devalue the currency by 33.5% and move to a USD-EUR basket to manage the exchange rate. Throughout 2015, amidst declining oil prices CBAR continued interventions in an attempt to keep this new peg, however, after spending more than $7 billion, the CBAR decided, on December 21, 2015, to abandon the peg and floated the AZN, which immediately depreciated by 48%. This move had been anticipated before, since in February 2015 Elman Rustamov, governor of CBAR, had considered introducing flexible exchange rates and a gradual move to an inflation targeting regime (Farchy and Barber 2015). The depreciation helped the Azerbaijan government to solve the budget deficit problems, however the general population was significantly hurt. Given the huge jump in the exchange rate, one can safely assume that floating had been long overdue; had the authorities moved to the flexible exchange rate earlier, the losses, monetary as well as social, would likely have been lower.

### *Kazakhstan*

Kazakhstan is another energy exporter hit hard by the decline in oil and other energy prices. Its problems started somewhat earlier than in other countries of the region, namely, in February 2014. With its closer ties to Russia, when the latter allowed the ruble to slide, it undermined Kazakhstan's "tightly-managed float" and caused the first devaluation since 2009, with the midpoint of the exchange rate target corridor shifting by 19% (Gordeyeva 2014). However, this early action did not alleviate the pressure on Kazakhstan Tenge (KZT); with the continuing decline in oil prices, causing a 40% fall in exports in January–July 2015, the Central Bank of Kazakhstan (CBK) was finally pushed to float its currency on August 20, 2015. The problem was exacerbated by the declining prices in other commodities (e.g. metals), which also constitute an important share of Kazakhstan exports.

During this period, CKB was sharply limiting short-term liquidity, in an attempt to support the currency, which somewhat nullified the introduction of the key policy rate, which the CBK set at 16%. In addition, the CBK declared that it would move to an inflation-targeting regime (Gordeyeva and Solovyov 2015). KZT immediately lost 35.5% against the USD and the slide, with some fluctuations, has continued ever since, with KZT/USD reaching almost 384 in January 2016.

As in case of Azerbaijan, the move to the floating rate might have come later than needed, thus causing excessive depreciation, which could have been avoided. The main problem with the CBK's monetary policy was the lack of effective interest rate instruments, which limited the bank to the use of the exchange rate as a main monetary instrument, as well as the primary objective. A high degree of dollarization made the management of system liquidity even more challenging (Epstein and Portillo 2014). The introduction of a key policy rate in September 2015, still did not properly signal the policy stance, and CBK was advised by the IMF to move to a more standard practice of monetary policy, using open market operations in order to anchor the key interbank rates. The decision to move to inflation targeting will definitely help the CBK in increasing its effectiveness, although according to the statement from Kazakh National Economy Minister Yerbolat Dosayev, a member of the central bank's board, the CBK has plans to introduce a flexible interest rate in 2016, which baffled market analysts and economists alike (Gordeyeva and Kelley 2015).

### *Moldova*

Moldova is significantly more dependent on remittances than most other countries in the world—according to World Bank data, only Tajikistan, Kyrgyz Republic, and Nepal have received more remittances as a share of GDP in 2014 than Moldova, whose remittances constituted 26.2% of GDP (World Bank n.d.). The poorest of all countries discussed herein, Moldova is heavily dependent on imports, with Ukraine and Russia being two of its largest trading partners, and remittances from Russia being an important source of foreign exchange. The problems in the Russian economy, war between Russia and Ukraine, import restrictions imposed by Russia on certain goods from Moldova, and structural regulations it put on migrants from states outside of the Eurasian Economic Union, have all caused a significant drop in both remittances (24% in the first 11 months of 2015) and exports (50%) (Stratfor 2015). This decline in foreign currency inflows created a significant depreciation pressure on the Moldovan Leu (MDL), which started losing value around August 2014, having previously fluctuated between 13 and 14 MDL/USD. The National Bank of Moldova (NBM) attempted to stop the depreciation by heavily intervening in the foreign exchange market, selling $640 million in 2014, and an additional $400 million in 2015 (Timpul n.d). Notably, throughout most of 2014 the NBM kept its main policy rate unchanged, at 3.5%, but increased it twice in December 2014 (to 4.5% and 6.5%) and then throughout 2015, first with a jump to 13.5% and then gradually to 19.5%. The situation in the country was further exacerbated by the huge banking fraud, which took place in 2014; the disappearance of $1 billion from country's leading banks significantly hurt the credibility of the NBM (Demytrie 2015).

Despite credibility problems, the monetary policy of the NBM was, as in other cases, based on attempts to defend the exchange rate with active sales of reserves—a policy clearly doomed to fail. In addition, the NBM kept the base policy rate too low for too long, and its increase came most probably too late to alleviate the pressure on MDL, despite a swing of 16 percentage points in around a year.

# Policy Response in Georgia—Monetary Policy

## *What was and should have been done*

When external shock is manifested through an effect on the current account, monetary authorities essentially have two choices—allow the currency to depreciate (provided that the country has not committed itself to a peg, in which case protecting the exchange rate is usually the first choice); or try to protect the exchange rate. The results in these cases can differ significantly:

1) If the exchange rate is allowed to respond freely, depreciation is almost inevitable. While there is a possibility of import-induced inflation (particularly for countries where the import share of the consumption basket is high), depreciation can be beneficial, both for exports and the competitiveness of local producers; imports are contained and finally adjust down, until balance is restored. Overall costs depend on the dollarization of the economy.

2) An opposite choice is to use monetary policy instruments to squeeze aggregate demand so that all adjustment comes from reduced imports (unlike choice 1, exports will not adjust). This is expected to cause a significant contraction of the economy, since it is impossible to target only imports. Therefore, population income will decline in real terms, weakened domestic demand will cause an increase in unemployment, and eventually, overall income losses of the population will be much larger than those coming from the increased loan payment burden.

It should also be mentioned that usually, in low-income countries, high dollarization of loans does not mean a high share of the population having loans in foreign currency. So, the social costs in the second case are not only larger, but also affect a much larger share of the population. On the whole, the first policy choice is a preferred alternative.

The position of the National Bank of Georgia was somewhat undermined by the populist demands of various "experts" to defend the exchange rate at all costs. The competence of such experts was easily seen from the fact that ever since the depreciation trend started they demanded selling foreign exchange reserves in order to prevent exchange rate shock. Both from a theoretical and practical point of view, this policy is futile, amounting to (a) the central bank essentially financing imports instead of letting them adjust, and, as such, (b) postponing the needed adjustment in the current account to restore balance, aggravating imbalance, increasing dollarization and augmenting inevitable depreciation, the magnitude of which will be higher than without any intervention by the central bank. It should be mentioned that foreign exchange interventions can indeed be useful in defending the exchange rate but if and only if (a) the international reserves of the central bank are vast enough to withstand the attack on the currency or (b) if the country is able to borrow in foreign exchange to replenish the depleted international reserves (that's in effect why and how the NBG was able to stop depreciation in August–September 2008).

The NBG was able to withstand such attacks, and the temptation of using reserves, and their chosen strategy proved to be effective (see cases of Moldova and Azerbaijan, above). Nevertheless, while the NBG did not use large-scale interventions in order to stop the depreciation, it had to resort to occasional interventions in order to curb the daily trading volatility of the exchange rate.

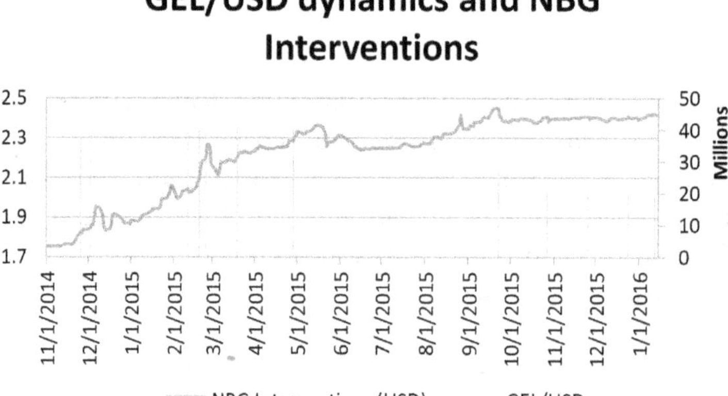


Figure 18: NBG forex Interventions and GEL/USD Dynamics

Given the high level of dollarization in the economy, the depreciation constituted a serious risk for financial stability as well and the NBG was ready to take relevant measures. However, unexpectedly, financial stability was not particularly hindered, as witnessed by the NPL ratio (Figure 20), so there appeared to be no particular need of serious use of macroprudential instruments. The stability of the NPLs can be explained by several factors, including relatively high nominal GDP growth, conservative supervisory practices (e.g. high capital adequacy ratio) of the NBG, and the fact that the depreciation, though large, did not occur overnight and was spread over a relatively long period of time (Figure 20), hence allowing banks/borrowers time to adjust. Nevertheless, both in order to prevent financial stability risks and curb inflation expectations, the NBG had to increase the monetary policy rate, from the all-time low of 3.75% in late 2013 to 8% in December 2015. As a result, inflation has been below the target almost throughout the depreciation period (aided, of course, by the significant decrease in fuel and transportation prices), only picking up in August 2015, but still remaining at a manageable level.

### *What the central banks should not do*

Evidence shows that the relatively passive (but watchful) policy of the NBG had been successful, not in stopping the depreciation (which would have been impossible), but in mitigating the consequences of the shock in an optimal way. In part, it was as much due to the policies that the NBG followed as to the policies it did not pursue. Namely, there are certain actions no central bank should take when facing external shocks like the one Georgia faced in 2014–2015.

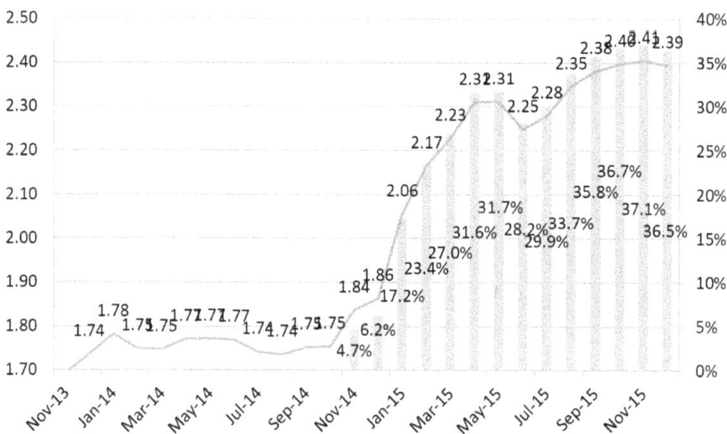


Figure 19:GEL/USD Exchange Rate and Depreciation Dynamics

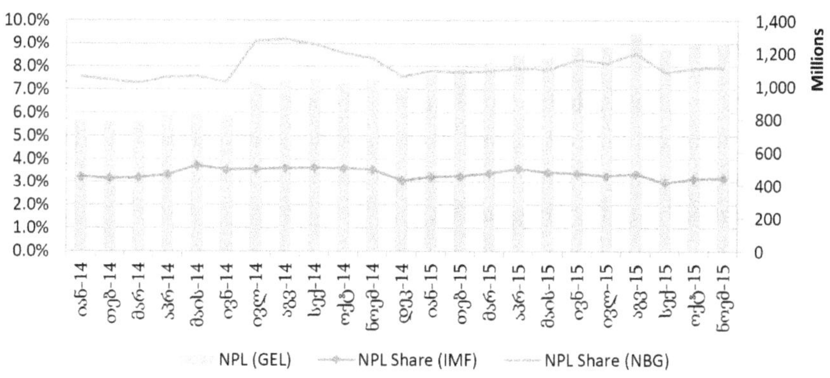


Figure 20: Nonperforming Loans

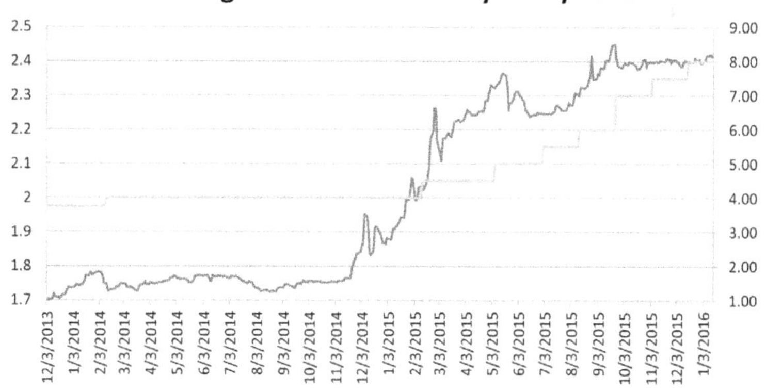


Figure 21: GEL/USD Exchange Rate and the Monetary Policy Rate

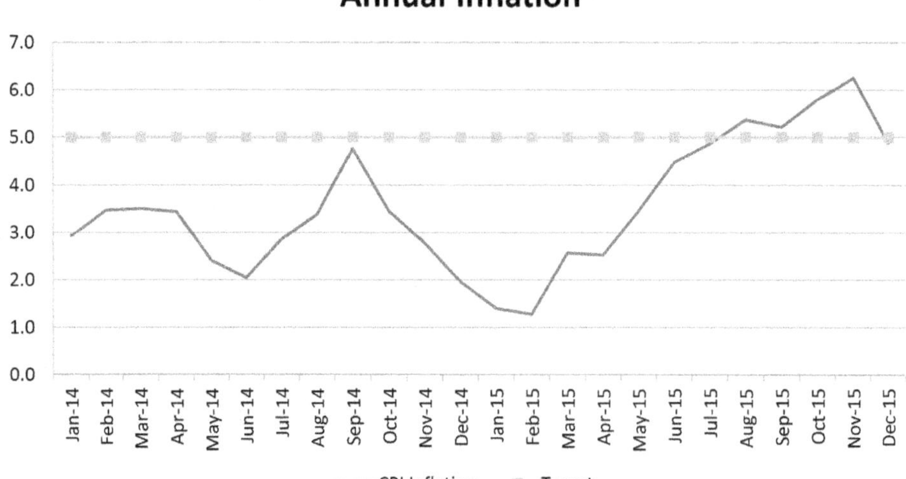


Figure 22: Annual CPI Inflation in Georgia

**Selling off Its FX Reserves**

Such a policy, as mentioned before, will only postpone the adjustment in the current account balance, increase dollarization and, eventually, cause depreciation that will likely be of a much larger magnitude, and happen in a much shorter period of time, creating significant problems for financial stability (Figure 23).

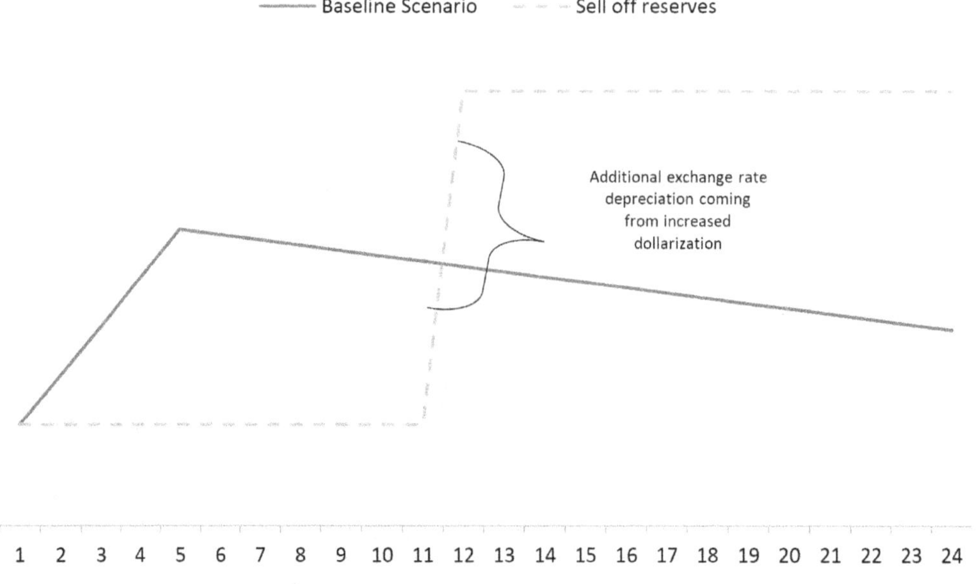


Figure 23: Reserves' Sale Versus Passive ER Policy

The scenario above was modeled by the NBG research team, however it can also be seen in real-life examples from 2008 to 2010 (Figure 24). Although Poland and Armenia may not be directly comparable given the significant differences between the two in economic development and size, one can see that the policy of not selling the FX reserves pursued by Poland was correct in the long run, since, despite the exchange rate volatility, dollarization was kept in place and the exchange rate, after peaking in March 2009, gradually appreciated further, whereas Armenia, which heavily intervened, was still forced to float the currency, and saw the dollarization levels almost double.

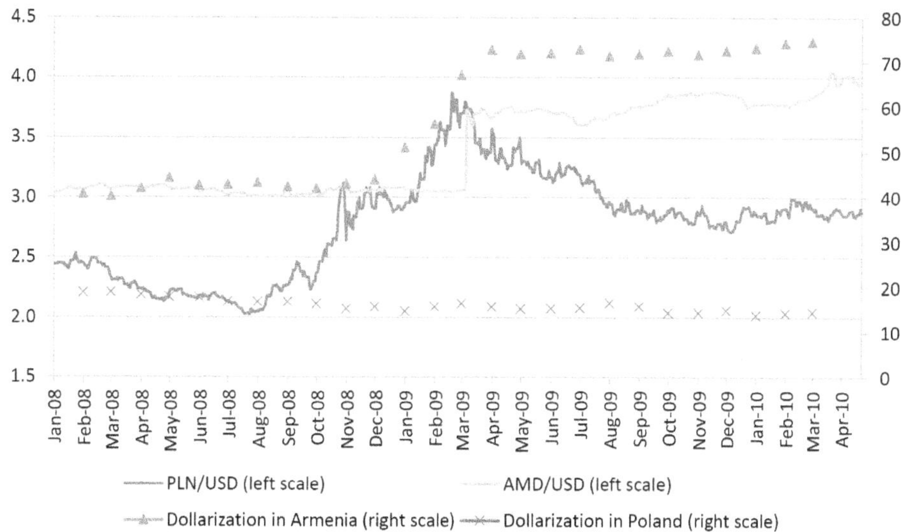


Figure 24: Armenia and Poland in 2008–2010 (National Bank of Poland; Central Bank of Armenia)

Active intervention in the foreign exchange markets was a mistake made by several countries hit by the recent shock, as well, with the notable examples being oil-rich Azerbaijan and Kazakhstan. Overall, the central banks should not forget that the floating exchange rate is a good shock absorber, as one can see on the following page, in Figure 25.

**Limit Short-Term Liquidity**

In no case should the central bank limit short-term liquidity provision to commercial banks. Such liquidity does not affect either the money supply or the exchange rate, and limiting it could create significant liquidity problems for the banks, causing, in the worst case, bank runs. Even if bank panic is prevented, shortage of liquidity will cause a dramatic rise in interest rates, affecting the loan portfolio and sending the economy into recession. Furthermore, the resulting confidence shock will add to economic decline, and make turnaround even more difficult. In order to replenish liquid assets, the commercial banks would likely try to sell government T-bills, resulting in a jump in interest rates for the latter, and widening the budget deficit. In the worst case the government would simply not be able to finance its expenditures and would have to cut them, thus adding to recession.

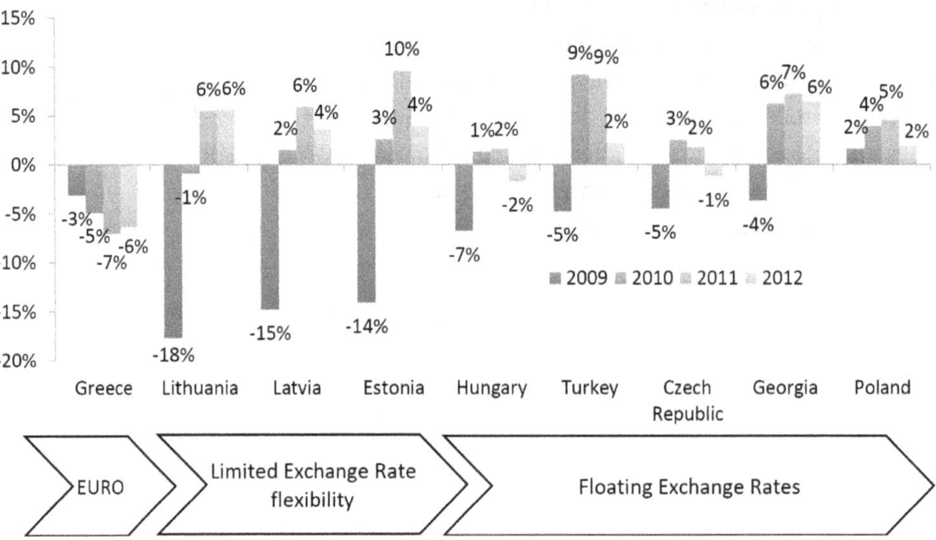


Figure 25: Floating Exchange Rate as a Shock Absorber (IMF World Economic Outlook, Central Banks of Respective Countries)

**Dramatic Increase in Policy Rate**

A gradual increase in policy rate will keep inflation expectations close to target, while at the same time curbing some financial stability risks. Dramatic increases in policy rates, though—akin to that implemented by the Russian Central Bank in December 2014—can cause significant decline in aggregate demand, affecting population income. Although the exchange rate will most likely appreciate, the drop in incomes, increase in unemployment and recession in the economy will eventually result in much higher social costs.

## Conclusions

The balance of payments shock of 2014–2015 was the greatest challenge that the Georgian economy has faced since 1998, and many agree that the National Bank of Georgia can be credited with managing the shock in the best way possible, given the circumstances. Namely, the monetary policy pursued by the NBG was supported by various international organizations, including the EBRD, and the IMF (The Clarion 2015).

At the same time the World Bank has positively assessed the NBG's management of foreign reserves (Agenda.ge 2015). The NBG's passive but watchful monetary policy, with emphasis made on long-term development and risk mitigation, rather than on short-term gains, proved to be successful, particularly when compared with the results of the shock in some other countries of the region that pursued more proactive, but eventually futile, policies. The NBG withstood temptation (and political pressure) to use its FX reserves in order to prevent depreciation, and kept providing commercial banks with ample short-term liquidity in order to keep interest rates down as much as possible and avoid dramatic drops in consumption or investment. The NBG also managed its policy rate without any drastic jumps that could have exacerbated the crisis; while (possibly) curbing the depreciation, such jumps could result in more prolonged repression of the economy. The experience of the NBG serves as an example of what the central bank in a developing country should likely do when facing an external shock of such magnitude.

The policy pursued by the NBG was in stark contrast to those implemented by other countries of the region in similar circumstances. There are several important reasons accounting for this difference. First and foremost, the level of central bank independence in Georgia was notably higher than in the other countries of the region and thus the NBG was able to withstand significant external pressure and pursue policy it deemed fit for the occasion. Secondly, the banking system in Georgia was much healthier and, despite dollarization in excess of 60%, was able to withstand even larger depreciation, which was a significant factor in policy decisions (figure 20 shows that even 40% depreciation had a relatively low impact on the level and share of non-performing loans). Another important factor helping the NBG in its policymaking was the high level of human capital at the bank (including both extensive training of the personnel directly working on monetary policy issues and experience of the mid and top-level management), so that the personnel were capable of developing and supportive of what would prove to be relatively effective, yet unpopular monetary policy. Finally, it should also be mentioned that, compared with other countries of the region, the inflation targeting instruments at the NBG's disposal are more advanced and better developed and, as such, were more suited for a monetary policy under a floating exchange rate.

## References

Agenda.ge. "World Bank Praises NBG's Reserve Management Policy." *agenda.ge*. June 4, 2015. http://agenda.ge/news/36457/eng

Al-Assaf, Ghazi, Alaaeddin Al-Tarawneh, and Mohammad Alawin. 2013. "Determinants of Currency Crisis in Jordan a Multinomial Logit Model." *European Scientific Journal* 9 (34): 354–369.

Amirkhanyan, Lilia. "2015 and the Economies of the Countries in the Region." *Armedia*. January 13, 2016. http://armedia.am/eng/news/28551/2015-and-the-economies-of-the-countries-in-the-region.html

Barbosa-Filho, Nelson H. 2012. "The Balance-of-Payments Constraint: From Balanced Trade to Sustainable Debt." *PSL Quarterly Review* 54 (219): 381–400.

Benford, James, Stuart Berry, Kalin Nikolov, Chris Young, and Mark Robson. 2009. "Quantitative Easing." *Bank of England. Quarterly Bulletin* 49 (2): 90.

Blecker, Robert A., and Carlos A. Ibarra. 2013. "Trade Liberalization and the Balance of Payments Constraint with Intermediate Imports: The Case of Mexico Revisited." *Structural Change and Economic Dynamics* 25: 33–47.

Chernyak, Oleksandr, Vasyl Khomiak, and Yevgen Chernyak. 2013. "The Main Triggers of the Balance of Payment Crisis in the Eastern Europe." *Procedia Technology* 8: 47–50.

Danielyan, Emil. "Armenian Central Bank Again Cuts Key Rate." *Azatutyun*. December 22 2015. https://www.azatutyun.am/a/27443404.html

Danielyan, Emil, and Sisak Gabrielian. "Russian Crisis Speeds Up Armenian Currency Depreciation." *Azatutyun*. December 16 2014. https://www.azatutyun.am/a/26746895.html

Danninger, Stephan, and Florence Jaumotte. 2008. "Divergence of Current Account Balances Across Emerging Economies." *World Economic Outlook* 2008: 197–239.

Demytrie, Rayhan. "Moldova Anger Grows Over Banking Scandal." *BBC*. September 14 2015. http://www.bbc.com/news/world-europe-34244341

Draghi, Mario. 2015. "ECB Announces Expanded Asset Purchase Programme." European Central Bank. https://www.ecb.europa.eu/press/pr/date/2015/html/pr150122_1.en.html

Epstein, Natan P., and Rafael Portillo. 2014. Monetary Policy in Hybrid Regimes: The Case of Kazakhstan. *IMF Working Paper.s* WP/14/108

European Central Bank. n.d. "ECB Euro Reference Exchange Rate: US Dollar (USD)." https://www.ecb.europa.eu/stats/policy_and_exchange_rates/euro_reference_exchange_rates/html/eurofxref-graph-usd.en.html

Fahrholz, Christian, and Andreas Freytag. 2012, January. "A Way to Solve the European Balance of Payments Crisis? Take a Chance on Market Solutions!." *CESifo Forum*, 13 (02): 77–82.

Farchy, Jack, and Tony Barber. "Azerbaijan Prepares to Drop Currency Peg to Dollar." *Financial Times*. February 15, 2015. https://www.ft.com/content/c1536126-b4f0-11e4-b186-00144feab7de#axzz3uqXRVYrt

Federal Reserve Bank of St. Louis. n.d. " Trade Weighted US Dollar Index." FRED database. https://fred.stlouisfed.org/series/TWEXB

Ghartey, Edward E. 1987. "Devaluation as a Balance of Payments Corrective Measure in Developing Countries: A Study Relating to Ghana." *Applied Economics* 19 (7): 937–947.

Glick, Reuven, and Michael Hutchison. 2011. "Currency Crises." *Federal Reserve Bank of San Francisco Working Paper Series. Working paper* 2011-22.

Gökçe, Atilla, and Erhan Çankal. 2013. "Balance-of-Payments Constrained Growth Model for the Turkish Economy." *Economic Modelling* 35: 140–144.

Gordeyeva, Mariya. "UPDATE 3-Kazakhstan Devalues Tenge by 19 Percent to Stymie Speculators." *Reuters*. February 11, 2014. http://www.reuters.com/article/kazakhstan-tenge-idUSL5N0LG07F20140211

Gordeyeva, Mariya, and Lidia Kelley. "Kazakhstan, Struggling with Low Oil Price, Revamps Monetary Policy." *Reuters*. December 8, 2015. http://www.reuters.com/article/us-kazakhstan-rate-idUSKBN0TR1XQ20151208

Gordeyeva, Mariya, and Dimitry Solovyov. "Kazakhstan Floats Tenge, Currency Tumbles." *Reuters*. August 20, 2015. http://www.reuters.com/article/us-kazakhstan-tenge-idUS KCN0QP0PN20150820

International Monetary Fund. 2005. *Balance of Payments Manual*. Washington: IMF.

International Monetary Fund. 2015. *World Economic Outlook*. October. Washington: IMF.

Kitco News. "ECB Leaves Door Open for QE After Cutting Interest Rates, Announcing New LTRO Package." June 5, 2014. https://www.forbes.com/sites/kitconews/2014/06/05/ecb-leaves-door-open-for-qe-after-cutting-interest-rates-announcing-new-ltro-package/#b63103337584

Krugman, Paul. 1979. "A Model of Balance-of-Payments Crises." *Journal of Money, Credit and Banking* 11(3): 311–325.

Kulkarni, Archana, and Bandi Kamaiah. 2015. "Predicting Balance of Payments Crises for some Emerging Economies." *Theoretical and Applied Economics* 22 (1 (602), Spring): 15–34.

Kumhof, Michael. 2000. "A Quantitative Exploration of the Role of Short-Term Domestic

Debt in Balance of Payments Crises." *Journal of International Economics* 51 (1): 195–215.

Kumhof, Michael, Shujing Li, and Isabel Yan. 2007. "Balance of Payments Crises under Inflation Targeting." *Journal of International Economics* 72 (1): 242–264.

Laeven, Luc, and Fabian Valencia. 2008. "Systemic Banking Crises: A New Database." *IMF Working Papers* WP08/224.

Moreno-Brid, Juan C. 1998. "On Capital Flows and the Balance-of-Payments-Constrained Growth Model." *Journal of Post Keynesian Economics* 21 (2): 283–298.

Moreno-Brid, Juan C., and Esteban Pérez. 1999. "Balance-of-Payments-Constrained Growth in Central America: 1950–96." *Journal of Post Keynesian Economics* 22 (1): 131–147.

Müller-Plantenberg, Nikolas A. 2010. "Balance of Payments Accounting and Exchange Rate Dynamics." *International Review of Economics & Finance* 19 (1): 46–63.

National Bank of Georgia. n.d. "Foreign Exchange Market." Statistical Data. https://www.nbg.gov.ge/index.php?m=304

Pacheco-López, Penélope. 2005. "The Effect of Trade Liberalization on Exports, Imports, the Balance of Trade, and Growth: The Case of Mexico." *Journal of Post Keynesian Economics* 27 (4): 595–619.

Park, Donghyun, Arief Ramayandi, and Kwanho Shin. 2014. "Capital Flows During Quantitative Easing and Aftermath: Experiences of Asian Countries." *Asian Development Bank Economics Working Paper Series no. 409.*

Prial, Dunstan. "Bernanke Offers Possible Timetable for Tapering." *Fox Business.* June 19, 2013. http://www.foxbusiness.com/politics/2013/06/19/fed-decision-on-tap.html

Remolona, Eli M., Mahar Mangahas, and Filologo Pante. 1986. "Foreign Debt, Balance of Payments, and the Economic Crisis of the Philippines in 1983–1984." *World Development* 14 (8): 993–1018.

Ricketts, Lowell R., and Christopher J. Waller. 2014. "The Rise and (Eventual) Fall in the Fed's Balance Sheet." *Federal Reserve Bank of St. Louis The Regional Economist* 22 (1): Online Extra. https://www.stlouisfed.org/publications/regional-economist/january-2014/the-rise-and-eventual-fall-in-the-feds-balance-sheet.

Sahakian, Nane. "Central Bank Moves to Shore Up Armenian Currency." *Azatutyun.* August 27, 2015. https://www.azatutyun.am/a/27212309.html

Sen, Partha. 2014. "The Impossible Trinity and Krugman's Balance of Payments Crisis Model." *International Economics* 139: 174–181.

Stratfor. "How Currency Woes Undermine Georgia, Moldova." *Worldview.* March 14, 2015. https://www.stratfor.com/analysis/how-currency-woes-undermine-georgia-moldova

Thanh, Nguyen N., and Kaliappa Kalirajan. 2006. "Can Devaluation be Effective in Improving the Balance of Payments in Vietnam?." *Journal of Policy Modeling* 28 (4): 467–476.

The Clarion. "IMF Assessments on Georgian Economy, Hit by 'Severe External Shocks'." *The Clarion*. March 5, 2015. http://new.civil.ge/clarion/news/1/922/eng

Thirlwall, Anthony P. 2011. "Balance of Payments Constrained Growth Models: History and Overview." *PSL Quarterly Review* 64 (259): 307–351.

Thirlwall, Anthony P. 2014. "The Balance of Payments Constraint as an Explanation of the International Growth Rate Differences." *PSL Quarterly Review* 32 (128): 45–53.

Timpul. "Latest News." n.d. http://www.timpul.org/en/news/detail/stiri110116-1.html

Wearden, Graeme. 2014. "Euro Slides After ECB 'Talks About' QE to Battle Stagnation." *The Guardian*. April 3. https://www.theguardian.com/business/2014/apr/03/european-central-bank-meets-as-deflation-fears-grow-business-live

World Bank. n.d. "Personal Remittances Received (% GDP)." http://data.worldbank.org/indicator/BX.TRF.PWKR.DT.GD.ZS

# CHAPTER 7
# Financial Sustainability of Regional Development in Georgia: Reforms, Flaws, and Challenges

**Archil Gersamia and Solomiya Shpak**

## Introduction

One of the most important pre-conditions for a country's development is the sustainable growth of its regions, where the financial strength and independence of local governments play a crucial role. Therefore, the establishment of relevant funding sources for municipal projects represents the foundation for steady regional development.

The Georgian government has taken several steps toward strengthening the role of local authorities. First, Decree N223, passed on March 1, 2013, introduced general principles of decentralization and development strategy for 2013–2014. In addition, the Georgian government has adopted the Regional Development Program (RDP) for 2015–2017, and a new "Local Self-Governance Code" in February 2014, with corresponding amendments to "budgetary code" and some improvements in local government finances.

Although the changes in legislation have introduced some enhancements to the system, significant gaps and flaws with regard to the sustainable provision of financial resources to regional budgets are still evident. Local governments remain fiscally weak and financial resources cannot be attained to fund priority projects of municipalities. Regions are mostly dependent on fund transfers from the central budget, the purpose and amounts of which are determined solely by the central government.

With respect to regional development, this chapter makes a distinction between the two levels of government in Georgia: (1) the central government, and (2) local governments, consisting of 76 municipalities. The purpose of this analysis is to consider whether the above-mentioned reforms have contributed to the improvement of conditions for steady regional development in Georgia. In particular, it considers whether the revenue sources of local governments have been diversified; if there are any opportunities to allocate relevant financial resources to local budgets; and whether there are any alternative mechanisms to finance priority projects through debt financing. Finally, mistakes that may have been made while conducting these reforms are taken into account.

The special emphasis of this chapter is to establish whether the Georgian government has considered either of two key internationally accepted aspects of regional development in its reform efforts:

1) Enhancement of fiscal decentralization

2) Utilization of debt financing through municipal bonds

The next two sections describe in detail the experience of other countries with these practices, as well as their applications in the Georgian context.

## International Practice

For proper assessment of recently conducted reforms, analysis of international practice is crucial. The latter includes a description of the levels of fiscal decentralization, the importance of debt financing, and the role of municipal bonds in regional development in the United States and European countries, with emphasis on southeastern European countries. In addition, government agency activities aimed at the promotion of regional development and the availability of debt financing are considered.

### *Fiscal Decentralization*

There are two common indicators of fiscal decentralization: the share of local public revenue in national GDP, which expresses the size of the local government sector in relation to a country's total economic activity; and the share of local public revenues in the consolidated public revenues (NALAS 2012, 19). The diversification of local government revenue sources is an additional indicator of importance.

A high level of fiscal decentralization can be observed in the United States, where about 43% of federal revenue is allocated to state and local government budgets (Hyman 2012, 21–25). In addition, national revenue sources are well diversified, coming from:

- Sales tax—accounts for about 22% of all receipts;
- Property tax—about 20% of all receipts;
- Shared taxes—about 20% (Personal income tax, Corporate profit tax);
- Other taxes—16%
- Federal grants—22%

An examination of European countries also gives significant insight into levels of fiscal decentralization. Figure 1 illustrates the comparison of local government revenues as a share of both total public revenues and GDP for Eastern European countries, and the rest of Europe and Georgia. The most important observation is that, on average, local governments in the European Union (EU) play a far more substantial role in economic activity than local governments in Eastern Europe, not to mention Georgia.

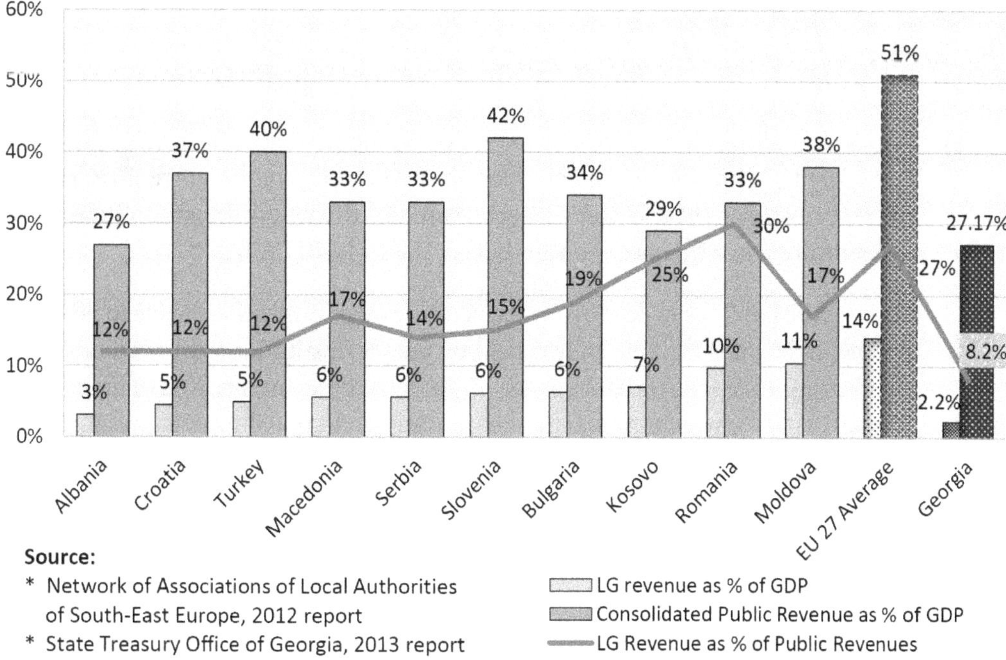


Figure 1. Local Government Revenue as Share of GDP and Total Public Revenue

Official statistics show that the size of the local government sector in Georgia before the 2014 reform was well below the average for both the EU and Eastern European countries. According to the Georgian State Treasury Office, in 2013 only 8.19% of the consolidated revenue (7,295,252,829 GEL) had been allocated to the budgets of territorial entities (GEL 597,679,401) (Ministry of Finance of Georgia, State Treasury, 2013). In addition, the share of local government revenue in GDP (GEL 26.4 b.) was only 2.23%, indicating the poor participation of the local government sector in the country's total economic activity.

The size of the public sector as a percentage of GDP in virtually all east European countries, and especially in Georgia, is well below the EU average. Total public revenues of less than 30% of GDP suggest both weak economies and poor tax collection. Local government revenues as a percentage of GDP are likely to be lower than one might expect simply because the entire public sector has difficulties in collecting the taxes needed to pay for public services (NALAS 2012, 20).

Additionally, in both the Eastern European group and in the rest of the Europe, the sources of local government revenues are well diversified, collected from local taxes and fees, property tax, shared taxes like personal income tax, payroll taxes, federal grants, etc. (NALAS 2012, 21–27). Before the 2014 reform, revenue sources of Georgia's local governments consisted of only property tax, municipal fees, and transfers from the central budget comprising more than 80% of local government budgets (Ministry of Finance of Georgia, State Treasury, 2016;). Details about the changes in fiscal decentralization after the reform are presented below.

***Debt Financing***

The existence of municipal debt in developed countries is accepted due to a couple of important arguments:

1) Borrowing allows a municipality to enjoy immediate benefit from capital improvements, which is not always possible when relying on current revenues. Current revenues (taxes, user fees, etc.) are usually not sufficient to fund large expenditures on a "pay-as-you-go basis" (UN-HABITAT 2009, 43).

2) Much of the holdings of debt of any particular local government is likely to be in the external debt category; that is, it is held by people/institutions not residing in the jurisdiction. This implies that issuance of the debt allows importation of funds (Hyman 2012, 514), which is essential for allocating additional financial resources to the regions. This is of special concern for Georgia because both human and financial resources are mostly concentrated in the capital.

3) Long-term debt financing by local governments can be justified on the basis of the benefits principle for financing capital projects. Because capital expenditures by local governments involve the construction of facilities (roads, public institutions, etc.) that will provide a stream of public services to future generations, it is reasonable to finance such expenditure through debt (Hyman 2012, 515).

Regarding these benefits, municipal bonds are widely accepted financial instruments of debt financing, and are successfully used to finance most important municipal projects both in EU countries and in the US (Istrates 2013, 4–10). Figure 2 illustrates the top 21 infrastructure purposes funded through municipal bonds in the United States in 2003–2012, which sheds light on the importance of municipal bonds for financing projects on the regional level.

In the United States, municipal bonds are a well-established, decentralized investment tool that allows for decision-making on the part of state and local leaders, in partnership with their residents. It allows Americans to diversify their retirement portfolios and provides them an opportunity to invest in their communities (Istrates 2013, 4). The latter is important for Georgia's efforts to implement pension reform and introduce a supplementary pension scheme (Ministry of Finance, 2016). A key feature of municipal bonds, which makes them attractive to private investors, is their tax-exempt status. Thus, as investors pay neither federal nor state taxes on the interest proceeds, this kind of security is more attractive than its counterparts (Hyman 2012, 514–515).

It is worth paying special attention to revenue bonds—a specific type of municipal bond. On the one hand, such bonds are risky securities (compared with general obligation bonds) as the returns depend on the success of a specific municipal project. On the other hand, the high risk is compensated with high returns and with the opportunity to convert on equity, which is another incentive for investors to invest in securities tied to specific municipal projects. As a result, these private-purpose bonds give investors access to municipalities' ability to borrow at tax-exempt rates (Bodie, Kane, and Markus 2013, 35–36).

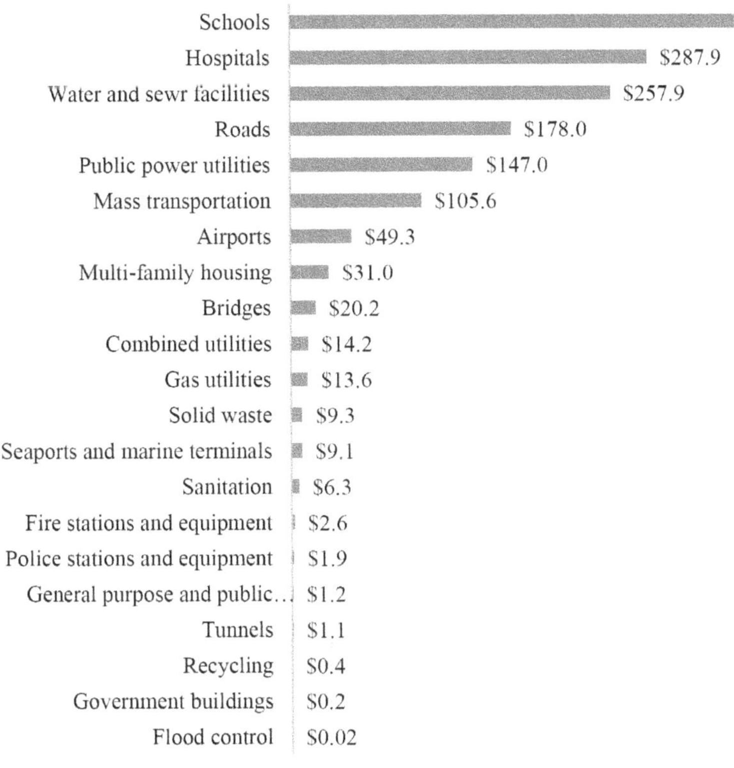


Figure 2. Municipal Bond Issuances for the 21 Largest Infrastructure Purposes (2003–2012)

The absence of such powerful debt-financing instruments in Georgia indicates the shortcomings of the recent reforms, as well as those of the Ministry of Regional Development and Infrastructure, and the "Municipal Development Fund," established with the purpose of enhancing the development of regions.

Federal agencies are critical in the promotion and popularization of such securities. In the US, for example, "Fannie Mae" (FNMA or Federal National Mortgage Association) and "Freddie Mac" (FHLMC or Federal Home Loan Mortgage Corporation) play a pivotal role in developing particular financial instruments (in this case mortgage-backed securities). An interesting approach for Georgia in this example is the practice of purchasing securities by the above-mentioned federal agencies from the initial issuer to further promote them on secondary markets (Bodie, Kane, and Markus 2013, 17–19). These organizations serve as an example for LEPL's (Georgia's Ministry of Internal Affairs) "Municipal Development Fund" to get engaged in the process of issuing municipal bonds for financing specific regional projects and investing in them in order to further promote them on the secondary market.

Another interesting example of debt financing is municipal projects financed through the European Bank for Reconstruction and Development (EBRD). For example, EBRD's Municipal Infrastructure Development Fund provides loan financing for projects in municipalities as well as utility companies in Albania, Bosnia, and Herzegovina, FYR Macedonia,

Montenegro, Kosovo and Serbia (the "Western Balkans" or the "Region") (EBRD 2013). The funding is used for infrastructure investments in water and wastewater, district heating, solid waste management, energy efficiency, public transport, and other municipal infrastructure (EBRD 2013).

This review of international practices for financing regional development projects allows us to consider how progressive the reforms passed in Georgia have been, and what mistakes may have been made on the way. For comparison, it is important to analyze the newly adopted "Local Self-Governance Code" of 2014 (with accompanying "budget code" amendments) and the official reports of budget fulfillment to assess the actual levels of fiscal decentralization and evaluation of budget processes at the regional level.

## Policy Implications in Georgia

Based on international practices described above, this article focuses on assessment of recent reforms regarding fiscal decentralization, availability of debt financing for municipalities and contributions of federal agencies to promote financial sustainability of regional development through optimization of local government revenues and promotion of municipal bonds.

### *Optimization of Local Government Revenues*

Before the 2014 reforms were passed, the revenue sources of local governments were poorly diversified. Revenue for about 80% of the municipal budget consisted of property tax, municipal fees, and transfers from the central budget (The Ministry of Finance of Georgia 2016). The reform has diversified revenue sources through the introduction of two important changes:

1) "Tax sharing": according to the new "Local Self-Governance Code" and corresponding amendments to "budgetary code," the revenue generated through the income tax will be shared between the central and local government budgets;

2) Local taxes: according to the new "Local Self-Governance Code," municipalities are authorized to levy local taxes.

The introduction of tax sharing is undoubtedly progressive and complies with international practice as described above. According to appendix N1 of the new "Budgetary Code," the following types of income tax will be allocated to local government budgets starting in 2016:

- Income tax on proceeds from activity of individual entrepreneurs;
- Income tax for non-residents on the proceeds from property sale;
- Income tax on proceeds from tangible asset sale by individuals;
- Individual income tax from the disposal of property;
- Income tax on inherited property;

- Income tax on proceeds from property leasing.

According to the official data provided by the "State Treasury Service" in 2015, this kind of income comprised GEL 274,431,310.47; that is about 3.5% of total revenue (Ministry of Finance of Georgia, State Treasury, 2013). Redirecting this amount from central to local government budgets clearly represents some progress in fiscal decentralization.

Local tax levy opportunities are also important, but difficult economic conditions in Georgian municipalities will likely hinder the possible effects of additional taxation on the increase in regional budgets. Moreover, international practice shows that local taxes represent only a minor part of local budget revenues (NALAS 2012, 18–25).

Regardless of these two significant changes, attaining essential improvements in fiscal decentralization is controversial. Budgetary projections for 2016–2019 show that local government revenue, as a share of GDP and consolidated revenue, is still expected to be considerably below the average of the EU and most east European countries, despite substantial improvement after the reform (Figure 3).

Indeed, it is fair to say that fiscal decentralization is still very much a work in progress. In spite of improvements, it is unlikely to lead to significant financial sustainability in the Georgian regions. In 2016 the central budget of Georgia still included "equalizing transfers" for nearly all municipalities, the purpose of which was ensuring the provision of very basic local services by municipalities. Interestingly, these equalizing transfers comprise more than 80% of local government revenue.

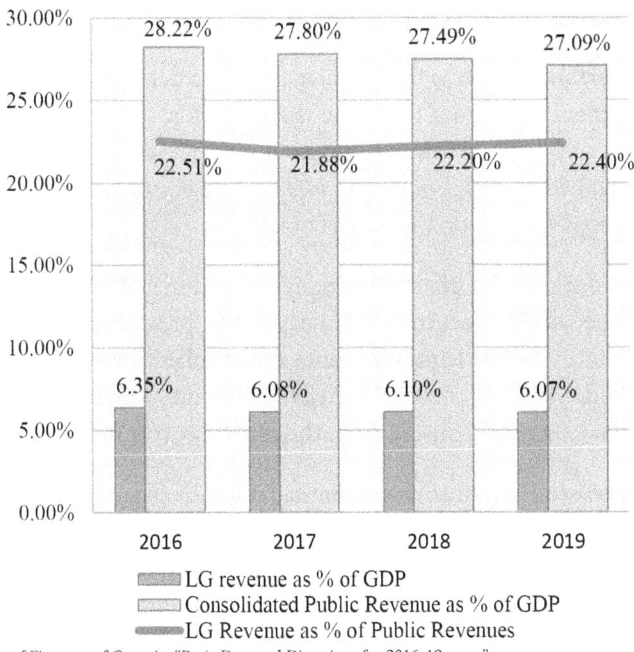


**Source**: Ministry of Finances of Georgia, "Basic Data and Directions for 2016-19 years"

Figure 3. Budgetary Projections for 2016–2019

The accumulation of more financial resources for local budgets is central to sustainable regional development. It is necessary to optimize the proportion of tax sharing, while further diversifying revenue sources, which is also crucial to ensuring the availability of debt financing through municipal bonds. Meanwhile, the creditworthiness of municipalities is another problematic issue in the framework of the current model.

One complication is that the process of redirecting more tax revenue to local budgets implies cuts to centrally planned projects. Therefore, it is necessary that the process be planned not all at once, but gradually, incorporating regions step by step until they all are introduced to the new system. This would prevent the government from abruptly curtailing centrally planned projects, as well as from experiencing other expected complications due to apparent management problems in municipalities. Moreover, by testing the new model, regions would enable the government to realize one of the advantages of decentralized government, which lies in the possibility to conduct government level experiments.

### *Availability of Debt Financing*

The 2014 reform and new "Self-Governance Code" introduced the availability of debt financing, which is an alternative source of funding priority projects for the regions. However, we do not observe utilization of debt instruments, partially because they are under the strict regulation of the central government in Georgia and need its continuous approval (the Budget Code, Article 21, paragraph 2). At the same time, there have been no attempts by the central government to facilitate the usage of this debt instrument by municipalities.

The main tool for debt financing is the municipal bond, the issuance of which is complicated in Georgia due to a variety of obstacles:

1) ***Low creditworthiness.*** While the municipalities are dependent on transfers from the central government in order to ensure the provision of basic municipal services, it is difficult to convince investors to invest in municipal bonds. These securities are potentially ranked as junk bonds and will require abnormally high coupon rates to compensate for high risk on the part of investors.

2) ***Flaws in legislation.*** The effective issuance of municipal bonds requires appropriate regulations with respect to coupon payments, procedures in case of default, tax exemptions, etc. Current legislation does not regulate these issues at the municipal level at all and, therefore, needs further refinements. Moreover, municipality code requires them to acquire consent from the central government to assume loans.

3) ***Lack of expertise.*** The issuance of municipal bonds is subject to complicated procedures, as well as being associated with high financial costs. It includes decisions about the volume of issuance, maturity, coupon rate and other financial parameters. Additional costly aspects of municipal bond issuance are the assessment of securities by rating agencies and organizing "road shows" by investment bankers to publicize the offering.

4) Considering the poor management skills in local governments, the lack of expertise and costly procedures of bond issuance, municipalities are not likely to be able to handle the process on their own. The issuance of such securities requires the active participation of different state agencies, which are reluctant to be involved.

5) ***The lack of coordination.*** Neither optimization of local budget revenues nor development of debt financing is a priority of the central government's regional development policy. The Ministry of Regional Development and Infrastructure of Georgia, as well as its sub-agency, LEPL's "Municipal Development Fund," are only implementing specific municipal projects instead.

   The establishment of a sustainable foundation for the efficient issuance of municipal bonds requires the engagement of different state agencies that can be expressed through their competencies:

   - The Ministry of Economy and Sustainable Development. The issuance of municipal bonds should be considered as part of other ongoing reforms related to capital market promotion, reforming the pension system, etc. The ministry has the potential to assist municipalities in finding investors through pension funds.
   - The Ministry of Finance. This agency should share planning expertise, organize auctions through its facilities, and share standards of registration and record-keeping procedures.
   - The Ministry of Regional Development and Infrastructure, together with its LEPL "Municipal Development Fund" should elaborate the criteria for assessment of municipal projects to be financed through bonds, the involvement of rating agencies, and "road show" activities.

To sum up, the formation of a successful foundation for municipal bond issuance requires complex actions and active engagement of several different state agencies. These agencies should create favorable conditions for local governments to plan priority projects for their regions, decide on means of financing, types of debt instruments, volumes, coupon rates, and other issues related to debt issuance.

## Conclusions and Implications for Future Research and Practice

This analysis of best practices in developed countries suggests that sustainable regional development can only be achieved through the enhancement of local government finances. Two components are crucial for this purpose: diversified revenue sources providing a substantial amount of income to local governments, and the availability of debt financing through municipal bonds.

Regarding the diversification of revenue sources, two new approaches are introduced by the Local Self-Governance Code of 2014: (1) the opportunity to levy local taxes; and (2) the tax sharing principle, meaning that a small portion of total revenue generated from income tax will be directed to the budgets of local governments.

Despite these changes, the 2016–2019 budget projections approved by the government show a low level of fiscal decentralization compared with the EU and east European countries. In the given time period the share of local government revenue in Georgia's GDP is projected to be only 6%, indicating poor participation of local governments in the total economic activity of the country. In addition, only about 22% of consolidated revenue will be allocated to regional budgets, which, for the most part, consists of equalizing transfers from the central budget.

Unfortunately, ensuring the availability of debt financing for municipalities is not on the priority list of the Georgian government. Municipal bonds are internationally acknowledged as a financial instrument that is the most powerful and effective mechanism for the self-financing of specific regional projects. Yet, in Georgia, the availability of debt financing for local governments is not considered a priority at all, and therefore, insufficient attention is paid to factors preventing the development of such debt instruments.

The issuance of municipal bonds is also complicated due to problems related to the low creditworthiness of municipalities. In addition, the imperfect legislative basis for municipal bond issuance; the absence of experience in municipalities; and the lack of coordination and engagement of corresponding federal agencies in the process of developing appropriate standards, are the main problems hindering the implementation of debt financing.

This analysis of international practices and recently introduced approaches in Georgia suggests that for ensuring sustainable regional development, it will be necessary to gradually enhance fiscal decentralization and introduce debt financing approaches on the basis of observation and thorough continued analysis.

Gradual redirection of tax revenues to regional budgets is crucial to avoid the painful process of sharp cuts in federal government spending. It will ensure the gradual improvement of municipalities' financial standing and will also provide an opportunity to further develop accessibility of debt financing through municipal bonds with the proper participation of corresponding federal agencies.

The issuance of municipal bonds should be considered as part of other ongoing reforms related to capital market development, most notably for the reform of the government pension system, that envisages the introduction of pension funds, the most common investors in municipal bonds according to international practice.

A gradual approach, including piloting of reforms, will provide an opportunity to monitor and analyze mistakes, to create effective mechanisms for the emission of municipal bonds, to consistently and meaningfully improve legislation, and to share appropriate expertise between different levels of government, encouraging cooperation, and, ultimately, ensuring sustainable regional development in the country.

## References

Bodie Z., Kane A., and Marcus A.J. 2013. *Investments*. 9th ed. New York: McGraw-Hill Education.

European Bank for Reconstrcution and Development (EBRD). 2013. "Municipal Infrastructure Development Fund." EBRD. http://www.ebrd.com/work-with-us/projects/psd/municipal-infrastructure-development-fund.html (accessed February 29, 2016).

Hyman D.N. 2012. *Public Finance, A Contemporary Application of Theory to Policy.* 10th ed. Boston: CENGAGE Learning.

Istrates E. 2013. *Municipal Bonds Built America.* National Association of Counties Policy Research Paper Series: (1). http://www.naco.org/sites/default/files/NACo-Research_Policy_MuniBonds_2013_0.pdf (accessed February 29, 2016).

Ministry of Finance of Georgia. 2016. *Basic Data and Directions Document for 2016-19 years.* http://mof.ge/4542 (accessed January 9, 2017).

Ministry of Finance of Georgia, State Treasury. 2013. "Consolidated Budget Revenues." http://treasury.ge/5465 (accessed February 29, 2016).

Network of Associations of Local Authorities of South-East Europe (NALAS). 2012. *Fiscal Decentralization Indicators for South-East Europe.* http://www.nalas.eu/knowledge-center/Fiscal-Decentralization-Indicators-for-South-East-Europe (accessed January 9, 2017).

UN-HABITAT. 2009. *Guide to Municipal Finance.* http://unhabitat.org/books/guide-to-municipal-finance/ (Accessed January 9, 2017).

# CHAPTER 8
# Regional Economic Cluster Development Opportunities in Georgia

**Keunwon Song, David Akhvlediani, Nikoloz Abuashvili and Natalia Partskhaladze**

## Introduction

Georgia boasts a rich history in trade and commerce. Situated by the Black Sea, at the juncture of Asia and Europe, Georgia flourished as part of the Great Silk Road that connected China and Byzantium. Today, Georgia remains an important regional trade corridor and now serves as a conduit for transporting energy from the Caspian basin to Europe. It is the only country in the central Caucasus that borders the sea, and its ports serve as a trade gateway to the region. Its Caucasus Mountains are abundant sources of minerals and serve as a barrier to cold air masses, creating an ideal agricultural environment. Georgia is well known for its tea, citrus, nuts, and vegetables, and, most of all, fine wine. In addition, Georgia has inherited from the Soviet Union a robust industrial sector, especially in machineries, various alloys of iron, and chemicals. Modern Georgia's principal economy consists of agricultural products, minerals, alcoholic and non-alcoholic beverages, machineries, chemicals, and tourism (The World Factbook 2017).

This chapter explores regional economic cluster development opportunities in Georgia. First, a theoretical framework of clusters is introduced and discussed in relation to Georgia's socioeconomic development goal, known as "Georgia 2020." Then, challenges of developing clusters are discussed in light of two historical clusters. The methods section introduces different analytical measures, such as revealed comparative advantage and total export share, which are used to analyze Georgia's cluster opportunities. In the findings section, products with comparative advantages based on our methodology are discussed. And, finally, policymakers' opportunities and challenges are discussed in the recommendations sections by delving into two cases, namely, the apparel/textile and wine tourism industries.

## Literature Review

### *What are Clusters?*

The benefits of geographic clustering in economic and social terms have long been studied. Alfred Marshall (1890) did seminal work on external economies of scale, which are realized through input sharing, labor market pooling, and knowledge spillovers. Joseph Schumpeter (1934) introduced the notion of the "recombination of resources," which is conducive to entrepreneurial and innovative ideas. Jane Jacobs (1961) supported urban developments that incorporate elements of diversity and concentration in building great American cities. The engine of innovation and economic growth as a result of agglomeration of talented individuals and resources in urban cities has remained a convincing idea (Bergman and Feser 1999; Florida 2002; Glaeser 2011). The term commonly known today as "Clusters" was popularized by Michael Porter, who defines it as "[ ... ] a geographically proximate group of interconnected companies and associated institutions in a particular field, linked by commonalities and complementarities" (1998, 199). One of Porter's most notable contributions to cluster research is the U.S. Cluster Mapping project done together with the Economic Development Administration (EDA). They were able to incorporate empirical data into cluster analysis that until then had been mostly theory-driven.

Clusters consist of an array of interlinked actors throughout the value chain (Porter 1985). The value chain can be vertical, including suppliers of various parts and processes in the upstream, and customers of products and services in the downstream. They also extend laterally to manufacturers and firms with complementary and substitutable skills and technology. In this ecosystem, firms are large and small, domestic, and multinational. The private business sector operates not in a vacuum but rather in interaction with governmental entities at the federal, state, or local levels, as well as with other institutions—such as, universities, laboratories, various agencies, trade associations, nonprofit organizations, banks, private equity firms, venture capital firms, and think tanks.

Being in clusters promotes competition and cooperation. Clusters affect cooperation and competition in three broad ways (Porter 2000): (a) increasing the current productivity of constituent firms and industries; (b) increasing the capacity of cluster participants' innovation and productivity growth; and (c) stimulating new business formation.

(a) Firms in a cluster are well positioned to take advantage of economies of scale and scope. Producers can minimize average total costs by sharing suppliers, storage centers, and logistics, especially for high-specialized industries. The costs are brought down by competition, usually horizontally, as firms in the same industry fight for market share. The cost savings are realized directly and indirectly. Some direct costs, such as in transportation, are minimized as the entire value chain positions itself close to each other. At the same time, there is a supportive structure and cooperation, especially on the vertical value chain among firms in related industries, which decreases indirect transaction costs.

(b) Agglomeration economies are poised for innovation through high volumes of exchange in ideas and knowledge. When firms compete for similar inputs, products and services, and segments of the market, clustering can minimize their costs associated with information asymmetry and coordination (Jacobs and De Man 1996). In clusters, ideas compete and only the best ideas survive, while best talents are often poached from each other. There are also the intangible benefits from closer interaction, such as better trust and coordination. Through continuous contact and interaction, buyer needs and trends, as well as supplier needs and trends, are more smoothly matched. As a result, the value chain becomes more responsive and stays more equilibrated from upstream to downstream.

(c) The very existence of a cluster signals an opportunity for many aspiring entrepreneurs and, over time, becomes a brand on its own. The access to information, technology, and human capital attracts more talent and essentially lowers the barrier to entry (Porter 2000). There are regular spinoffs by employees who have innovative ideas. Often, access to specialized technology, suppliers of materials, equipment and services maintenance can be costly and limited to laboratories or universities who often serve as facilitators of high technology innovation and knowledge spillovers (Anselin, Varga, and Acs 1997). These hubs not only give access to certain technology-dependent products or services but also serve as creators of a high-skilled workforce (Florida 1999). To benefit from such spillover effects, many entrepreneurs and small and medium enterprises (SMEs) choose to locate near large corporations, a research institution, or even a governmental institution (Jacobs and De Man 1996).

In the past few decades, cluster initiatives have proliferated across the globe as a means for developing regional economies and cultivating competitive advantages (Reinhold and Mirko 2015). In the process, some questions regarding the role of government have become important. "How much government intervention is appropriate?" or "What kind of government intervention is successful?" are pertinent questions. While the goals may be the same, there are pronounced differences based on who initiates these clusters, and policies differ accordingly. As illustrated in Figure 1, Ann Markusen (1996) categorizes industrial clusters into four types: (1) Marshallian; (2) Hub-and-spoke; (3) Satellite; and (4) State-anchored. Marshallian and Hub-and-spoke models are initiated bottom-up by the private sector, which is the most natural, market-driven, and recommended means of cluster formation (Ferreira et al. 2012). Hence, the government plays a minor role in assisting the needs of businesses, such as by decreasing regulations or taxes. Marshallian clusters are formed by natural market forces, primarily driven by SMEs, usually over a long period of time. Satellite clusters are driven by large corporations and their subsidiaries and branches. These corporations tend to be domestic in developed countries, and foreign, multinational corporations (MNCs) in developing countries. Governments in such clusters are responsible for attracting MNCs. Meanwhile, state-anchored initiatives are top-down approaches that often involve high government intervention and regulation in the market (Ferreira et al. 2012). State-anchored clusters are government-owned (state-owned enterprises, or SOEs) or government-supported firms (e.g. whether through indirect control of Chaebol companies in Korea or through direct share ownerships of Gazprom & Rosneft in Russia) and governments. Governments may spearhead protectionist policies such as export promotion or import substitution. Also, they can establish state-owned enterprises (SOEs) that fill in the missing links in the value chains.

The Cluster Initiative Greenbook published in 2003 was an early study of cluster initiatives (CI) around the world, mainly focused on OECD countries. The research found strong evidence that companies' economic productiveness and competitiveness rose after being registered in relevant clusters. The Cluster Initiative Greenbook 2.0, a decade later, revealed an additional benefit: enhancement of innovation (Lindqvist, Ketels, and Sölvell 2013). Innovation is what allows clusters to minimize costs and maximize competitiveness and productivity.

There is an element of art required of policymakers. Some emphasize outcomes, that is, the successful harnessing of various relevant factors yielding competitive advantages and innovation, while others give emphasis to the process (Feser 1998). Clusters are a powerful concept because of linkages, relationships, interactions, and the exchange of goods, services, and knowledge (Simmie and Sennett 1999; Van den Berg, Braun, and Van Winden 2001). However, while clusters may generate agglomeration and spillover effects, they may also pose dangers, such as isomorphism in technologies and inflation of labor, land, and housing costs (Martin and Sunley 2003).

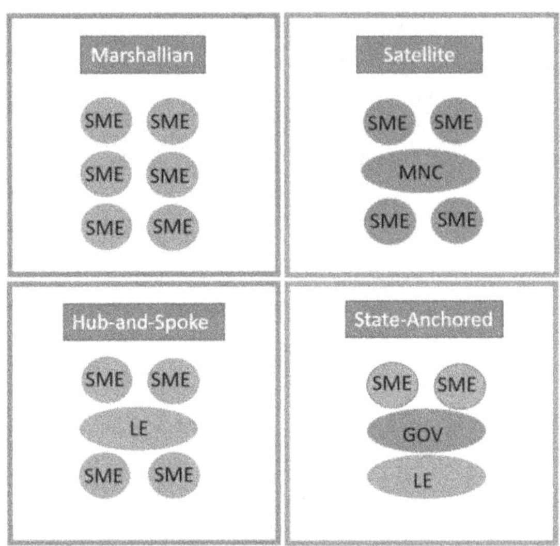


Figure 1: Markusen's Typology of Clusters

Source: Adopted from Markusen (1996). Note: Blue refers to private, domestic; yellow refers to private, foreign. SMEs refer to small and medium enterprises; LE refers to large enterprises; GOV refers to government.

In developed countries, cluster initiatives focus on advanced, high-tech industries, such as biotech and information and communication technologies (Lindqvist, Ketels, and Sölvell 2013). A good practice of developed countries that developing countries can adopt is to foster a national economic geography characterized by specialization and dispersion. Germany, Italy, and the United States are good examples of domestic specialization by regions and metropolitan areas, and also industrial dispersion based on regional comparative advantages across the country. This setup appears to be more effective than having one or two large metropolitan areas that account for the majority of production, but obviously, this type of development is a luxury for policymakers in the developing countries and will need to be incorporated in the long-term vision of regional economic development.

Developing countries have vastly different competencies from developed countries. Hence, policymakers' role in building strategies adapted to local contexts that are based on proper assessment of a region's core competencies are critical. That is, policymakers need to identify bottlenecks and opportunities for growth. In developing countries, clusters usually specialize in basic industries such as agriculture, textiles, and other labor-intensive sectors. The McKinsey Global Institute estimates that over 70% of developing country exports are concentrated in six industries: agribusiness, mining, light manufacturing, tourism, information and communications technology, and retail distribution (Shakya 2009). Most developing countries require modernization in labor and technological capital. Hence, government policies needed are straight-forward: "improving education and skill levels, building capacity in technology, opening access to capital markets, and improving institutions" (Porter 1998, 86).

Implementation of these policies, however, is often lagging and ineffective due to lack of institutions and corruption. This is exacerbated by the fact that the availability of resources and capabilities tend to be geographically concentrated around capitals that are exponentially ahead of other regions. While agglomeration around major metropolitan areas is a common pattern observed in many developed countries, in developing countries the disparity tends to be even more pronounced. Often, basic provision of infrastructure such as highways, roads, water, and electricity worsens markedly outside of the metropolitan areas. However, as seen in Figure 2, the most pressing concern of businesses in Georgia is political instability. Since its independence in 1991, Georgia has become an arena of geopolitical interest, with increasing economic and political influence from the United States, and Russian support of the separatist regions of Abkhazia and South Ossetia. Political instability makes attracting foreign investment more difficult and the Georgia's pivot to the West has often resulted in the loss of trade with countries in the region, most notably, Russia, but also with the member countries of the Eurasian Economic Union.

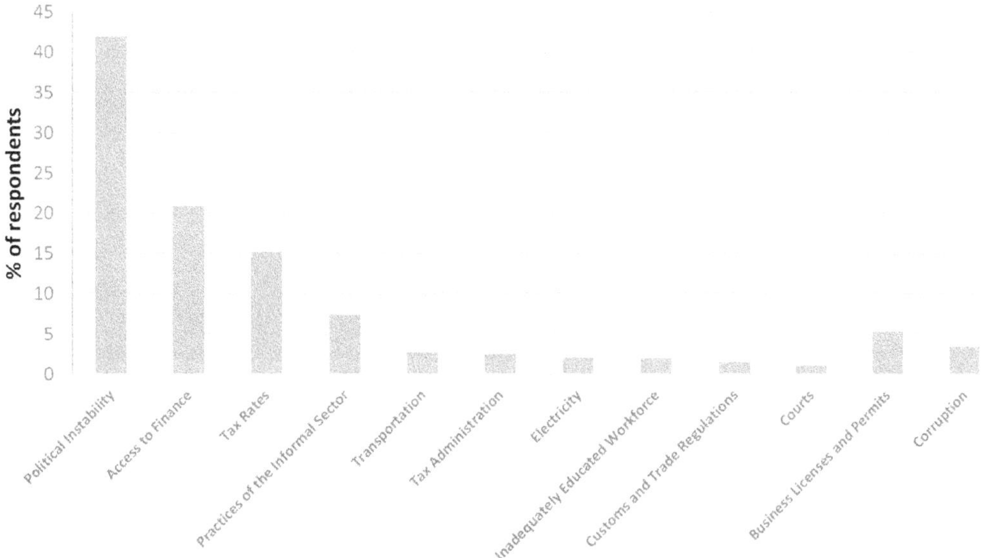


Figure 2: Main Obstacles to Economic Development Identified by Georgian Firms
Source: Data from World Bank Enterprise Surveys 2013. Authors' calculations.

One of critical indicators of successful clusters that developing countries lag behind in is the performance of small and medium enterprises (SMEs), employing no more than 250 employees. In developed economies, such as countries in the Organization for Economic Cooperation and Development (OECD), 60%–70% of GDP is generated by small and medium enterprises with a maximum of 50 employees (OECD 1997). Semi-developed countries, such as those in Latin America or the post-communist region, have a lower number of small and medium enterprises, which is considered a sign of structural weakness (World Bank 2002). Dalberg Global Development Advisors (2011) found that share of employment generated by the SME sector as a percentage of total employment increased as one went from low income (16%) to high income (51%).

A World Bank study (2002) has examined post-communist transition countries, all of which started with few small enterprises, and discovered that these countries have taken two very different trajectories. Countries in the first group, including Georgia, the Czech Republic, Hungary, Latvia, Lithuania, and Poland, obtain 50%–60% of their GDP from small enterprises—almost as much as in the industrialized West. According to 2008 data from the National Statistics Office of Georgia, SMEs employing a hundred or fewer employees had a significant presence in the trade sector (40.4%) and services sector (36.8%) but less so in manufacturing (16.7%) and agricultural/other (6.0%). The second group, comprised only of Russia and Kazakhstan, on the contrary, generates only 20% of GDP from small enterprises.

According to the World Bank (2002), a critical mass of small entrepreneurs is reached once the officially registered enterprises account for somewhere around 40% of GDP. They refer to this as the political "tipping point" because once tax-paying entrepreneurship rises above this level, the group becomes politically stronger and less likely to be expropriated of its property. When below 40%, small businesses remain politically vulnerable to expropriation, and their influence is limited in the face of government and larger corporations.

### *Georgia 2020*

Georgia has successfully transformed a Soviet legacy economy into a vibrant market-driven economy and continues its efforts to modernize. The 2012 parliamentary elections brought new leadership to Georgia—the "Georgian Dream"—a coalition of six parties united by a billionaire businessman, Bidzina Ivanishvili. The Georgian Dream under the helm of President Giorgi Margvelashvili has continued many policies initiated by the United National Movement, favoring closer ties to NATO and the EU (Waal 2012). The amendments to the constitutions in 2013 greatly reduced the powers of president in favor of the prime minister and the government. In 2014, the Government of Georgia outlined its Socio-economic Development Strategy of Georgia also known as "Georgia 2020" emphasizing fast and efficient economic growth through a broadening of private sector liberty and focusing government's commitment to ensuring market competition. This strategy has greatly minimized government intervention in the market, except for periods or cases of market failures. A particular emphasis was given to inclusiveness of economic growth and sustainability of the environment (Government of Georgia 2014). The Strategy identifies and sets measurable goals to overcome three main obstacles to the country's economic growth:

1) Competitiveness of the Private Sector

- Improve investment and business environment;
- Innovations and technologies;
- Facilitate the growth of exports;
- Develop infrastructure, fully realizing the country's transit potential;

2) Human Capital Development
    - Develop the country's workforce to meet labor market requirements;
    - Tighten the social security net;
    - Ensure accessible and quality health care;

3) Access to finance
    - Mobilization of investments
    - Development of financial intermediation

Regional economic cluster development is most closely aligned to the first objective of improving Georgia's private sector competitiveness. Over the past decade, its investment and business environment have continuously improved. In 2005, the government eliminated 84% of licensing requirements. Georgia climbed in the World Bank's *Doing Business* rankings from 100th in 2006 to 8th place in 2014. Armenia, which ranked above Georgia in 2006 at 46th place, peaked at 32nd place in 2013, and since then has not much improved, remaining at 38th in 2017. Azerbaijan, ranked at 98th in 2006, peaked at 33rd in 2009, but has reversed its trajectory since then, remaining at 65th in 2017. According to the latest *Doing Business* report (2017), Georgia's business environment clearly outperforms that of its regional counterparts, like Armenia and Azerbaijan. Out of 190 countries represented in the report, Georgia ranks third in the East for registering property, seventh in protecting minority investors, eighth in starting businesses, and eighth in dealing with construction permits. However, its bottleneck is in resolving insolvency, for which it ranks 106th. A good bankruptcy system is essential for economic growth. That is, in a healthy economy, there is an efficient reallocation of capital from unproductive to productive firms.

Georgia's foreign direct investment (FDI) flows have increased dramatically in three waves (1997–1998, 2003–2004, and 2006–2008). The first two waves were associated with Baku–Supsa and Baku-Tbilisi-Ceyhan oil pipeline projects that connected Caspian oil and gas to European markets, while the third wave was from a historic privatization of state-owned enterprises as part of economic reforms (U.S. Department of State 2014). However, geopolitical conflict with Russia in August 2008 and the global financial crisis temporarily reduced FDI inflows. Unlike other former Soviet countries, Georgia pivoted its economic development strategies toward the West. A Bilateral Investment Treaty in 1994 signed between Georgia and the United States has made many of Georgia's exports duty-free under the Generalized System of Preferences (GSP) program. In 2014, Georgia signed an Association

Agreement (AA) to establish a Deep and Comprehensive Free Trade Area (DCFTA) with the EU. The AA removed almost all trade barriers and quantitative restrictions between the two entities, as well established visa-free travel to member countries.

Georgia needs to continuously explore opportunities to modernize and diversify its economy. Georgia's top five fields of technology filing patent applications recorded in the World Intellectual Property Organization (WIPO) are (i) pharmaceuticals, (ii) food chemistry, (iii) other special machines, (iv) engines, pumps, turbines, (v) civil engineering, (vi) materials, metallurgy, (vii) transport, (viii) medical technology, (ix) measurement, and (x) mechanical elements (Onugha et al. 2013).

There is one indicator that may potentially be signaling something worrisome about Georgia's long-term economic development trajectory. Figure 3 depicts high-technology exports as a percent of manufactured exports, and Georgia has demonstrated a reverse trend in high-technology manufactured exports. Georgia's technology exports (measured as a percent of manufactured exports) grew exponentially from 1.61% in 1996 to 4.58% in 1998 and 23.89% in 1999; they dipped to 10.85% in 2000, before jumping to 38.14% in 2001 and reaching their zenith of 41.1% in 2002; subsequently, with the exception of one peek in 2004 (equivalent to 89 million in current US Dollars), this figure has been in decline; and since 2007 has stayed under 10%. A counter example in the same period among former Soviet countries is Kazakhstan. Kazakhstan went from 3.24% in 2001 to a sustained growth, which reached 37.17% in 2014. Kazakhstan was not very different from other former Soviet countries until about 2004 (at 49 million US dollars) but it reached the impressive milestone of 3.32 billion in 2014. While its large territory and vast natural resources must have played a role, Azerbaijan, with similar endowments, has mostly remained the same, peaking at about 14% in 1998 and 2013 but still under 5% in most years.

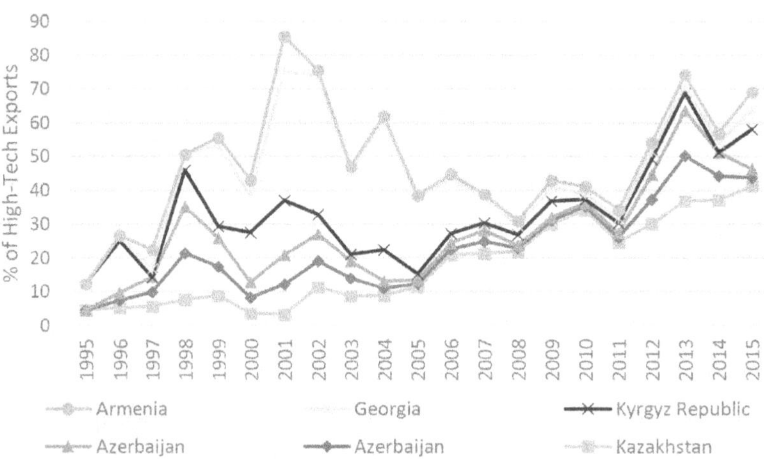


Figure 3: High-Technology Exports as Percent of Manufactured Exports (1995–2015) Source: Data from World Bank. Authors' calculations. Note: Turkmenistan and Uzbekistan are excluded from the figure due to lack of data. Data on Azerbaijan is unavailable for 1995. Data on Kyrgyz Republic is unavailable for 1997 and 2014. Data on Georgia is unavailable for 1995. Data on Armenia is unavailable for 1995, 1996, and 1998.

One of Georgia 2020's goals is to establish Georgia as a transportation and logistics regional hub by investing in its infrastructure. It is the only country in the central Caucasus that borders the sea, and can serve as a conduit for transporting energy from the Caspian basin to Europe. Special importance is therefore being given to raising cargo turnout of the airports, building additional storage capacity, and building a harbor in Anaklia. Georgia's container port traffic has experienced a 57.7% increase, from 184,792 in 2007 to 291,364 in 2014, as measured in 20-foot equivalent units (TEUs), a standard-size container. Air transport freight is measured by the volume of freight, express, and diplomatic bags carried on each flight stage, measured in metric tons times kilometers traveled. While correlated to population, Uzbekistan experienced tremendous growth, from a low of 8.2 million ton-km in 1997 to 110.24 million ton-km in 2014. Azerbaijan was once a leader with 92.5 million ton-km in 1998, but came down to 31.29 million ton-kms in 2014. Georgia was never a major player, with a peak of only 8.7 million ton-km in 1998 and 0.42 million ton-km in 2014.

### *Georgia's Historical Clusters*

The historic Dezertirebi Market in the center of Tbilisi is one example of a cluster that transformed itself during the 1990s from a mere bazaar to a main hub for agricultural goods. The 2,000-m$^2$ open-air market featuring various retailers, wholesalers, importers, farmers, warehouses, financial institutions, caterers, and other suppliers, attracted about 1.3 million consumers from Tbilisi and Rustavi city (about 30% of the Georgian population,). In 2007, the city demolished the old Soviet-era building at the Dezertirebi Market and pushed out a number of sellers to neighboring areas. When the new building was completed in 2012, only a few traders returned. Today, many large retailers, such as Passage 200, Georgian Trade Centre, Old and New Kidobani, and Uptown Tbilisi have transformed the economic sector that Dezertirebi Market had once dominated. Lilo Market of Tbilisi is another noteworthy example a marketplace or bazaar transformed into a significant cluster of economic activity. It became the largest market in the Caucasus, to which even Abkhazians and South Ossetians came to trade. The government took notice of this opportunity and designated it as the first free economic zone (FEZ), even before Tbilisi or Kutaisi. Additionally, the European Bank for Reconstruction and Development, along with some Georgian banks, allocated $60 million for construction of Lilo-Mall to modernize the market (Kalatozishvili 2012). These are Marshallian clusters that emerged naturally, without government or other outside assistance.

In both cases, though, the government intervened in ways that greatly altered these clusters. And while Tbilisi's total economy has grown continuously, the role of the Dezertirebi and Lilo Markets has diminished over time, as newer malls and developments replace them. It is unclear to what extent this trend can be attributed to government intervention or private sector interests. Overall, however, it seems such traditional marketplaces have only so much to contribute to Georgia's future. In this light, government's modernization projects can be considered reasonable interventions in historical clusters. A major task for policymakers and researchers is to determine how best to leverage capabilities and assets of these bazaars for regional economic development. FEZs are a valiant attempt at promoting trade, but their impact appears less conclusive.

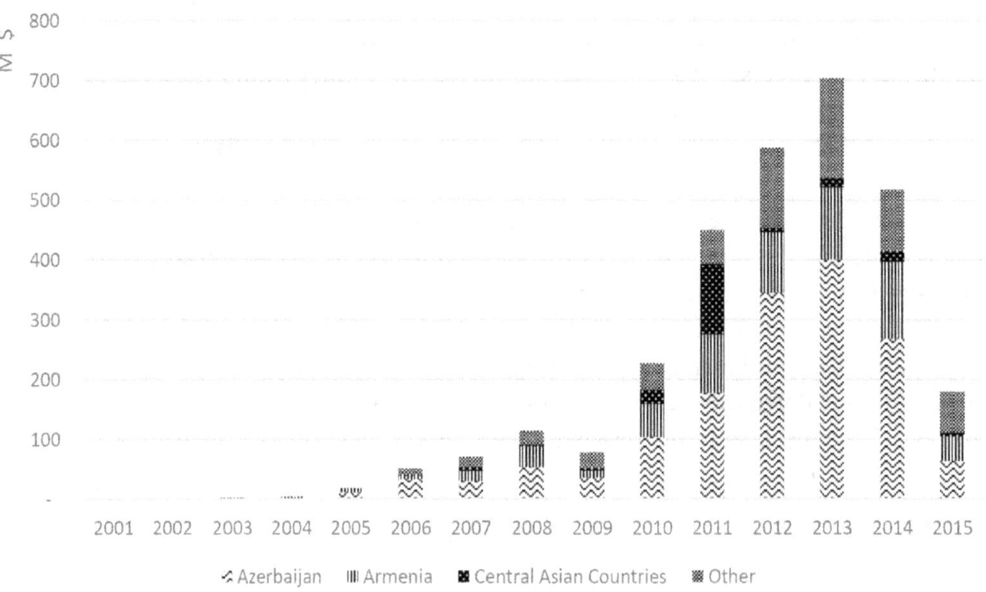


Figure 4: Georgia's Export of Cars by Countries (2001–2015)
Source: Data from UN COMTRADE. Authors' calculations.

The city of Rustavi's secondary car market presents another example of a cluster that was developed primarily by the private sector. The market grew as an important trade destination not only for Georgia but also for Armenia and Azerbaijan and many other Central Asian countries. The spike in export of cars to these countries, especially between 2010 and 2014, is depicted in Figure 4. Secondary car exports made up a substantial portion of the growth in Georgia's' total exports, depicted in Figure 6. One of the determinants of this success was arguably the free and transparent business environment in Georgia, which became useful in mitigating common problems of information asymmetry in used car markets (e.g. lemon cars). Its growth, however, was also significantly hampered for a number of reasons, including the devaluation of the Georgian Lari against the US dollar, and stricter import regulations from customer countries (Miller 2015). In 2012, Armenia and Kyrgyzstan joined the Eurasian Economic Space, an economic integration initiative, originally formed by Belarus, Kazakhstan, and Russia. Kazakhstan and Armenia raised their duties on car imports as required by the agreement in the Russia-led European Economic Space. Car imports from Azerbaijan have also decreased precipitously. In April 2014, Azerbaijan transitioned to environmental standard Euro-4, which significantly increases restrictions on used car imports (Zeynalli, Ahmedova, and Safarova 2014). As a result of exogenous political changes, this cluster has been disappearing as quickly as it arose. Major changes in its strategy, perhaps through government guidance, may be necessary. But, as in the case of the Dezertirebi and Lilo Market clusters, this cluster has not played a significant role in modernizing the Georgian economy or acting as a stepping-stone for building its capacity.

# Methodology

This chapter attempts to identify Georgia's comparative advantages and subsequent cluster opportunities by analyzing: (1) Descriptive statistics; (2) stock and flow measures of total export shares and revealed comparative advantages; and (3) diversity and ubiquity measures that together form a product complexity index (PCI).

The first method employed is a simple survey of descriptive statistics: Georgia's exports are analyzed by country; Georgia's economic performance is compared with its immediate neighbors, like Armenia and Azerbaijan, as well as other former Soviet countries.

The second method more narrowly analyzes Georgia's exports and products by industry to identify its competitive industries. Georgia's export shares of specific products relative to the world's total exports are analyzed. Then, a more advanced method of revealed comparative advantage index, which identifies products that a country exports more of relative to other countries, is identified. In a sense, it is a classical measure of David Ricardo's comparative advantage. The index measures the relative weight of a percentage of total export of commodities in a nation over the percentage of world export in that commodity (Balassa 1965). Revealed comparative advantage is represented in the following way:

$$\mathrm{RCA}_{ij} = \frac{\left(\frac{X_{ij}}{\sum_j X_{ij}}\right)}{\left(\frac{\sum_i X_{ij}}{\sum_i \sum_j X_{ij}}\right)}$$

There is a country *i* exporting good *j*. In the numerator, represents country *i*'s export of good *j* while represents country *i*'s total exports of all goods. In the denominator, represents world's export of good *j* while represents the world's total exports of all goods When RCA is >1, it means that country *j* has a revealed comparative advantage on commodity or product *k*. When RCA is <1, it means that country *j* has a revealed comparative disadvantage on commodity *k*.

While RCA analyses above depict a "stock" of export products in a particular year, we have employed a method similar to the SWOT framework in order to examine the "flow" of Georgia's export baskets as well. Using the available RCA data from 1995 to 2013, we attempt to estimate the flow as shown in Table 1. Strengths denote products in which Georgia had the highest export RCAs—the country has specialized in these goods and has been dependent on these exports for income. Likewise, weaknesses denote products in which Georgia has had the highest import RCAs—the country has been highly reliant upon these products and hence vulnerable to the global supply and price fluctuations. Threats and Opportunities stand for losses and gains in these products over time. Threats to strengths are related to products in categories in which Georgia has long specialized and capitalized on for exports, but, over time, has lost its competitive edge. Opportunities to strengths are products in which Georgia has demonstrated comparative advantage and over time strengthened its position. Threats to weaknesses are products in which Georgia has been importing in large quantities and over time its vulnerability worsened. Opportunities to weaknesses are products in which Georgia has become less import-dependent.

Table 1: SWOT Analysis based on Export and Import RCAs

| | Threats (losses) | Opportunities (gains) |
|---|---|---|
| Strengths | Largest export RCA (−) | Largest export RCA (+) |
| Weaknesses | Largest import RCA (+) | Largest import RCA (−) |

The third method employs two measures, ubiquity and diversity adopted from Hausmann et al. (2014), to build the product complexity index, which is useful in mapping Georgia's economic capacity and comparative advantages. "Ubiquity" measures the number of countries that can produce a given product. In the matrix $M$, $c$ indexes countries in rows and $p$ indexes products in columns. If a country $c$ produces good $p$, it is given a value of 1 and 0 otherwise. Summing across columns, we get a measure of how ubiquitous the specific good is. The underlying assumption is that more ubiquitous goods are low value-adding, and hence harder to differentiate from competitors and lower in profit-margins. Also, products high in ubiquity tend to be simple in production, contributing little to the collective "know-how" in a country's capacity for innovation.

$$\text{UBIQUITY} = \kappa_{p,0} = \sum_c \mathrm{M}_{cp}$$

"Diversity" measures how diversified a country's export basket is, or, put differently, how many different goods a country can make. A country that is able to produce many different goods and export them with a comparative advantage is well-diversified. A diversified economy has high capacity for different production methods and hence a high pool of collective "know-how" that can interact for recombination and innovation. Similar to the ubiquity measure, in the matrix $M$, $c$ indexes countries in rows and $p$ indexes products in columns. If a country $c$ produces good $p$, it is given a value of 1 and 0 otherwise. Summing across rows, we get a measure for a country's diversification.

$$\text{Diversity} = \kappa_{c,0} = \sum_c M_{cp}$$

The product complexity index is a ranking of products by the level of complexity. Products such as chemicals and machinery are considered of high product complexity while vegetable products or minerals are considered of low product complexity. The PCI computation involves taking the average diversity of countries producing the specific product, and the average ubiquity of the other products that these countries make.

$$\widetilde{M}^{p}_{p,p'} = \sum_c \frac{M_{cp} M_{cp'}}{\kappa_{c,0}\ \kappa_{p,0}}$$

# Findings

## *Georgia's Cluster Opportunities*

In this section, Georgia's competitive advantages based on revealed comparative advantage and total export share will be presented, but first, it is worth understanding what products Georgia exports and to which countries. Georgia's export products can be categorized into four types: capital, consumer, intermediate, and raw materials. For economic development purposes, a country wants to diversify its export product basket. And over time, a county would want to move from low-value-added to high-value-added exports that usually offer greater profit margins and are more differentiable in the competitive global market. Based on Figure 5, over half (57%) of Georgia's exports in 1996 were low-value-adding raw materials and intermediate goods. By 2014, consumer goods and capital goods became the majority of exports (50.5%). This shift was possible due to large growth in the consumer goods category that rose from 37.5% to 45.7% (+22% growth).

A more detailed breakdown of Georgia's export product share is presented in Figure 6. Largest gains in export product share were in transportation (+1,062%), animal (+411%), stone and glass (+191%), food products (+61.1%). Largest losses in export product share were fuels (−86%), wood (−85%), hides and skins (−71%), footwear (−54%), and vegetable (−51%).

Over the past two decades, the destinations of Georgia's exports have become well-diversified. Today, roughly speaking, a third of its exports go to the EU countries, a third to other countries, and a third to Commonwealth of Independent States (CIS) countries (refer to Figure 7). This transformation reflects Georgia's commitment to pivot to the West. Trade with EU member countries has increased, while trade with CIS countries has diminished. Nonetheless, in the case of many export products, CIS countries still make up a large portion its exports. In 1995, 63% of exports went to CIS countries, 28% to other countries, and 9% to EU countries. In 2015, 38% of exports went to CIS countries, 33% to other countries, and 29% to EU countries. Essentially, its trade dependence on CIS countries has been halved.

The largest export growth over the observed period of time were in EU countries: Czech Republic (+3,713-fold increase), Spain (+3,106), Belgium (+438), Lithuania (+389), Poland (+304), Latvia (+239), Austria (+79), Germany (+63), United Kingdom (+49), Netherlands (+37), Bulgaria (+37), Greece (+28), Italy (+26), France (+23), and Estonia (+16). There were also large export growths in other countries: Canada (+2,130), Lebanon (+974), Jordan (+492), Israel (+465), Singapore (+194), China (+189), the United States (+165), Japan (+55), Iran (+44), India (+44), Afghanistan (+11), Turkey (+4), Switzerland (+4), Mongolia (+3), and Taiwan (+3). The largest export growths among CIS countries were in Uzbekistan (+120), Moldova (+43), Kazakhstan (+24), Azerbaijan (+17), Tajikistan (+17), Kyrgyzstan (+12), Ukraine (+9), Armenia (+9), Belarus (+9), Russia (+2), and Turkmenistan (+1).

Georgia's top export destinations in 1995 were (in 1000$): 1. Russia (48,634) 2. Turkey (34,288) 3. Armenia (18,040) 4. Azerbaijan (13,384) 5. Turkmenistan (6,536) 6. Switzerland

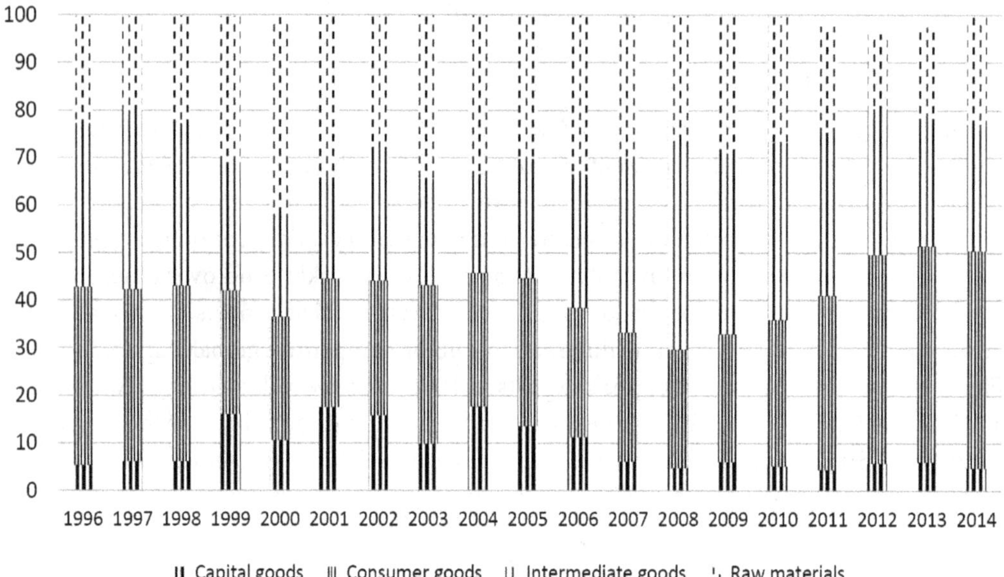


Figure 5: Georgia's Export Product Share, in % (1996–2014)
Source: Data from World Bank's World Integrated Trade Solutions (WITS). Authors' calculations.

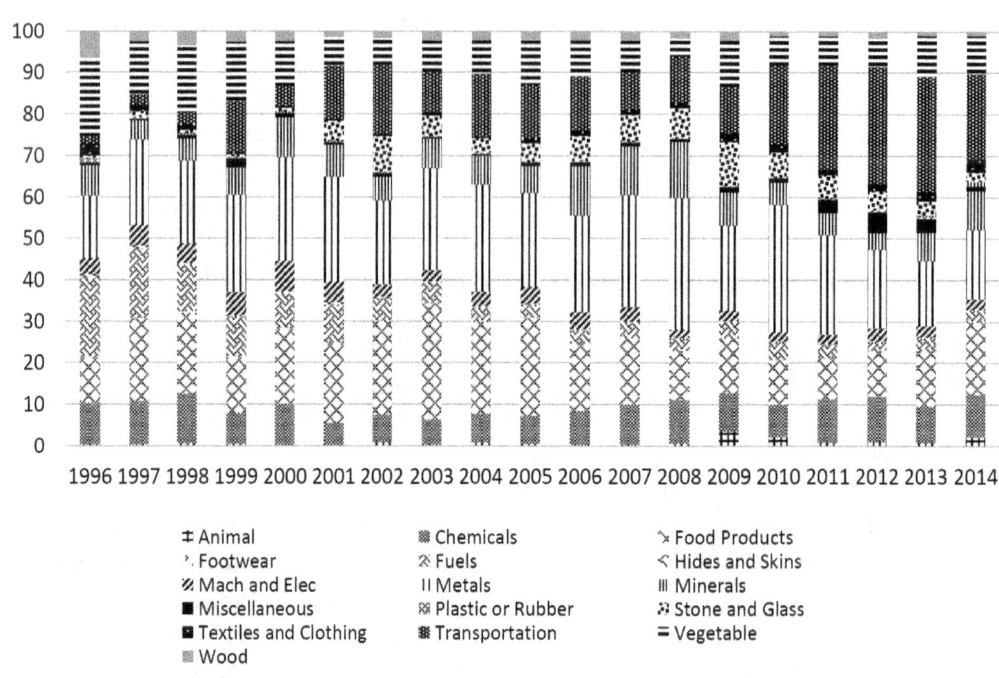


Figure 6: Georgia's Export Product Share, in % (1996–2014)
Source: Data from World Bank's World Integrated Trade Solutions (WITS). Authors' calculations.

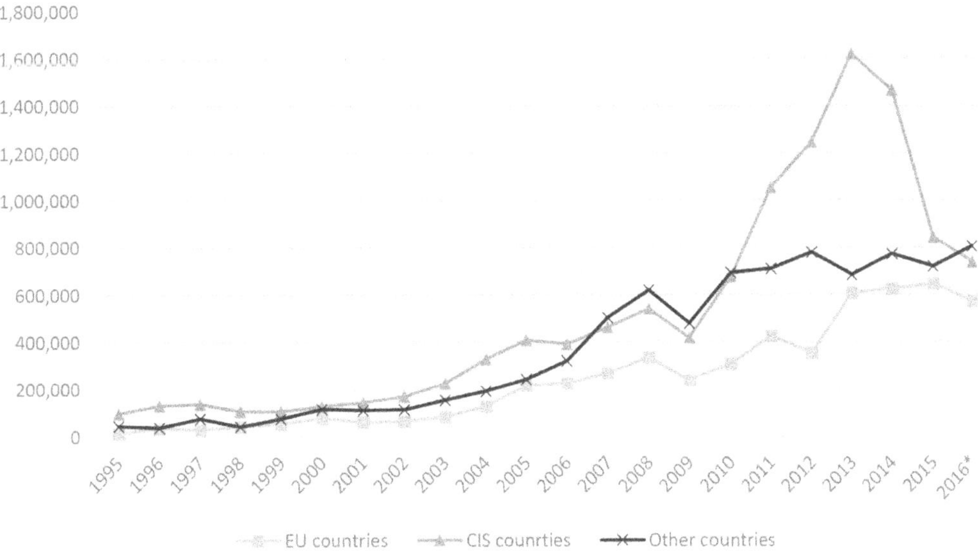


Figure 7: Georgia's Exports by Region, in 1000$ (1995–2016)
Source: Data from National Statistics Office of Georgia (NSO). 2016. Authors' calculations. Note: * Preliminary data for 2016. CIS Countries consist of Armenia, Azerbaijan, Belarus, Kazakhstan, Kyrgyzstan, Moldova, Russia, Tajikistan, Turkmenistan, Ukraine, and Uzbekistan. EU countries consist of Austria, Belgium, Bulgaria, Croatia, Cyprus, Czech Republic, Denmark, Estonia, Finland, France, Germany, Greece, Hungary, Ireland, Italy, Latvia, Lithuania, Luxembourg, Malta, Netherlands, Poland, Portugal, Romania, Slovakia, Slovenia, Spain, Sweden, and United Kingdom. The other countries refer to all the rest.

(6,137) 7. Ukraine (5,774) 8. Bulgaria (5,657) 9. Italy (2,758) 10. Belarus (2,134). These top 10 countries made up 92.4% of Georgia's total exports in 1995. Bulgaria and Italy were the only EU countries, while most other countries were from the CIS. In 2015, Georgia's top export destinations (in thousand $) were: (1) Azerbaijan (240,430), (2) Bulgaria (214,247), (3) Turkey (186,014), (4) Armenia (180,104), (5) Russia (162,866), (6) China (125,800), (7) United States (104,181), (8) Uzbekistan (97,124), (9) Germany (75,811), and (10) Italy (74,407). These top 10 countries made up 66.3% of all export destinations, and the top 30 countries made up 91.0% of Georgia's total exports in 2015.

In 2014, about half of exports to Azerbaijan were in secondary car sales. Exports to Bulgaria primarily consisted of gold content (49%) and crude petroleum oils (40%). About a quarter of exports to Turkey were in apparel-related goods, another quarter related to semi-finished products of metal and ferroalloys, and another quarter were in nitrogenous minerals or chemical fertilizers. Over half of exports to Russia were wine and other alcoholic and non-alcoholic beverages. Exports to the United States primarily consisted of refined petroleum oil (47%), ferroalloys (38%), nitrogenous minerals, or chemical fertilizers (9%). Exports to China consisted of copper waste and scrap (47%), gold content (18%), wine from fresh grapes (8%), and refined copper and copper alloys (7%). Exports to Canada primarily consisted of gold (53%), ferroalloys (34%), and petroleum coke (6%).

According to data from 2014, Georgia's exports with the highest values were in secondary cars—a product category that made up less than a million in 2008, but by 2014 had grown to over $500 million (refer to Table 2). Intermediate petroleum and metals (e.g. ferro-alloys, copper ores, and minerals) have been more consistent product categories. Two industries, wine and apparel, which will be discussed more in detail later, were in 5th place (hs07 code: 2204) and 15th (hs07 code: 6109), respectively.

Georgia's exports with the highest revealed comparative advantages are in chemicals, machinery, metals, and food products (refer to Table 3). Many of the products in the top 10 in Table 3 were initiated during the Soviet Era under the famous Soviet industrialization plans, which aimed at capitalizing endowments in the most strategic ways. More than two decades after leaving the Soviet Union, many of these sectors remain competitive in the global market.

First, Georgia has several chemical products that rank highly. In 2008, isotope exports (hs07 code: 2845) held over 14% of the global market share and in 2014 still held 5.25%. Cyanides (hs07 code: 2837) made up 1.52% in global market share. As part of the Soviet legacy, Georgia is home to a decommissioned nuclear reactor and three nuclear research institutes. Sukhumi I. Vekua Institute of Physics and Technology (SIPT) once housed isotope production reactors that produce nuclear and radiological materials requiring highly sophisticated technology and facilities (Daughtry and Wehling 2000). These materials are dangerous and the government has had to fight against illicit trafficking. Another example is manganese oxides (hs07 code: 2820). Chiatura boasts one of the richest manganese deposits in the world and Georgia's exports made up almost 2% of the global market share.

Second, Georgia's machinery and metal industries demonstrated continued growth in exports. Chemical and metallurgical production in Rustavi dates back to 1947 and includes some of the largest production plants in the country. The railway locomotive factory in Tbilisi was established back in 1883, and transformed into the only state-of-the-art manufacturer of its type in the Soviet Union. Rail locomotives (hs07 code: 8601) made up 2.3%, ferro-alloys (hs07 code: 7202) made up 1% and precious stones (hs07 code: 7116) made up 1.2% of the global market share. Third, Georgia's several food-related products take up a substantial part in the global market share. In the past two decades, arguably the largest growth in exports was mineral water (hs07 code: 2201), whose production had been concentrated in the Borjomi area during the Soviet era but spread throughout Georgia following its independence. Its global market share rose from 0.3% in 2008 to 3.9% in 2014. Exports of live sheep and goats (hs07 code: 104) made up 1.5% of global market share and exports of nuts made up 1.1%.

Table 4 shows the results of the SWOT analysis on Georgia's change of import and export RCAs between 1995 and 2013. Seven of its largest export RCA losses were in metals, which are low in PCIs but also important intermediate products for more advanced machineries. This drop could be interpreted in two ways: Georgia's industrial legacy is rusting away, or Georgia is capitalizing its "know-how" to move into more complex products. The largest

Table 2: Georgia's 25 Products with Highest Export Value, in $ (ordered by 2014)
Source: Data from UN COMTRADE. Authors' Calculations. Note: HS07 are Harmonized Commodity Description and Coding Systems (HS) with amendments from 2007.

| hs07 | Description | 2008 | 2009 | 2010 | 2011 | 2012 | 2013 | 2014 |
|---|---|---|---|---|---|---|---|---|
| 8703 | Motor cars and other motor vehicles principally designed for the transport of persons (other than those of heading 87.02), including station wagons and racing cars. | 770,871 | 80,412,109 | 212,271,849 | 455,090,476 | 584,460,868 | 678,431,842 | 515,618,055 |
| 2710 | Petroleum oils and oils obtained from bituminous minerals, other than crude; preparations not elsewhere specified or included, containing by weight 70 % or more of petroleum oils or of oils obtained from bituminous minerals, these oils being the basic con | 452,121,478 | 166,943,943 | 399,444,009 | 597,606,471 | 364,233,564 | 110,777,374 | 297,900,895 |
| 7202 | Ferro-alloys. | 255,145,054 | 135,302,766 | 260,939,265 | 265,305,994 | 263,712,809 | 226,396,376 | 293,769 994 |
| 2603 | Copper ores and concentrates. | 152,866,834 | 99,911,784 | 194,921,384 | 236,285,103 | 179,356,836 | 200,268,484 | 243,481 231 |
| 2204 | Wine of fresh grapes, including fortified wines; grape must other than that of heading 20.09. | 23,104,285 | 45,811,821 | 58,213,055 | 53,943,225 | 95,910,265 | 135,434,021 | 188,669,701 |
| 802 | Other nuts, fresh or dried, whether or not shelled or peeled. | 34,519,158 | 72,725,959 | 68,997,630 | 128,784,536 | 94,708,350 | 169,236,288 | 183,704,934 |
| 2709 | Petroleum oils and oils obtained from bituminous minerals, crude. | - | - | 131,252,274 | 56,301,795 | 173,944,520 | - | 154,483,504 |
| 3102 | Mineral or chemical fertilisers, nitrogenous. | - | - | 85,408,938 | - | 146,465,445 | 138,672,091 | 146,485,544 |
| 2201 | Waters, including natural or artificial mineral waters and aerated waters, not containing added sugar or other sweetening matter nor flavoured; ice and snow. | 9,538,247 | 24,490,206 | 31,165,815 | 47,508,681 | 59,383,864 | 106,251,382 | 137,969,540 |
| 2208 | Undenatured ethyl alcohol of an alcoholic strength by volume of less than 80 % vol; spirits, liqueurs and other spirituous beverages. | 7,691,513 | 53,334,344 | 53,921,405 | 65,214,490 | 75,040,912 | 98,369,360 | 98,518,357 |
| 3004 | Medicaments (excluding goods of heading 30.02, 30.05 or 30.06) consisting of mixed or unmixed products for therapeutic or prophylactic uses, put up in measured doses (including those in the form of transdermal administration systems) or in forms or packin | 3,784,710 | 23,635,015 | 34,996,038 | 41,482,135 | 50,162,316 | 50,426,928 | 88,814,150 |
| 7214 | Other bars and rods of iron or non-alloy steel, not further worked than forged, hot-rolled, hot-drawn or hot-extruded, but including those twisted after rolling. | 8,391,789 | 2,497,126 | 39,585,129 | - | 53,332,723 | 59,466,063 | 77,716,214 |
| 7108 | Gold | - | - | - | - | - | - | 75,472,005 |
| 7207 | Semi-finished products of iron or non-alloy steel. | - | - | 5,462,942 | 1,044,525 | 10,780,391 | - | 66,216,875 |
| 6109 | T-shirts, singlets and other vests, knitted or crocheted. | 484,170 | 2,997,181 | 11,341,721 | 10,890,074 | 15,380,047 | 29,288,215 | 50,064,993 |
| 7404 | Copper waste and scrap. | 8,719,436 | 19,234,804 | - | - | 43,634,412 | 39,784,138 | 31,268,307 |
| 2202 | Waters, including mineral waters and aerated waters, containing added sugar or other sweetening matter or flavoured, and other non-alcoholic beverages, not including fruit or vegetable juices of heading 20.09. | 7,716,282 | 10,811,650 | 14,221,801 | 15,288,797 | 21,312,815 | 18,315,136 | 30,184,045 |
| 102 | Live bovine animals. | - | 16,902,540 | 16,041,504 | 1,844,673 | 37,989,196 | 318,216 | 28,619,322 |
| 8704 | Motor vehicles for the transport of goods. | 35,791 | 1,789,150 | 12,049,930 | - | 32,269,460 | - | 26,345,156 |
| 7304 | Tubes, pipes and hollow profiles, seamless, of iron (other than cast iron) or steel. | 3,771,487 | 864,984 | 320,137 | 3,959,973 | 3,858,435 | - | 24,811,741 |
| 7116 | Articles of natural or cultured pearls, precious or semi-precious stones (natural, synthetic or reconstructed). | - | 38,414 | - | 26,859 | 1,280 | - | 24,495,274 |
| 8601 | Rail locomotives powered from an external source of electricity or by electric accumulators. | 983,270 | 13,980,863 | 15,216,220 | 10,733,375 | 25,392,962 | - | 24,355,062 |
| 104 | Live sheep and goats. | - | - | 7,551,712 | 15,322,119 | 18,111,799 | 14,919,047 | 20,802,076 |
| 6201 | Men's or boys' overcoats, car-coats, capes, cloaks, anoraks (including ski-jackets), wind-cheaters, wind-jackets and similar articles, other than those of heading 62.03. | 1,473 | 48,277 | 22,558 | 99,676 | 830,383 | 7,508,351 | 20,046,239 |
| 7601 | Unwrought aluminium. | - | 3,891,527 | 11,333,150 | - | - | - | 19,416,913 |

Table 3: Georgia's 25 Products with Highest Revealed Comparative Advantage (Ordered by RCA Index 2014)
Source: Data from UN COMTRADE. Authors' Calculations.

| hs07 | Description | 2008 | 2009 | 2010 | 2011 | 2012 | 2013 | 2014 |
|---|---|---|---|---|---|---|---|---|
| 2845 | Isotopes other than those of heading 28.44; compounds, inorganic or organic, of such isotopes, whether or not chemically defined. | 1,140.20 | 381.58 | 487.97 | 403.15 | 245.85 | 246.94 | 256.72 |
| 2201 | Waters, including natural or artificial mineral waters and aerated waters, not containing added sugar or other sweetening matter nor flavoured; ice and snow. | 23.21 | 58.04 | 63.38 | 81.07 | 105.22 | 164.94 | 190.22 |
| 8601 | Rail locomotives powered from an external source of electricity or by electric accumulators. | 7.05 | 62.11 | 47.87 | 46.66 | 133.02 | 143.24 | 112.71 |
| 2820 | Manganese oxides. | 3.10 | 42.44 | 79.63 | 71.81 | 81.08 | 97.09 | 83.96 |
| 104 | Live sheep and goats. | - | 98.47 | 30.14 | 46.59 | 53.54 | 38.55 | 74.57 |
| 2837 | Cyanides, cyanide oxides and complex cyanides. | 15.43 | 23.90 | 14.53 | 49.82 | 121.61 | 62.27 | 63.63 |
| 7116 | Articles of natural or cultured pearls, precious or semi-precious stones (natural, synthetic or reconstructed). | - | 0.42 | - | 0.16 | 0.01 | - | 58.32 |
| 802 | Other nuts, fresh or dried, whether or not shelled or peeled. | 32.51 | 55.41 | 36.15 | 53.33 | 37.15 | 57.86 | 53.30 |
| 7202 | Ferro-alloys. | 48.48 | 47.24 | 49.39 | 40.43 | 44.33 | 42.66 | 48.58 |
| 1106 | Flour, meal and powder of the dried leguminous vegetables of heading 07.13, of sago or of roots or tubers of heading 07.14 or of the products of Chapter 8. | 47.08 | 16.00 | 29.41 | 40.12 | 39.10 | 39.82 | 30.27 |
| 2204 | Wine of fresh grapes, including fortified wines; grape must other than that of heading 20.09. | 6.01 | 11.40 | 11.46 | 8.53 | 15.47 | 20.03 | 26.39 |
| 3102 | Mineral or chemical fertilisers, nitrogenous. | 41.02 | 25.24 | 22.46 | 25.12 | 23.58 | 24.73 | 26.10 |
| 2603 | Copper ores and concentrates. | 36.40 | 20.90 | 23.90 | 23.47 | 17.71 | 18.95 | 22.19 |
| 1504 | Fats and oils and their fractions, of fish or marine mammals, whether or not refined, but not chemically modified. | 2.38 | 0.11 | 5.69 | 3.69 | 1.56 | 18.03 | 18.56 |
| 7214 | Other bars and rods of iron or non-alloy steel, not further worked than forged, hot-rolled, hot-drawn or hot-extruded, but including those twisted after rolling. | 2.08 | 1.07 | 13.15 | 15.36 | 12.02 | 13.56 | 18.00 |
| 2208 | Undenatured ethyl alcohol of an alcoholic strength by volume of less than 80 % vol; spirits, liqueurs and other spirituous beverages. | 2.58 | 16.64 | 12.80 | 12.27 | 13.52 | 16.87 | 15.93 |
| 4406 | Railway or tramway sleepers (cross-ties) of wood. | 1.23 | 13.27 | 4.91 | 4.00 | 2.07 | 9.50 | 15.69 |
| 6809 | Articles of plaster or of compositions based on plaster. | 0.03 | 0.05 | 3.35 | 7.03 | 13.30 | 13.75 | 15.57 |
| 2205 | Vermouth and other wine of fresh grapes flavoured with plants or aromatic substances. | 3.90 | 30.30 | 29.23 | 23.00 | 14.44 | 14.59 | 14.89 |
| 7008 | Multiple-walled insulating units of glass. | - | - | - | 0.01 | 0.03 | 20.00 | 14.77 |
| 910 | Ginger, saffron, turmeric (curcuma), thyme, bay leaves, curry and other spices. | 5.53 | 12.01 | 10.60 | 9.03 | 15.09 | 13.07 | 14.60 |
| 102 | Live bovine animals. | - | 17.87 | 12.11 | 1.17 | 21.86 | 0.19 | 14.40 |

| | | | | | | | | |
|---|---|---|---|---|---|---|---|---|
| 4404 | Hoopwood; split poles; piles, pickets and stakes of wood, pointed but not sawn lengthwise; wooden sticks, roughly trimmed but not turned, bent or otherwise worked, suitable for the manufacture of walking-sticks, umbrellas, tool handles or the like; chipwo | - | 0.16 | - | - | 0.21 | 2.66 | 14.09 |
| 7806 | Other articles of lead. | - | 0.12 | 1.10 | 7.46 | 25.17 | 24.97 | 12.77 |
| 2301 | Flours, meals and pellets, of meat or meat offal, of fish or of crustaceans, molluscs or other aquatic invertebrates, unfit for human consumption; greaves. | 3.83 | 1.52 | 3.19 | 2.78 | 1.10 | 11.21 | 12.00 |

export RCA gains were in chemicals and foodstuffs (e.g. natural water and wine). There is some indication that the Soviet industrial legacy survived; while $12 million is too small of a number in global trade, many of these chemical products rank high in PCI, meaning that they are complex products requiring high levels of human capital and technology that can potentially lead to spillover benefits or become a "know-how" capacity for other complex goods. Likewise, a rise in export RCA of rail locomotives, highly complex machinery, is a positive sign that somewhat compensates for losses in metal export competitiveness.

In contrast, there are some categories of goods in which import RCAs have increased. These increases could be benign if these intermediate or raw imported goods are sourced for production of more complex finished goods, but they could equally be signs of increased dependence. Three categories appear to have risen in import RCAs: mineral products, machinery/electrical, and miscellaneous products. The loss in railway passenger coaches is significant given its high product complexity and given its relatedness to rail locomotives, which experienced increases in export RCAs. This divergence could be a benign result of upgrading technologies or a real loss in competitiveness of a product. Another category of loss is hydraulic turbines, water wheels, and presses (crushers used in the manufacture of wine, cider, and fruit juices). These machineries are the very capital used to produce wines and other foodstuffs on which Georgia already has comparative advantages. One interpretation is that Georgia fell behind in process innovation, which could have greater negative consequences on the economy. On the other hand, Georgia has become less dependent on three product categories: animal and animal products, vegetable products, and foodstuffs. While these goods rank low in product complexity, decrease in import RCAs implies that Georgia's internal economy has become more resilient; perhaps, internal production output has grown and prices fallen for these goods to sufficiently supply domestic consumers.

Figure 8 is a visual plot of Table 4, showing the flow of export RCAs over the years 1995–2013, disaggregated by PCI. Clear winners in Figure 8 are "rail locomotives powered from electricity" and "isotopes not elsewhere specified." A case study on these two products would serve Georgia's trade interests and potentially be informative to deliberations on cluster initiatives. Other growth sectors were wine from fresh grapes and "waters, natural". Proportionally speaking, "waters, natural" has experienced a far greater RCA growth but wines are far more specialized goods with higher profit margins.

Table 4: SWOT Analysis of Georgia's Exports and Imports (1995–2013)

Source: Data from UN COMTRADE. Authors' Calculations. Note: All export and import products above made up at least a million $ in trade. If Georgia ceased all trade of the good, meaning that its export or import values dropped to zero, they were excluded from ranking. The RCA (+/–) is the net change in the export or import RCA between 2013 and 1995. Products in the top 15 rankings that had relevance to Section 5 were bolded and italicized.

| The Largest Export RCA Losses | | | | | | The Largest Export RCA Gains | | | | | |
|---|---|---|---|---|---|---|---|---|---|---|---|
| # | HS4 | Name | PCI | EX_RCA | RCA (+/-) | # | HS4 | Name | PCI | EX_RCA | RCA (+/-) |
| 1 | 7202 | Ferroalloys | -0.31 | 43.45 | -97.98 | 1 | 2845 | Isotopes not elsewhere specified | 2.19 | 238.84 | 178.76 |
| 2 | 7204 | Ferrous waste and scrap | -0.34 | 1.98 | -92.47 | 2 | 2201 | Waters natural | 0.80 | 165.03 | 162.81 |
| 3 | 7207 | Semifinished products of iron or nonalloy steel | 0.45 | 12.35 | -41.73 | 3 | 8601 | Rail locomotives powered from electricity | 2.26 | 127.15 | 127.15 |
| 4 | 7404 | Copper waste and scrap | -0.98 | 7.92 | -28.60 | 4 | 2820 | Manganese oxides | 0.77 | 95.46 | 95.46 |
| 5 | 1209 | Seeds, fruits and spores for sowing | -0.34 | 1.43 | -13.16 | 5 | 2837 | Cyanides | 0.42 | 69.42 | 69.42 |
| 6 | 7112 | Scrap of precious metal | 0.25 | 4.98 | -10.34 | 6 | 104 | Sheep | -0.35 | 60.00 | 60.00 |
| 7 | 7403 | Refined copper and copper alloys | -0.41 | 0.13 | -9.24 | 7 | 802 | Other nuts | -2.89 | 59.24 | 47.29 |
| 8 | 7215 | Other bars and rods of iron or nonalloy steel | 0.75 | 2.64 | -9.23 | 8 | 1106 | Flour or meal of dried legumes | -1.95 | 38.17 | 38.17 |
| 9 | 902 | Tea | -3.04 | 1.79 | -6.19 | 9 | 7802 | Lead waste or scrap | -1.07 | 35.89 | 35.89 |
| 10 | 2206 | Fermented beverages (cider, perry, mead, etc) | 1.62 | 8.13 | -5.83 | 10 | 7806 | Other articles of lead | 1.55 | 25.89 | 25.89 |
| 11 | 2009 | Fruit juices | -1.05 | 2.14 | -5.55 | 11 | 7008 | Multiple-walled insulating glass | 2.06 | 19.81 | 19.81 |
| 12 | 2710 | Petroleum oils, refined | -1.35 | 0.68 | -3.94 | 12 | 2204 | ***Wine of fresh grapes*** | 0.81 | 19.89 | 18.62 |
| 13 | 6202 | ***Womens overcoats, not knit*** | -0.17 | 3.23 | -3.78 | 13 | 2603 | Gold content | -3.43 | 18.05 | 18.05 |
| 14 | 7304 | Tubes, pipes and hollow profiles, seamless, of iron or steel | 1.81 | 4.69 | -2.87 | 14 | 1504 | Fats and oils of fish or marine mammals | -1.45 | 18.86 | 17.46 |
| 15 | 8474 | Machinery for working earth, stone, and other mineral substances | 1.90 | 0.41 | -1.62 | 15 | 2205 | Vermouth and other flavored wines | 1.03 | 13.81 | 13.81 |

| The Largest Import RCA Losses | | | | | | The Largest Import RCA Gains | | | | | |
|---|---|---|---|---|---|---|---|---|---|---|---|
| # | HS4 | Name | PCI | IM_RCA | RCA (+/-) | # | HS4 | Name | PCI | IM_RCA | RCA (+/-) |
| 1 | 2520 | Gypsum | -1.21 | 55.60 | 55.50 | 1 | 1101 | Wheat or meslin flour | -1.36 | 3.30 | -331.51 |
| 2 | 8605 | Railway passenger coaches | 2.76 | 31.62 | 31.62 | 2 | 2102 | Yeasts, active | 0.48 | 5.67 | -51.00 |
| 3 | 8435 | Presses, crushers used in the manufacture of wine, cider, fruit juices | 1.09 | 30.75 | 30.75 | 3 | 407 | Birds eggs, in shell | 0.71 | 1.89 | -40.63 |
| 4 | 2602 | Manganese of 47 percent or more by weight | -4.38 | 23.53 | 23.53 | 4 | 1517 | Margarine, not liquid | -0.79 | 10.26 | -40.18 |
| 5 | 8410 | Hydraulic turbines, water wheels | 1.66 | 17.97 | 17.97 | 5 | 2207 | Ethyl alcohol > 80% by volume | -1.51 | 2.26 | -37.57 |
| 6 | 7313 | Barbed wire of iron or steel | -1.06 | 17.03 | 17.03 | 6 | 2202 | Waters flavored or sweetened | -0.12 | 2.58 | -33.94 |
| 7 | 6309 | ***Used clothes and textiles*** | 0.28 | 13.90 | 13.41 | 7 | 2203 | Beer | 0.66 | 1.26 | -27.94 |
| 8 | 4413 | Densified wood | -1.02 | 12.54 | 12.45 | 8 | 1516 | hydrogenated animal and vegetable fats, oils | -1.00 | 1.10 | -25.17 |
| 9 | 4503 | Articles of natural cork | 0.66 | 12.40 | 12.30 | 9 | 1001 | Wheat and meslin | 0.84 | 7.62 | -24.70 |
| 10 | 2818 | Artificial corundum | 0.35 | 12.30 | 12.30 | 10 | 6305 | Sacks and bags, used for packing goods | -2.29 | 3.32 | -16.91 |
| 11 | 4504 | Agglomerated cork | 1.83 | 11.77 | 11.77 | 11 | 1806 | Cocoa powder, sweetened | 1.05 | 5.10 | -16.12 |
| 12 | 3916 | Monofilament | 1.79 | 11.75 | 11.75 | 12 | 402 | Milk and cream, concentrated | -0.57 | 1.80 | -14.86 |
| 13 | 6405 | Other footwear | -0.95 | 12.02 | 11.55 | 13 | 713 | Dried legumes | -2.45 | 1.89 | -12.94 |
| 14 | 4814 | Wallpaper | 2.45 | 12.60 | 10.97 | 14 | 1704 | Confectionery sugar | -0.11 | 4.11 | -9.53 |
| 15 | 2704 | Coke etc of coal, lignite or peat, retort carbon | 0.47 | 9.94 | 9.94 | 15 | 1904 | Cereal foods | 0.22 | 0.73 | -9.29 |

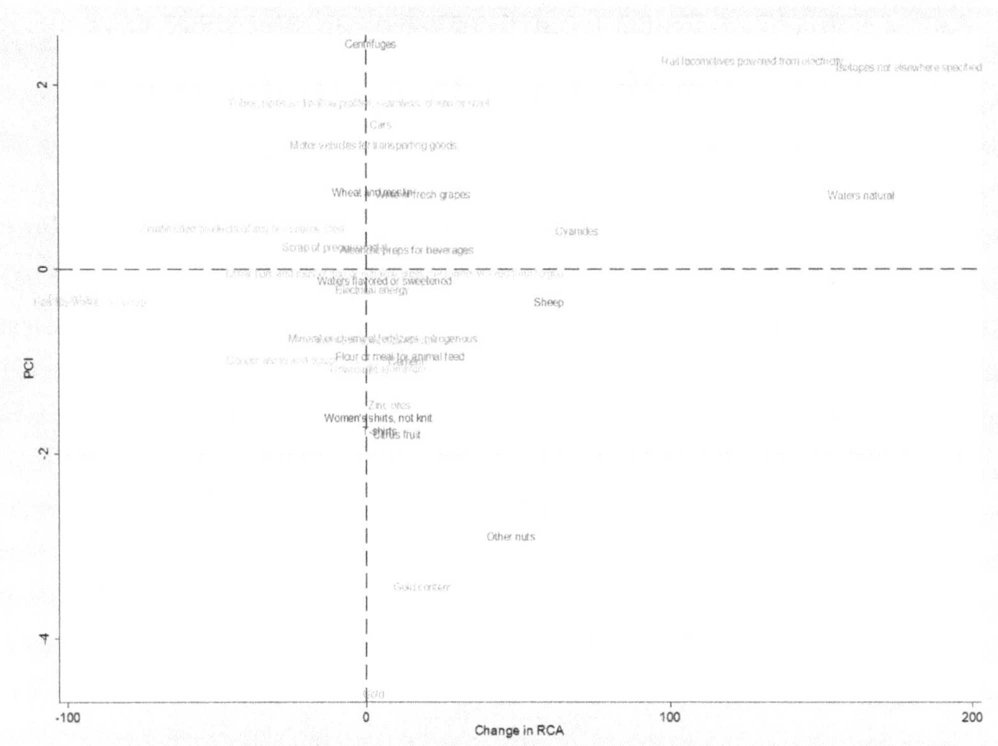


Figure 8: Change in Export RCAs of HS4 Products, Disaggregated by the Product Complexity Index (1995–2013)

Source: Data from UN COMTRADE. Authors' calculations. Note: Only export products with a minimum trade of $10 million and export RCA >1 are included. The x-line and y-lines trace Change in RCA=0 and PCI=0, respectively. There are 1,018 unique product codes in the HS4 classification. HS4 codes are color-coded into 15 different categories: (1) animal and animal products, (2) vegetable products, (3) foodstuffs, (4) mineral products, (5) chemicals & allied industries, (6) plastics & rubber, (7) raw hides, skins, leather & furs, (8) miscellaneous, (9) textiles/footwear/headgear, (10) wood & wood products, (11) stone/glass, (12) metals, (13) machinery/electrical, (14) transportation, and (15) service.

## Discussion

This chapter's primary contributions have been the theoretical exposition of cluster initiatives, and empirical analysis of Georgia's trade capabilities, in an attempt to link theory to data. Below we further explore Georgia's economic potential by examining in some detail two promising economic clusters in Georgia: textiles and wine. These two product sectors have a special relevance in the clusters discourse because of the Government's preferential investments and interests. While some insights are offered on the basis of the analysis in the present chapter, Onugha et al. (2013) offer more comprehensive recommendations where the industrial sector is concerned. Both Gazadze and Nakashidze (2014) and Anderson (2013) offer a more detailed analysis of Georgia's wine industry. And for further insights and analysis of Georgia's apparel and textile industry, see PricewaterhouseCoopers (2012) or Steinheim (2016). Our analysis suggests that developing wine clusters is a good path. The wine industry has much potential to carve its niche in the global market and become a national brand attracting tourism. We are less optimistic about the apparel/textile industry which has gained little ground on strengthening its comparative advantage. But given the current cooperation and investment from Turkish producers, it also has some potential.

## *Apparel and Textile Industry*

### History and Background

Georgia has had a long history in the textile and apparel industry, dating back to the Soviet era. Most noteworthy are its fine silk and wool blend fabrics. The collapse of the Soviet Union saw the sector abandoned, but a resurgence came in the early 2000s through investments from Turkish textile companies that acquired and modernized Georgia's Soviet-built textile factories. Between 2003 and 2014, the number of workers employed in this sector grew by 65%; between 2006 and 2014, exports increased 7 fold from \$11.8 to \$89.8 million (WTO Secretariat 2015). Turkish businesses that have invested in Georgia are well-established in their industry and have long-term contracts with the European fashion houses. Most notable Turkish textile factories are found in Georgia's Adjara region, which abuts Turkey. As depicted in Figure 9, in 2016, over 90 percent of Georgia's produced goods are exported to Turkey. The other markets consist of European Union (EU) and Commonwealth of Independent States (CIS) member countries. The following companies have contracts with Adjarian textile factories: Tommy Hilfiger, Zara, Moncler, Marks & Spencer, Kotton, Puma, Mexx, Next, George, Miss Etam, Lotto, Per Una, Autograph, Lebek, Hawes & Curtis, Dainese, and Primark.

Based on data from the World Trade Organization (WTO), trade in textiles has grown from \$476 billion in 2006 (Adhikari and Yamato 2007) to \$705 billion \$ in 2011 (Fukunishi, Goto, and Yamagata 2013). China is the top exporter, accounting for 40% of global textile exports, while the United States is the top importer, accounting for 25% of global textile imports (PricewaterhouseCoopers 2012). The other top exporters are: Italy (6%); Turkey (4%); India (3%); and France (3%). The other major importers are: Germany (11%); Japan (8%); United Kingdom (7%); and France (7%). All importers on the list are developed countries. Among importers, Italy garners the top end apparel of the industry, while China, India, and Turkey are mostly beneficiaries of outsourcing from developed countries' apparel companies.

According to PricewaterhouseCoopers (2012), the largest share of value in the apparel industry value chain is captured by retailers (65%), followed by wholesalers (13%) and apparel manufacturers (11%). Georgia's role in the value chain shown in Figure 10 falls under apparel manufacturers, and the materials supplier category represents a facet of the apparel industry in which Georgia could potentially expand its presence. However, its capture of value and bargaining power are low, as many of its contracts are awarded via Turkish and European intermediaries who are in direct contact with the European fashion houses.

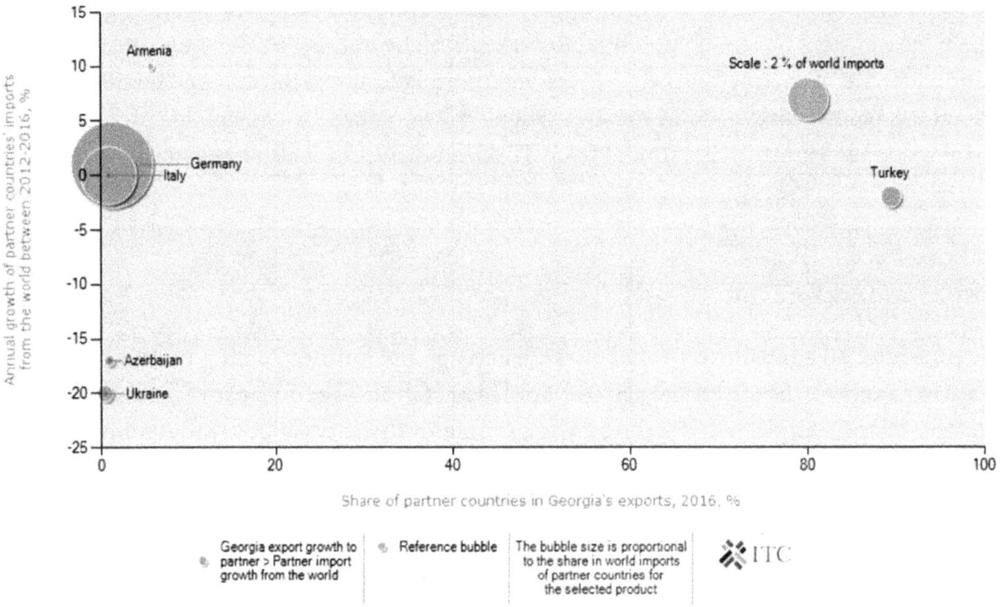


Figure 9: Prospects for Market Diversification for Apparel Exported by Georgia (2016) Source: Data and trade map provided by the International Trade Center. ITC calculations based on UN COMTRADE and ITC statistics. Note: The full product name is 61 Articles of apparel and clothing accessories, knitted or crocheted.

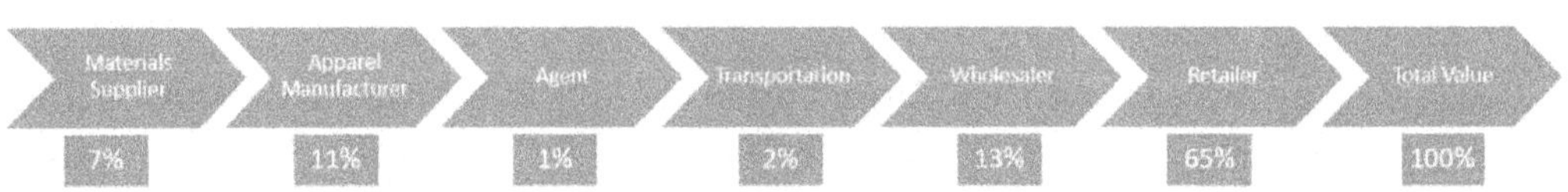


Figure 10: The Value Distribution in the Apparel Industry
Source: Adopted from PricewaterhouseCoopers (2012).

There are four stages of value chain development in apparel manufacturing (Fernandez-Stark, Frederick, and Gereffi 2011). The first stage is known as Cut, Make, and Trim (CMT) in which the manufacturer is responsible for cutting and sewing woven or knitted fabric, or knitting apparel directly from yarn. Currently, Georgia's apparel and textile manufacturers fall under this stage. As shown in Figure 10, their capabilities are in sewing, stitching, and printing. The second stage is known as original equipment manufacturing (OEM) in which the manufacturer is responsible for all production activities, including CMT and finishing. These manufacturers are able to cover all the upstream activities belonging to material suppliers in Figure 11, whether through self-production or procurement. Currently, Georgian manufacturers do not have these capabilities, as there is no local production of other components such as buttons, threads, labels, and zippers. The third stage is known as original design manufacturing (ODM) which is a business model that has design capabilities in addition to production capabilities. The fourth stage is known as original brand manufacturing (OBM) in which the manufacturer is capable of branding and the sale of its own brand products. Georgia's potential opportunities lie in all three stages. By modernizing the manufacturing facilities and logistics, Georgian manufacturers should develop full OEM capabilities. In the long-term, by investing in fashion education and training its workforce, Georgian manufacturers can claim a bigger share of the value chain and its profits by having ODM capabilities.

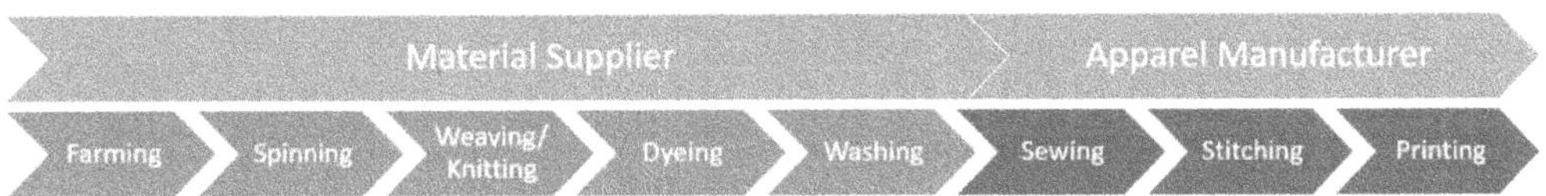


Figure 11: Georgia's Value Chain Potential
Source: Adapted from Steinheim (2016) and supplemented with authors' contribution.

**Policy Recommendations**

Georgia's competitive advantage in the apparel industry stands on four important factors. First, it boasts low costs in labor, land, and energy. Fabric and other materials make up about 56% of total costs in the apparel production process, while labor costs makes up about 17%. Georgia's workforce is educated and relatively cheap, with good labor laws and low levels of unionization for foreign investors. According to the Georgian Investment Agency (2015), the average salary of the Georgian workforce in 2015 was $411, which is almost double what it was in 2007. However, Georgia's labor market and apparel industry do not meet many standards related to quality, safety, health and sustainability (e.g. Ethical Trading Initiative (UK), the Business Social Compliance Initiative (BSCI) and Fair Wair Foundation (EU)). If Georgia wants to expand its exports to the EU market, these shortfalls will need serious attention and investment. Second, its geographic proximity to Turkey and the major European market has played a vital role in its rapid growth. Georgia is located at an advantageous route to the European market in comparison to its Asian competitors. The time advantage is about 1 week, which itself is a cost-saving. Thirdly, Georgia benefits from preferential access to the EU market. For instance, in 2011, Georgia's exports enjoyed 0% apparel-related import duties from France, Germany and the United Kingdom. What is also unexpectedly playing in Georgia's favor are security concerns regarding Asian suppliers, such as those in Bangladesh. Fourth, the Georgian government has created a business-friendly environment, along with an infrastructure and transportation logistics that compensate for its late entrance back into this market. Georgia is in the process of transitioning from the generalized system of preferences (GSP) status, a preferential tariff system which provides exemption from the more general rules of the WTO (GSP has allowed Georgia access to countries like the USA, Canada, Japan, Norway, and Switzerland), to a Deep and Comprehensive Free Trade Agreement (DCFTA) status which will further integrate Georgia into the EU member countries' markets. In fact, the Georgian government has a program called "Produce in Georgia" that allows apparel and textile companies eligible for loan subsidies to use these funds toward creation or expansion of their business operations (WTO Secretariat 2015).

For policymakers in Georgia, the textile and apparel industry is a potential cluster candidate. Many of today's developed countries (e.g. Great Britain, the United States, and Japan), as well as many of the newly industrialized countries (e.g. South Korea and Taiwan) went through a stage of high textile and apparel exports (Adhikari and Yamato 2007; Keane and te Velde 2008). It is also an industry that can accelerate Georgia's labor force participation rate by easing more women into the workforce.

However, there are legitimate concerns, too. Low barrier of entry and threat of substitutes make it a very competitive market. This industry is characterized by cost-competition more than competition based on differentiation. High-end fashion markets may use high technology and highly paid professionals, but the market segment that Georgia's apparel industry captures is the lower end. While Georgia's apparel industry has resurged and found its competitive edge in the global value chain, its textile industry will need long-term investments to find its place. Entrance to the apparel industry has been relatively easy, as it is not particularly capital-intensive and does not require sophisticated production skills. Also, Georgia's Soviet legacy played in its favor. Based on Figure 9, building capacity for activities of material suppliers and the agents are possible expansion paths. A 2016 study of Georgia's apparel and textile industry conducted by the Deutsche Gesellschaft für Internationale Zusammenarbeit (GIZ) GmbH recommended that Georgia expand its investments in the apparel industry, but not the textile industry (Steinheim, 2016) citing high upfront investment costs that outweigh the potential benefits (see also Figure 8. Note that women's shirts, not knit and shirts appeared in the SWOT Analysis with all the cutoffs but essentially remained stagnant). It is a compelling argument given that the textile industry is usually more capital-intensive than the clothing industry. Spinning, weaving, and finishing are integrated by high-technology equipment that produces large, standardized volumes to take advantage of economies of scale (Nordås 2004). Georgia's short-term objectives should focus on expanding its manufacturing capabilities from just CMT to ODM and OBM. And, in the long-term, Georgia should aim to develop its textile/material supplier value chain in order to have more productive capabilities and bargaining power over the downstream players.

Currently, Georgian apparel manufacturers are either Georgian or Turkish-owned. For example, seven of the largest players in the sector are Georgian-based Turkish producers, who operate through their satellites (Steinheim 2016). Based on Figure 1, Georgia's apparel industry falls under Satellite clusters in Markusen's typology. Most of the 200 apparel enterprises employ 5–10 employees, while the top 10 largest employ between 25–40 or 50–150, which from an international perspective is still small (Steinheim 2016). Georgia will need a critical mass, a mixture of large enterprises, as well as small and medium enterprises, to grow its competitiveness in the global markets. That is, Georgian apparel manufacturers in the CMT stage, will need significant capital and know-how to expand to ODM and OBM.

While some Georgian apparel manufacturers are already experimenting with ODM and OBM, there are limitations in capital and scale. There are also limitations with what Turkish satellites will be willing to contribute in this expansion process. Going back to Markusen's typology, much like in Figure 1's Hubs-and-Spokes model, Georgia should develop its own large enterprises that will have the capital and scale to invest in ODM and OBM capabilities.

### *Wine and Tourism Industry*

#### History and Background

During the Soviet era, Georgian wine was widely exported to today's CIS countries and commanded a premium over other wines. Under the Soviet command economy, Georgian wineries were agglomerated into collective farms with standardized wine making. Georgia's wine production became efficient and its production volume peaked at about 7 million cases of wine per year, which some claim is more than what is produced today (Anderson and Signe 2009). The cost, however, was that some of Georgia's tacit traditions, passed down generationally, were lost. Following the collapse of the Soviet Union, Georgia's wine exports continuously increased between 1990 and 2005 from 4.7 to 41.6 million liters or \$3.7 to \$81.3 million (refer to Figure 12). However, in 2006, Russia, Georgia's largest importer of wine, imposed an embargo, citing sanitary and quality concerns, in a move widely considered to have been politically motivated in objection to Georgia's pivot to the West. In addition, Georgia was embroiled in a war with Russia in August 2008 that further distanced the two countries. Since Russia's embargo in 2006, Georgia's main export destinations were redirected to two other CIS countries, Ukraine and Kazakhstan. Since 2013, Russia has dropped its embargos and regained its place as the largest importer. Since early 2014, Ukraine has been in turmoil due to the Crimea Crisis and its imports suffered as a result. Georgia has made a decision to pivot to the EU market and its wine sector continuously probes for opportunities to expand its presence there. Among many areas, the industry needs immediate attention to improvements in its wine quality and sanitary standards in production.

Today, the global wine industry is dominated by large wine producers in the Old and the New World. The New World (e.g. Argentina, Australia, Chile, New Zealand, South Africa, and the United States), in competition against the Old World (e.g. European countries) took advantage of its large land endowments and new technology for economies of scale and, its global share of wine exports rose from a mere 2% to almost 40% (Anderson 2004). Georgia cannot compete in volume as its wine production is dwarfed by countries like Italy, France, Spain, the US, Argentina, and Australia (refer to Figure 13). Georgia's wine producers do not have a comparative advantage in economies of scale; neither do they have the state-of-the-art technologies for high production and quality capabilities.

Georgia's endowment of the finest grapes and rich tradition in wine making offer unique comparative advantages that can be cultivated. Kym Anderson (2013) of the Wine Economics Research Centre published a paper entitled, "Is Georgia the Next 'New' Wine Exporting Country?" Anderson names Georgia's three comparative advantages, which he sums up as the "three Ts": terroir, tradition, and technology. Terroir refers to the environment

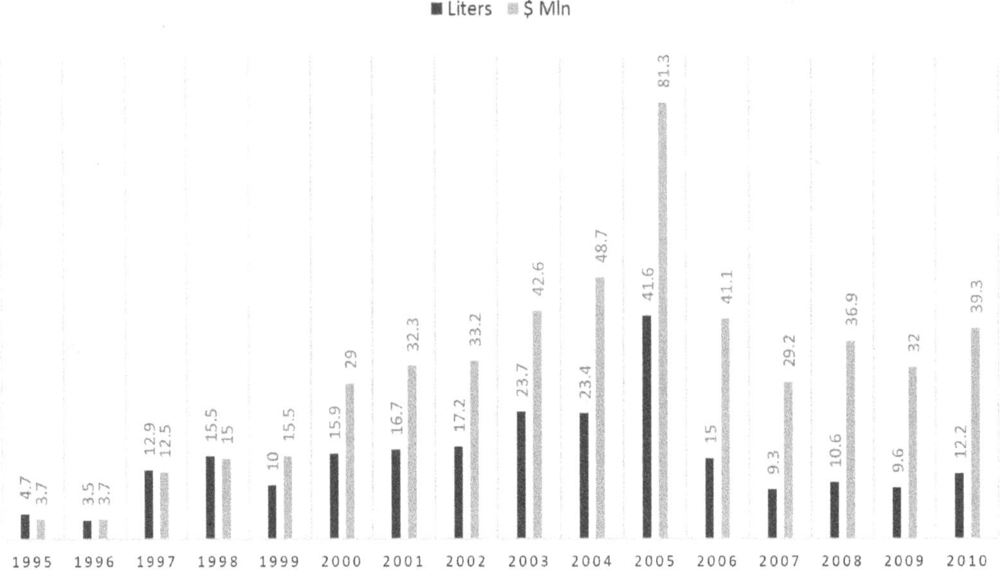


Figure 12: Georgia's Wine Exports (1995–2010)
Source: Data from Georgian Wine Association.

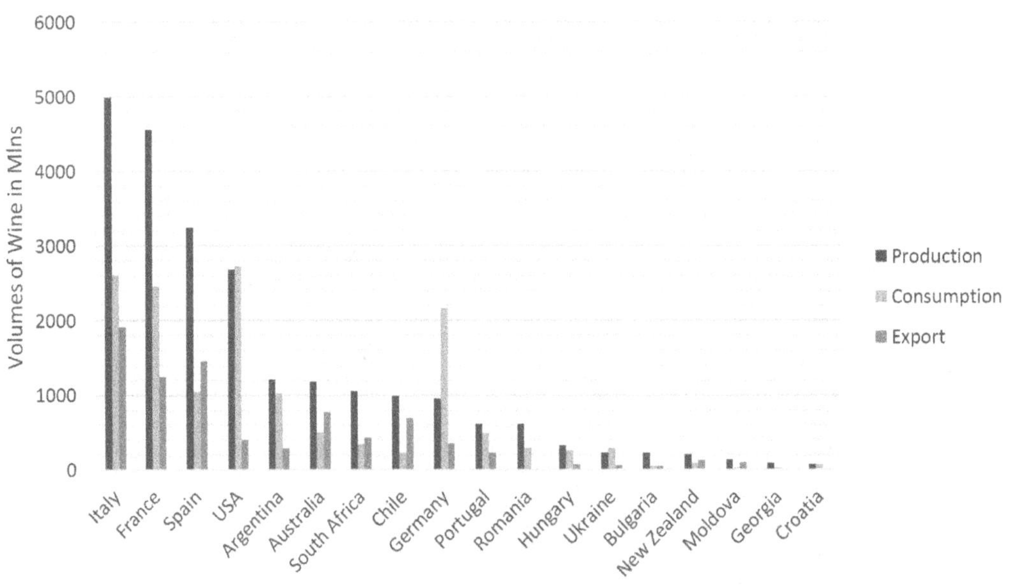


Figure 13: Production, Consumption, and Export
of Wine in Selected Countries (2009)
Source: Data from Wine Economics Research Centre.

where the wine is grown, including climate, topography, and soil. Situated at the same latitude as California (United States), Tuscany (Italy), and La Rioja (Spain), Georgia is endowed with a climate and terrain that is ideal for production of the finest grapes. Its Caucasus Mountains serve as a barrier to cold air masses and its long, dry, and hot summers are ideal for vineyards. Some 525 unique varieties of grapes are cultivated in Georgia in 10 viticulture zones, including: Kakheti, Kartli, Meskheti, Imereti, Racha, Lechkhumi, Guria, Samegrelo, Abkhazia, and Adjara. Tradition refers to how wine producing and consumption are deeply ingrained in Georgia's history and culture. There is a level of authenticity and uniqueness to Georgia's wine as a result of its production and consumption that have kept tradition intact. Technology refers to the extent formal investment is made in private and public research and development (R&D). While Georgia does not have modernized R&D centers, facilities or equipment, it does have a Soviet legacy of equipment and production facilities in place. These facilities and equipment served a particular market, namely, the former Soviet republics, with cheap, low-quality wine. Georgia benefits from experience in serving this market and CIS still makes up the largest export destination today. This non-premium market is just one market on which the Georgian wine industry might hope to capitalize, and in this particular sector, it already has a running start.

**Policy Recommendations**

With good leadership and strategic vision, Georgia's wine sector has the potential for expansion. Establishing a "Made in Georgia" brand to compete in the global market, and integrating the wine sector with the tourism sector, could help in this development. A concerted effort across the entire value chain is needed. Following Markusen's typology in Figure 1, grape and wine producers could benefit from transforming themselves from a Marshallian to a State-anchored type of a cluster. It is in government's best interest to be part of this industry's transformation, especially if it wants to build a "Made in Georgia" brand. The Kakheti Region, which produces 70% of Georgian grapes and is home to many great wineries is already a natural cluster (Government of Georgia 2013). On an industry level, horizontal or vertical consolidation through mergers or acquisitions is recommended. In this section, seven detailed recommendations propose how the value chain can be improved.

Georgia's wine production value chain can be largely divided into three parts: primary production (grape growing), manufacturing (wine production), and services (e.g. transportation and marketing). In Figure 14, one can see the interlinkages between the grape and wine sectors. Also evident is the extent to which the Georgian government has come to the assistance of the sector by establishing relevant institutions that protect rights, ensure quality, and promote exports.

First, Georgia must raise the quality of grape production. Grapes produced by households tend to be inconsistent in quality. Dissatisfied Georgian wine producers have begun to plant their own vineyards to raise the quality standards and to have more control over the whole value chain (Anderson 2013). Hence, either farmers will have to increase quality and production capacities or become irrelevant. Most vineyards can benefit from denser spacing, which can help raise grape quality and also, many vineyards need modernized irrigation systems to support production through dry seasons (Anderson 2013).

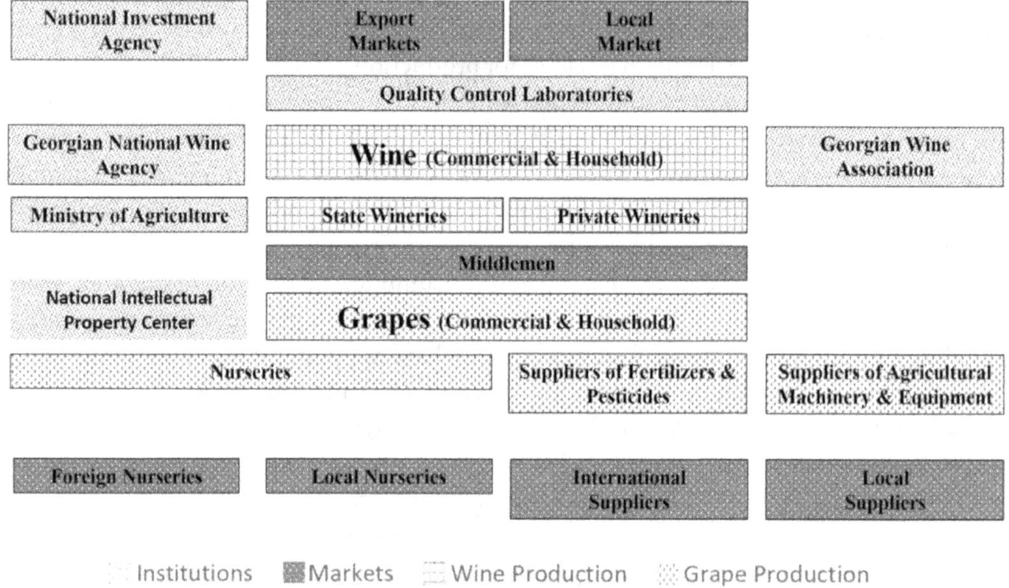


Figure 14: Value Chain of Grape and Wine Production in Georgia
Source: Adapted Bank of Georgia and supplemented by authors.

Second, Georgia's grape and wine producers should coordinate with each other in order to identify and specialize in varieties that are best suited for wines in demand in the market. Even though Georgia boasts over 500 varieties of grapes, commercial wine producers are permitted by regulation to use only 38 of these varieties, and in the market, most wines are made from just 1 of 20 (Taber 2009). Georgia grows some of grapes that are more generic, such as, Cabernet Sauvignon. But more interesting is the fact that, unlike many of its competitors, Georgia widely uses grapes like Saperavi and Rkatsiteli. For example, Alazani Valley wine is made from Rkatsiteli and Kindzmarauli is made from Saperavi grapes. Saperavi is the most commonly used red grape for wine production, and Rkatsiteli, a variety that is highly acidic and used for both dry and sweet wines, is the most common white grape used for wine production in Georgia (Taber 2009).

Third, Georgia's wine producers should strategically select wine categories in which to compete. The Wine Economics Research Centre categorizes wine into three categories: non-premium, commercial premium, and super premium. Table 5 indicates that Georgia has a revealed comparative advantage in non-premium and commercial premium. The non-premium category serves the CIS countries and the commercial premium category serves the European markets. These are the two categories that Georgian wine producers would be best advised to hone in on. Historically, Georgia's exports focused on semi-sweet, low-quality red wines with less alcohol content than dry wines, such as Alazani Valley and Kindzmarauli, which reflected CIS and Eastern European customer preferences (Taber 2009). Little attention was given to quality as consumers in the Soviet Union preferred cheaper wine, and similarly, grape varieties with the highest yield were preferred over grape varieties that are best for wine. To this day, half of wines produced are sweet and serve the CIS market due to Georgia's experience with the market and understanding of its customer preferences (Taber 2009). Meanwhile, Georgian wine producers are relatively new to the Western market. Western customer preferences are generally for higher quality, dry wines—a product segment flooded by competition from the New World. Wines like Cabernet Sauvignon, Chardonnay, Pinot Noir and the like have been historically dominated by countries like the US, Australia, and France, which have established markets and loyal customer bases.

Table 5: Index of RCA in Wine, by Quality, 2009 (Selected Countries)

Source: Data from Wine Economics Research Centre. Note: Wine is categorized as FAO CODE 0564, SITC 112.12, and Harmonised System Tariff Heading 2204. Bottled still wine is categorized in three sub-categories based on quality: still grape wines traded in containers of two liters or less (which are further sub-divided as 'commercial premium' or "CP" and "super premium" or "UP" wines); and still grape wines traded in containers exceeding two liters (also called "non-premium" or "NP" wine); and Sparkling wine.

| | Still wine | | | | |
|---|---|---|---|---|---|
| Country | NP | CP | UP | Sparkling wine | Total wine |
| France | 3.36 | 4.49 | 16.37 | 15.92 | 8.19 |
| Italy | 4.86 | 7.06 | 5.32 | 4.12 | 6.05 |
| Portugal | 4.49 | 9.90 | 16.77 | 0.70 | 8.94 |
| Spain | 13.55 | 5.64 | 2.01 | 6.67 | 6.10 |
| Germany | 0.37 | 0.59 | 0.21 | 0.34 | 0.46 |
| Bulgaria | 2.54 | 3.05 | 0.42 | 0.61 | 2.17 |
| Croatia | 0.21 | 0.69 | 1.18 | 0.02 | 0.61 |
| **Georgia** | **5.03** | **8.27** | **1.14** | **3.45** | **5.95** |
| Hungary | 1.59 | 0.49 | 0.07 | 0.43 | 0.54 |
| Moldova | 133.31 | 56.53 | 3.87 | 16.48 | 49.99 |
| Romania | 0.62 | 0.26 | 0.09 | 0.04 | 0.24 |
| Ukraine | 2.72 | 0.47 | 0.07 | 1.45 | 0.82 |
| Australia | 7.27 | 7.93 | 2.83 | 1.20 | 5.92 |
| New Zealand | 10.16 | 6.93 | 46.98 | 0.85 | 12.93 |
| USA | 0.90 | 0.49 | 0.17 | 0.08 | 0.42 |
| Argentina | 4.15 | 8.80 | 1.22 | 0.84 | 5.73 |
| Chile | 18.15 | 17.74 | 6.33 | 0.56 | 13.12 |
| South Africa | 12.55 | 6.96 | 1.46 | 1.18 | 5.75 |

Georgia essentially has a legacy market in the former Soviet republics, and a growing Western market for which a separate strategy is needed. For the CIS market, Georgian wine producers need to consolidate vineyards and standardize production, not unlike in the Soviet days, in order to scale up the production and increase cost efficiencies. For the Western markets, Georgian wine producers should focus on increasing quality and creating a premium niche market through a differentiation strategy, whether by producing wines with unique grape varieties or using unique production methods.

Giorgi Tevzadze, a young Georgian wine maker, believes Georgia's future is not in traditional wine but in finding Georgia's niche in the global market through differentiated product. He wants to preserve Georgia's traditions and celebrate its deep history, but also understands that Georgian wine producers need to focus their resources on wine products that appeal to global demand and can differentiate themselves from competitors, many of whom have far greater land and capital endowments.

Fourth, Georgian wine producers need to prioritize R&D, which can guide differentiation strategy. R&D Centers can serve as a great resource for product development and understanding customer preferences. For a developing country like Georgia to expand into developed markets that have high standard requirements and higher income consumers, continuous R&D may become the decisive factor in determining its wine sector's long-term fate. California's wine producers benefit from research done by the Robert Mondavi Institute Center for Wine Economics (CWE), and, similarly, Australia benefits from the Australian Wine Research Institute (AWRI). President Saakashvili announced in 2011 that a new Georgia Wine Institute will be established in Tsinandali, Kakheti (Anderson 2013). Since the announcement, there has been little news on the progress of the Institute. Following the leadership transition, it is unclear if the project has continued. A real opportunity that Georgia appears to have identified is that in the near future, China's wine market is expected to grow significantly, as shown in Figure 15.

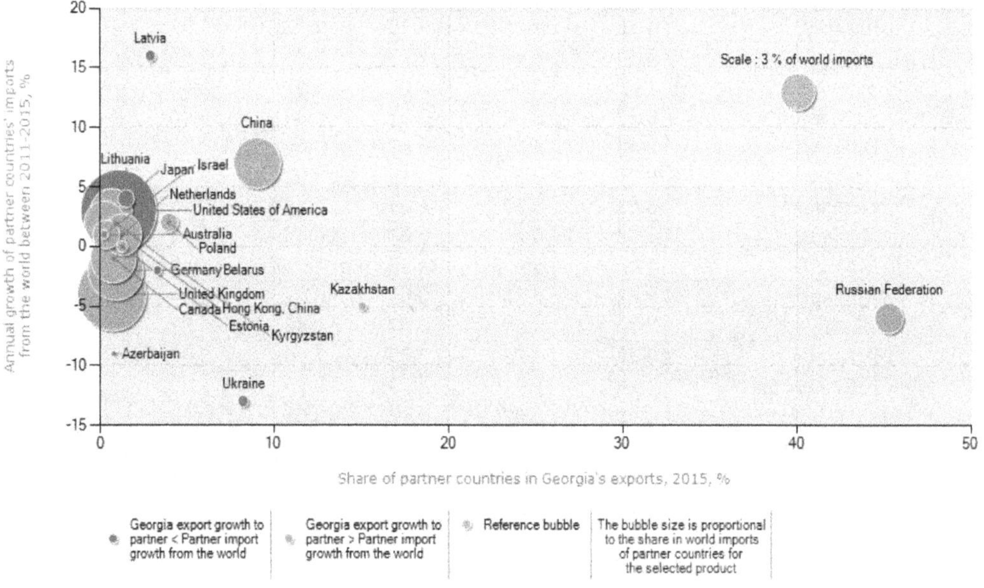


Figure 15: Prospects for Market Diversification for Wine Exported by Georgia (2015) Source: Data and trade map provided by the International Trade Center. ITC calculations based on UN COMTRADE and ITC statistics. Note: The full product name is 2204 Wine of fresh grapes, including fortified wines; grape must, partly fermented and of an actual alcohol strength of >0.5% or grape must with added alcohol of an actual alcoholic strength of >0.5% vol.

Currently, wine production in Georgia is done by two groups: households and commercial wineries. The first group consists of hundreds of thousands of Georgian households that produce their own grapes and wine in "family cellars," as Georgia remains a poor country, with roughly half of its population residing in the countryside. Most of the rural population runs small, private, family farms with an average plot of 1.2 hectares, and 93% cultivate <2 hectares (Anderson 2013). Grapes account for around two-fifths of the volume of all fruit produced in Georgia, and between 92% and 95% of the country's grapes are grown on family farms, out of which about 90% go for wine production. (National Statistical Office of Georgia 2011a, b). These households usually harvest grapes from their own vineyards, sell some to commercial wineries, and also produce an estimated 20–1,000 liters of wine on average themselves, which adds up to nearly 50–80 million liters of wine (Georgian Wine Association 2011).

The second group is made up of commercial wine producers that sell wine domestically and internationally. There are state-owned and private wineries. Together they produce between 90,000 (2002) and 227,000 (2005) tons of grapes annually, of which about one-fifth are used for wine production by registered wineries. Only a few dozen of hundreds of thousands of Georgian wineries are export-capable (Anderson 2013). Between 2000 and 2009, wine exports made up, on average, about 6.67% of Georgia's total exports, with a high of 10.1% in 2001 and a low of 2.4% in 2007. Georgia's percentage of wine exports from total production are relatively low when compared with other major wine-exporting countries. As shown in Figure 16, countries like Chile and Moldova export 70% of their wine. In fact, countries like Ukraine, Bulgaria, and Hungary ranked higher than Georgia in 2009.

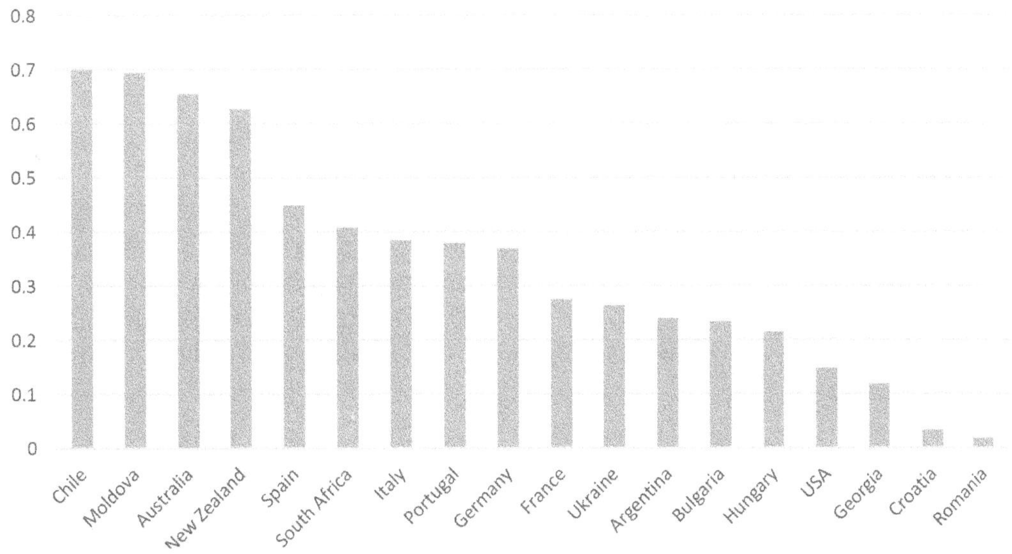


Figure 16: Percentage of Wine Production Exported in Selected Countries (2009)
Source: Data from Wine Economics Research Centre. Authors' calculations.

Fifth, the Government can play an important role by putting in place regulatory and property right institutions to ensure Georgia's wine quality. The Government already has been active in assisting the industry, but more can be done. Georgia was the first among former Soviet republics to create its national patent service "Sakpatenti" in 1992. This service was later transformed into the National Intellectual Property Center, which is tasked to review and maintain a registry of all authorized appellations of origin (AO) and geographic indication (GI). For example, Bordeaux and Napa Valley are widely recognized as GIs associated with fine wine, and to build a brand, property rights must first be clearly designated and enforced. A major step taken by the Government was the adoption of the Law on Appellations of Origin and Geographical Indication in 1999, which made development of the wine sector a national economic priority. In 2004, Georgia signed the Lisbon Agreement for the Protection of Appellations of Origin administered by the World Intellectual Property Organization (WIPO). By signing this Agreement, Georgia has registered and protected its AOs at the international level. In 2010, wine producers established the Georgian Wine Association, a forum of mutual support to promote Georgia's wine internationally. In 2011, an agreement was signed with the EU on the mutual recognition of GIs—a crucial move to branding Georgia's wine. Also, in the same year, the Ministry of Agriculture, the Georgian Wine Association and the National Investment Agency jointly developed the Sector Export Market Development Action Plan. In 2014, the Georgian National Wine Agency was founded under the Georgian Ministry of Agriculture whose mission became to ensure that Georgian wine producers comply with established standards by granting quality certification and granting rights to use registered AOs.

While the Government has initiated the promotion of wine tourism, which takes advantage of three of Georgia's prominent assets: wine, beautiful nature, and cultural heritage, it has been the private sector that has practically led in this effort. Wine tourism is not a novel idea. In fact, many of world's leading wine producers attract large number of wine tourists annually. Wine tourism, simply put, refers to tourism (e.g. vacation, health, entertainment, artifacts, retirement, and education) that incorporates wine-related activities in the package. These activities include wine tastings and tours of wine-making processes, vineyards and historical sites. While the Government might have channeled resources or set strategic goals, a true leader in Georgian wine tourism has emerged from the private sector. Over the past 10 years, Georgia's largest wine producer Badagoni, which produces 1.2 million cases per year from 750 acres of vineyards, has been running the Badagoni Tours business that has specialized in wine tourism packages since 2007 (Taber 2009). As shown in Figure 17, international arrivals to Georgia have increased 11-fold, from about 560,000 in 2005 to over 6.35 million in 2016.

Sixth, the private sector, the wine and grape producers, in cooperation with government institutions such as the Georgian Investment Agency and the Georgian National Wine Agency, should build a "Made in Georgia" brand. Georgia could emphasize tradition and health benefits to promote its brand. For example, a 7,000-year-old tradition of wine-making in qveri, an oval-shaped earthenware vessel where it is stored and fermented, was added to the UNESCO Heritage List in 2013 as part of the Intangible Cultural Heritage of Humanity. Some preliminary scientific research suggests that qvevri-made wine is healthier than conventionally produced wine in the west (Diaz 2011; Shalashvili et al. 2011). Prominent wine producers like Josko Gravner and Elisabetta Foradori are now using qvevri-like methods to let their wine mature. The benefits are that the wines find their identity much sooner than in conventional containers and the complexity of the flavor is enhanced, but the downside is its cost at $8,000, which is about 10 times of conventional price of a barrique barrel (Feiring 2011).

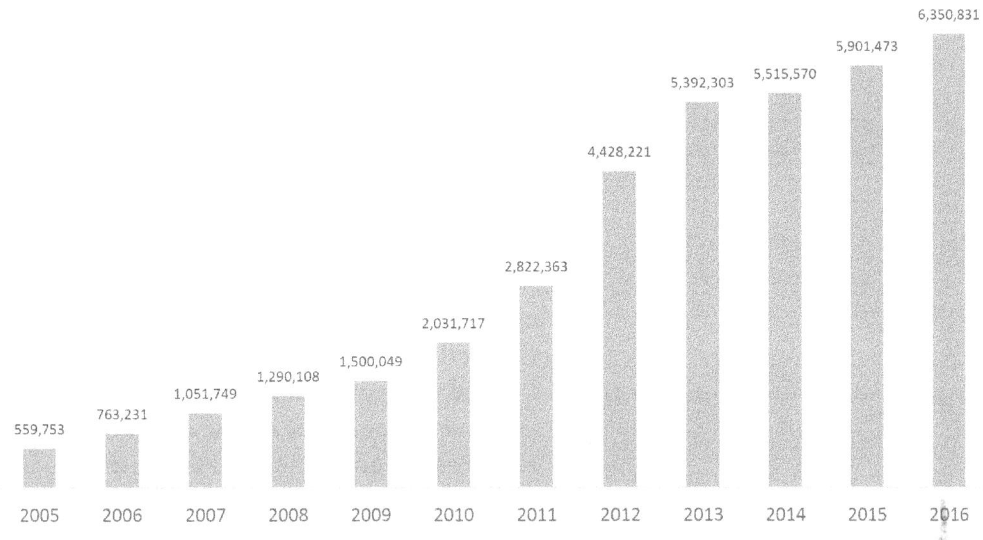


Figure 17: International Arrivals by Year
Source: Data from Georgian National Tourism Administration (2015).

Seventh, Georgia's tourism sector needs major investments in its infrastructure, from roads to accommodations to tourist-friendly restaurants, and should work closely with the wineries to design quality tour packages. Georgia has had the most international arrivals in 2016 from Azerbaijan and Armenia, which sent about 1.5 million each; another 1.25 million visited from Turkey and a million from Russia (refer to Table 6). These are the only four countries from which there are at least a million visits. Visits from Azerbaijan and Armenia are not of primary interest because many of these visits are likely to be family-related or business-related. Of greater importance are visitors from Russia and the EU member countries, whose consumers have discretionary income and are tourist-sending countries. According to the report "Georgian Tourism in Figures: Structure & Industry Data" (2015), 242,172 EU citizens (4.1% more than the previous year) arrived in Georgia, which is 4.1% of total arrivals.

In 2010, the Georgian National Tourism Administration (GNTA) was established in order to promote tourism in Georgia. While international arrivals have been increasing exponentially, only a small fraction of these arrivals were for tourism purposes. According to the National Statistics Offices of Georgia, the main purpose of visits in 2015 were the following: visiting friends/relatives (54.5%), shopping (11.4%), health and medical care (10.3%), holiday/leisure/recreation (7.6%), visit to second home (6.6%), business or professional

(6.0%), religion (1.8%), education or training (0.6%), and other (1.2%). However, GNTA (2015) register's official count is at a total of 1,765 accommodation units with a total of 57,049 beds.

Table 6: Top International Arrivals from Selected Countries (2005–2016)
Source: Data from Georgian National Tourism Administration (2015).

| Country | 2005 | 2006 | 2007 | 2008 | 2009 | 2010 | 2011 | 2012 | 2013 | 2014 | 2015 |
|---|---|---|---|---|---|---|---|---|---|---|---|
| Azerbaijan | 153,467 | 198,062 | 281,629 | 344,936 | 418,992 | 497,969 | 714,418 | 931,933 | 1,075,857 | 1,283,214 | 1,393,257 |
| Armenia | 100,508 | 180,550 | 243,133 | 281,463 | 351,049 | 547,510 | 699,382 | 921,929 | 1,291,838 | 1,325,635 | 1,468,888 |
| Turkey | 109,796 | 146,696 | 248,028 | 351,410 | 384,482 | 535,593 | 738,085 | 1,533,236 | 1,597,438 | 1,442,695 | 1,391,721 |
| Russia | 90,176 | 88,538 | 91,361 | 114,459 | 127,937 | 170,584 | 278,458 | 513,930 | 767,396 | 811,621 | 926,144 |
| Ukraine | 12,288 | 22,436 | 28,932 | 32,988 | 39,339 | 47,596 | 58,966 | 76,610 | 126,797 | 143,521 | 141,734 |
| Iran | 5,033 | 5,379 | 7,986 | 10,038 | 9,848 | 21,313 | 60,191 | 89,697 | 85,598 | 47,929 | 25,273 |
| Israel | 6,316 | 8,229 | 16,450 | 17,413 | 16,757 | 19,447 | 25,438 | 30,851 | 39,922 | 42,385 | 59,487 |
| Germany | 8,840 | 11,076 | 14,081 | 13,267 | 15,351 | 17,619 | 22,204 | 26,448 | 30,815 | 33,446 | 36,826 |
| USA | 12,922 | 12,801 | 14,818 | 15,652 | 16,934 | 20,081 | 24,236 | 28,513 | 26,713 | 28,272 | 31,147 |
| Greece | 7,098 | 10,344 | 12,380 | 12,914 | 14,300 | 16,424 | 17,664 | 19,777 | 22,024 | 21,464 | 19,221 |
| UK | 6,677 | 8,901 | 9,775 | 8,951 | 10,633 | 10,985 | 10,695 | 14,805 | 16,672 | 18,586 | 19,191 |

## Conclusion

Georgia's socioeconomic development goal, "Georgia 2020," is an ambitious vision for a country with committed leadership. Cluster initiatives, if executed properly, can be a useful tool in achieving regional economic development. But for such initiatives to work, government will need help from the nation's most creative and entrepreneurial individuals and companies. The current government's push toward the wine tourism sector makes a lot of sense. Georgia has fine grapes, long traditions in wine making, and is already establishing its niche in the global market. To leverage this sector in creating a national brand and fostering a tourism sector may be the best strategy there is. However, less evidence is found for the long-term benefits of developing the textile/apparel industry, for which there are fewer comparative advantages. Several analyses presented in this chapter suggest that Georgia's chemical and machinery sectors have been surging, particularly in products such as cyanides, isotopes, and rail locomotives. Policymakers could benefit from further studies on these sectors, especially given that these industries present opportunities to diversify and modernize Georgia's economy.

## References

Adhikari, Ratnakara, and Yumiko Yamato. 2007. "The Textile and Clothing Industry: Adjusting to the Post-Quota World." In *Industrial Development for the 21st Century*. New York: United Nations, 183–205.

Anderson, Kym. (ed.) 2004. *The World's Wine Markets: Globalization at Work*. Cheltenham, UK: Edward Elgar.

Anderson, Kym. 2013. "Is Georgia the Next 'New' Wine-Exporting Country?" *Journal of Wine Economics* 8 (1): 1–28.

Anderson, Kym, and Nelgen Signe. 2009. *Global Wine Markets, 1961 to 2009: A Statistical Compendium*. Adelaide: Wine Economics Research Centre. http://www.adelaide.edu.au/wine-econ/databases/GWM/ (accessed February 20, 2017)

Anselin, Luc, Attila Varga, and Zoltan Acs. 1997. "Local Geographic Spillovers Between University Research and High Technology Innovations." *Journal of Urban Economics* 42 (3): 422–448.

Balassa, Bela. 1965. "Trade Liberalisation and 'Revealed' Comparative Advantage." *The Manchester School* 33 (2): 99–123.

Bergman, Edward M., and Edward J. Feser. 1999. *Industrial and Regional Clusters: Concepts and Comparative Applications*. Morgantown, WV: WVU Regional Research Institute Web Book, 4–16.

Dalberg Global Development Advisors. 2011. *Report on Support to SMEs in Developing Countries Through Financial Intermediaries, SME Briefing Paper*, EIB Draft Version. Geneva: European Investment Bank. http://www.eib.europa.eu/attachments/dalberg_sme-briefing-paper.pdf (accessed February 20, 2017).

Daughtry, Emily E., and Fred L. Wehling. 2000. "Cooperative Efforts to Secure Fissile Material in the NIS." *The Nonproliferation Review* 7 (1): 97–111.

Diaz, C. 2011. "Studies of Traditional Winemaking Methods Based on Spontaneous Fermentation." Paper presented at the 1st Qvevri Wine Symposium, Georgia.

Feiring, Alice. 2011. "Winemakers Go Wild for Qvevri." *Newsweek*, October 23. http://www.newsweek.com/winemakers-go-wild-qvevri-68217 (accessed February 7, 2017).

Fernandez-Stark, Karina, Stacey Frederick, and Gary Gereffi. 2011. *The Apparel Global Value Chain*. Durham, N.C.: Duke University, Center on Globalization, Governance and Competitiveness http://www.cggc.duke.edu/pdfs/2011-11-11_CGGC_Apparel-Global-Value-Chain.pdf (accessed February 7, 2017).

Ferreira, M. P., F. Ribeiro Serra, B. Kramer Costa, E. A. Maccari, and H. Ritor Couto. 2012. "Impact of the Types of Clusters on the Innovation Output and the Appropriation of

Rents from Innovation." *Journal of Technology Management & Innovation* 7 (4): 70–80.

Feser, Edward J. 1998. "Old and New Theories of Industry Clusters." In *Clusters and Regional Specialization*, ed. Michael Steiner. London: Pion, 18–40.

Florida, Richard. 1999. "The Role of the University: Leveraging Talent, Not Technology." *Issues in Science and Technology* 15 (4): 67–73.

Florida, Richard. 2002. *The Rise of the Creative Class: And How It's Transforming Work, Leisure, Community and Everyday Life.* New York: Basic Books.

Fukunishi, Takahiro, Kenta Goto, and Tatsufumi Yamagata. 2013. *Aid for Trade and Value Chains in Textiles and Apparel.* Survey, Organisation for Economic Co-operation and Development (OECD). https://www.oecd.org/dac/aft/AidforTrade_SectorStudy_Textiles.pdf (accessed February 7, 2017).

Gazadze, Ekaterine, and Giorgi Nakashidze. 2014. "Georgia's Wine Sector: Wine is Bottled Poetry." Bank of Georgia, April 16. http://research.investingeorgia.org/userfiles/admin_files/88.pdf (accessed February 13, 2017).

Georgian Investment Agency. 2015. "Labor." https://www.investingeorgia.org/en/georgia/labor (accessed February 20, 2017).

Georgian National Tourism Administration. 2015. *Georgian Tourism in Figures: Structures & Industry Data.* Tbilisi, Georgia: Ministry of Economy and Sustainable Development of Georgia. http://gnta.ge/wp-content/uploads/2016/06/2015-eng.. .pdf (accessed March 15, 2017).

Georgian Wine Association. 2011. "Sector Export Market Development Action Plan (SEMDAP): Wine Sector." http://www.gwa.ge/upload/file/ENG_Sector_Export_Market_Development_Action_Plan.pdf (accessed February 20, 2017).

Glaeser, Edward. 2011. *Triumph of the City: How Our Greatest Invention makes us Richer, Smarter, Greener, Healthier, and Happier.* London: Macmillan.

Government of Georgia. 2013. *Kakheti Regional Development Strategy 2014–2020.* Tbilisi, Georgia: Deutsche Gesellschaft für Internationale Zusammenarbeit (GIZ) GmbH. http://static.mrdi.gov.ge/52f9bedc0cf298a857ab7d55.pdf (accessed February 7, 2017).

Government of Georgia. 2014. "Social-economic Development Strategy of Georgia 'Georgia 2020.'" http://static.mrdi.gov.ge/551e4a570cf24147438b1727.pdf (accessed February 7, 2017).

Hausmann, Ricardo, Cesar A. Hidalgo, Sebastian Bustos, Michele Coscia, Sarah Chung, Juan Jimenez, Alexander Simoes, and Muhammed A. Yildirim. 2014. *The Atlas of Economic Complexity: Mapping Paths to Prosperity.* MIT Press.

Jacobs, Jane. 1961. *The Death and Life of American Cities.* New York: Random House.

Jacobs, Dany, and Ard-Pieter De Man. (1996). "Clusters, Industrial Policy and Firm Strategy." *Technology Analysis & Strategic Management* 8 (4): 425–438.

Kalatozishvili, Georgy. 2012. "First Free Economic Zone in Georgia." March 15. http://vestnikkavkaza.net/articles/economy/24213.html (accessed February 13, 2017).

Keane, Jodie, and Dirk W. te Velde. 2008. *The Role of Textile and Clothing Industries in Growth and Development Strategies.* London: Overseas Development Institute. https://www.odi.org/sites/odi.org.uk/files/odi-assets/publications-opinion-files/3361.pdf (accessed February 22, 2017).

Lindqvist, Göran, Christian Ketels, and Örjan Sölvell. 2013. *The Cluster Initiative Greenbook 2.0.* Stockholm: Ivory Tower Publishers.

Markusen, Ann. 1996. "Sticky Places in Slippery Space: A Typology of Industrial Districts." *Economic Geography* 72 (3): 293–313.

Marshall, Alfred. 1890. *Principles of Economics.* London: Macmillan.

Martin, Ron, and Peter Sunley. 2003. "Deconstructing Clusters: Chaotic Concept or Policy Panacea?" *Journal of Economic Geography* 3 (1): 5–35.

Miller, Matthew J. 2015. "Georgia: Once an Economic Driver, Used Car Market Turning Into a Lemon." *EurasiaNet,* September 30. http://www.eurasianet.org/node/75331 (accessed February 13, 2017).

National Statistical Office of Georgia (NSO). 2011a. *Agriculture of Georgia 2010.* www.geostat.ge

National Statistical Office of Georgia. 2011b. *Households' Income and Expenditure 2010.* www.geostat.ge

National Statistics Office of Georgia (NSO). 2016. "External Trade: Georgian Exports by Countries 1995–2016." www.geostat.ge

Nordås, Hildegunn K. 2004. *The Global Textile and Clothing Industry Post the Agreement on Textiles and Clothing.* Geneva: World Trade Organization Publications, Discussion Paper No 5.

Onugha, Ifeyinwa, Mariana Iootty, Austin Kilroy, and Vincent Palmade. 2013. *Georgia Competitive Industries Preliminary Sector Diagnostic.* Washington, D.C.: World Bank, 16069.

Organisation for Economic Co-operation and Development (OECD). 1997. *Small Businesses, Job Creation and Growth: Facts, Obstacles and Best Practices.* Paris: OECD. https://www.oecd.org/cfe/smes/2090740.pdf (accessed February 7, 2017).

Porter, Michael E. 1985. *Competitive Advantage: Creating and Sustaining Superior Performance.* New York: Simon and Schuster.

Porter, Michael E. 1998. "Clusters and the New Economics of Competition." *Harvard Business Review* 76 (6): 77–90.

Porter, Michael E. 2000. "Location, Competition, and Economic Development: Local Clusters in a Global Economy." *Economic Development Quarterly* 14 (1): 15–34.

PricewaterhouseCoopers. 2012. *Apparel Production in Georgia–Greenfield Investment Opportunity.* Tbilisi: PricewaterhouseCoopers Central Asia and Caucasus B.V. Georgia Branch. http://researchgeorgia.ge/userfiles/admin_files/117.pdf (accessed February 7, 2017).

Schumpeter, J. A. (1934). *The Theory of Economic Development: An Inquiry into Profits, Capital, Credit, Interest, and the Business Cycle* (Vol. 55). New Brunswick: Transaction Publishers.

Shakya, Mallika. 2009. "Clusters for Competitiveness: A Practical Guide and Policy Implications for Developing Cluster Initiatives." Washington, DC: World Bank. http://siteresources.worldbank.org/INTLAC/Resources/clusterinitiativetext.pdf (accessed February 7, 2017).

Shalashvili, A., D. Ugrekhelidze, I. Targamadze, N. Zambakhidze, and L. Tsereteli. 2011. "Phenolic Compounds and Antiradical Efficiency of Georgian (Kakhethian) Wines." *Journal of Food Science and Engineering* 1 (5): 361–365.

Simmie, James, and James Sennett. 1999. "Innovative Clusters: Global or Local Linkages?" *National Institute Economic Review* 170 (1): 87–98.

Sölvell, Örjan, Göran Lindqvist, and Christian Ketels. 2013. *The Cluster Initiative Greenbook.* Stockholm: Ivory Tower Publishers.

Steinheim, Philipp. 2016. *Textile and Apparel in Georgia.* Tbilisi: Deutsche Gesellschaft für Internationale Zusammenarbeit (GIZ) GmbH. http://qartuli.ge/uploads/editor/Textile_and_Apparel_in_Georgia1.pdf (accessed February 7, 2017).

Taber, George M. 2009. "Kakheti, Georgia—the Last Frontier." In *In Search of Bacchus: Wanderings in the Wonderful World of Wine Tourism.* New York: Simon and Schuster, Ch. 13.

The World Factbook. 2017. Washington, DC: Central Intelligence Agency. https://www.cia.gov/library/publications/the-world-factbook/index.html

United Nations Statistics Division. 1990–2014. *UN COMTRADE.* New York: International Merchandise Trade Statistics, United Nations Statistics Division. http://comtrade.un.org/.

U.S. Department of State. 2014. "2014 Investment Climate Statement." https://www.state.gov/documents/organization/229020.pdf (accessed February 13, 2017).

Van den Berg, Leo, Erik Braun, and Willem Van Winden. 2001. "Growth Clusters in European Cities: An Integral Approach." *Urban Studies* 38 (1): 185–205.

Waal, Thomas de. "Georgia Holds Its Breath." *Carnegie Endowment for International Peace*. http://carnegieeurope.eu/2012/09/26/georgia-holds-its-breath-pub-49508 (accessed February 13, 2017).

World Bank. 1996–2014. World Integrated Trade Solution (WITS). http://wits.worldbank.org/wits/

World Bank. 1995–2015. "High-technology Exports (% of Manufactured Exports)." World Development Indicators. http://data.worldbank.org/indicator/TX.VAL.TECH.MF.ZS

World Bank. 2002. *Transition: The First Ten Years. Analysis and Lessons for Eastern Europe and the Former Soviet Union.* Washington, DC: World Bank. http://siteresources.worldbank.org/ECAEXT/Resources/complete.pdf (accessed February 7, 2017).

World Bank. 2013. *Enterprise Surveys. Georgia Country Profile. International Finance Corporation.* Washington, DC: Enterprise Analysis Unit. http://www.enterprisesurveys.org/~/media/GIAWB/EnterpriseSurveys/Documents/Profiles/English/Georgia-2013.pdf (accessed June 2, 2017).

World Bank. 2017. *Doing Business 2017: Equal Opportunity for All.* Washington, DC: World Bank. DOI: 10.1596/978-1-4648-0948-4. License: Creative Commons Attribution CC BY 3.0 IGO.

World Trade Organization Secretariat. 2015. "Trade Policy Review of Georgia." November 10. https://www.wto.org/english/tratop_e/tpr_e/s328_e.pdf (accessed February 20, 2017).

Zeynalli, Nazakat, Shahnaz Ahmedova, and Gunel Safarova. 2014. "Rustavi Car Market after Euro 4 Standard." *StoryBuilder*, July 22. https://storybuilder.jumpstart.ge/en/rustavi-car-market-after-euro-4-standard (accessed February 13, 2017).

# Acknowledgements

It was our pleasure to work with a dedicated array of faculty from the Georgian Institute of Public Affairs, as well as their faculty and doctoral student collaborators from the Schar School at George Mason University, in putting together this volume. We are grateful to the US State Department and the US Embassy in Tbilisi, whose support for an initiative aimed at strengthening scholarship and pedagogy brought us all together.

We are indebted to our Schar School colleagues who were gracious, helpful, and thorough in reviewing chapters and making recommendations for revisions in several rounds. These stalwart souls include Timothy Conlan, John Marvel, Eric McGlinchey, Robert J. McGrath, Paul Posner, Priscilla M. Regan, and Frank Shafroth.

We are also grateful to Paul Rich and Daniel Gutierrez-Sandoval of the Policy Studies Organization and Westphalia Press for their encouragement of this project and support for publication.

**Nino Dolidze** wishes to thank the GIPA research team participating in the project, which included: Levan Samadashvili, Zhana Antia, Tinatin Kldiashvili, Ana Gorgodze, Nino Kochiashvili, Tornike Kapanadze, Meri Pantsulaia, Nino Murjikneli, Natia Kapanadze.

**Giorgi Bakradze, Nino Rusieshvili,** and **Kurt Birson** would like to express their sincere gratitude to the wonderful team of the National Bank of Georgia professionals and, in particular, to Archil Mestvirishvili, Vice-President; Giorgi Barbakadze, Head of the Macroeconomics and Statistics Department; Zviad Zedginidze, Head of the Macroeconomic Research Division; and Archil Imnaishvili, Head of the Monetary Policy Division, for their valuable input and advice, without which their chapter would never have been written.

**Tamar Koberidze** would like to thank Diane Maye for her editing assistance on an early version of her current chapter.

We enjoyed collaborating with all contributors in Tbilisi and in Virginia, and via Skype and email. It has truly been a rewarding, interdisciplinary, international project born of mutual enthusiasm and respect.

Bonnie Stabile and Nino Ghonghadze
*Editors*

# About the Authors

**David Akhvlediani** is Program Coordinator of the Master of Public Administration program at the Georgian Institute of Public Affairs. His MPP degree is from the Korean Development Institute, and his MA in International Relations is from Collegium Civitas in Poland.

**Nikoloz Abuashvili** is Professor of Business and Economics in the School of Government at the Georgian Institute of Public Affairs, where he is also Head of Marketing. He delivers training and lectures both in the private sector and for Georgian and foreign students.

**Giorgi Bakradze** is a Lecturer at the Georgian Institute of Public Affairs and several other Georgian universities. He has a MA in Economics from the Center for Economic Development of Williams College, a MA in Economics from Georgetown University in the United States, and a MSc in Physics from Tblisi State University.

**Kurt Birson** is a PhD student in Public Policy at the Schar School of Policy and Government at George Mason University. His research interests include international development, economic geography, and political economy of Latin America. He received an MA in Economics at the New School for Social Research.

**Nino Dolidze** is Professor, Head of Public Administration, and Deputy Head of Research at the Georgian Institute of Public Affairs. Professor Dolidze conducts classes in Public Administration and Organizational Management, and supervises research at the doctoral level, and in the Master's and undergraduate programs.

**Sheldon M. Edner** is a term Professor of Public Administration, at the Schar School of Policy and Government at George Mason University. He teaches courses in Public Policy Process, Third Party Governance, Ethics and Administration, and Emergency Management.

**Archil Gersamia** is Head of Administration at the Georgian Institute of Public Affairs, supervising strategic planning, budgeting and other administrative issues. He delivers two main lecture courses at GIPA's School of Government, in Economics, and Public Finance.

**Nino Ghonghadze** is a Professor at the Georgian Institute of Public Affairs and teaches courses in Public Policy Analysis and Research Methodology in the Master's and PhD degree programs. Her research focuses on integrity issues in public governance.

**Tamar Koberidze** is invited professor at the Georgian Institute of Public Affairs, where she teaches undergraduate and graduate courses on Civil Society and its Role in Democratic Development, Non-Profit Management, and Political Lobbying and Advocacy.

**Lali Khurtsia** is Assistant Professor at Tbilisi State University, on the faculty of Economics and Business, in the Department of Economic Policy. She is author of several articles concerning economic policy issues.

**Yulia Krylova** holds a PhD degree in Political Science from George Mason University and a PhD degree in Economics from Saint Petersburg State University. She is currently affiliated with the Terrorism, Transnational Crime, and Corruption Center at George Mason University.

**Nino Loladze** is Assistant Professor at the Georgian Institute of Public Affairs. She conducts classes in local economic development and budgeting, and supervises research in the Master's program.

**Natalia Partskhaladze** is Coordinator of the Master's Program in Environmental Management and Policy at the Georgian Institute of Public Affairs. Her MPA degree is from GIPA and MA from the Sorbonne in Paris.

**Paul L. Posner** has served as Professor and Director of the Master of Public Administration Program, and the Center on the Public Service, in the Schar School of Policy and Government at George Mason University. He is Past President of the American Society for Public Administration and was Chairman of the Board of the National Academy of Public Administration through 2016.

**Priscilla Regan** is a Professor in the Schar School of Policy and Government at George Mason University. Along with Paul Posner and Eric McGlinchey, she has led the US State Department funded GIPA-Mason Public Administration Partnership.

**Nino Rusieshvili** works in the Public Relations and International Cooperation division of the National Bank of Georgia. Her MPA degree is from Caucasus University in Tbilisi, Georgia.

**Raja M. Ali Saleem** worked as a civil servant in the Ministry of Finance, Pakistan for six years before graduating with a PhD degree from George Mason University. His first book "State, Nationalism and Islamization: Historical Analysis of Turkey and Pakistan" is being published by Palgrave Macmillan in 2017.

**Levan Samadashvili** currently serves as a Deputy Chief of Party for the USAID Good Governance Initiative (GGI), in Georgia. His prior employment was at the UNDP Georgia in the capacity of the Public Administration Reform Coordinator. He holds a Master of Public Administration from the University of Georgia School of Public and International Affairs in Athens, Georgia in the US.

**Keunwon Song** is a PhD student at the Schar School of Policy and Government, George Mason University. His research revolves around labor markets, political economy, firm performance, entrepreneurship and regional economic development in Russia and the United States.

**Elisabed (Liza) Sopromadze** is Assistant Professor in the Georgian Institute of Public Affairs. Professor Sopromadze conducts classes in local self-government and public participation in decision-making processes, and supervises research in the Master's and undergraduate programs.

**Solomiya Shpak** is a PhD student at the Schar School of Policy and Government at George Mason University. She received her MA in Economic Analysis from Kyiv School of Economics and MA in International Economics from Ivan Franko National University in Lviv.

**Bonnie Stabile** is Research Assistant Professor, and Director of the Master of Public Policy Program in the Schar School of Policy and Government at George Mason University, where she also directs a Gender and Policy initiative. She is Co-Editor of *World Medical & Health Policy*, a peer-reviewed academic journal sponsored by the Policy Studies Organization and published by Wiley Blackwell.

**Jessica N. Terman** is Assistant Professor at the Schar School of Policy and Government at George Mason University. She studies implementation issues in state and local governments.

**Vano Tsertsvadze** is a researcher at the Georgian Institute of Public Affairs, School of Government. He is author of several articles on cost-effectiveness in addiction and drug policy.

www.ingramcontent.com/pod-product-compliance
Lightning Source LLC
Chambersburg PA
CBHW081408270326
41931CB00016B/3409